EFFECTIVE MEDICAL LEADERSHIP

BRYCE TAYLOR

Effective Medical
Leadership

UNIVERSITY OF TORONTO PRESS
Toronto Buffalo London

© University of Toronto Press Incorporated 2010
Toronto Buffalo London
www.utppublishing.com
Printed in Canada

ISBN 978-1-4426-4200-3

Printed on acid-free, 100% post-consumer recycled paper
with vegetable-based inks

Library and Archives Canada Cataloguing in Publication

Taylor, Bryce, 1944–
Effective medical leadership / Bryce Taylor.

Includes bibliographical references and index.
ISBN 978-1-4426-4200-3

1. Health services administration.   2. Hospitals – Administration.
3. Leadership.   I. Title.

RA971.T39 2010   362.1068   C2010-902227-0

University of Toronto Press acknowledges the financial assistance to
its publishing program of the Canada Council for the Arts and Ontario
Arts Council.

  Canada Council   Conseil des Arts    ONTARIO ARTS COUNCIL
      for the Arts   du Canada   CONSEIL DES ARTS DE L'ONTARIO

University of Toronto Press acknowledges the financial support for its
publishing activities of the Government of Canada through the Canada
Book Fund.

To Marie-France, Chris, Marie-Noëlle, Michel,
Alexandra, Jean-François, Lily, Ben, and Will

Contents

Figures and Situational Examples

Figures

Situational Examples

Foreword

This leadership guide challenges would-be medical leaders to go beyond an aspiration to control their working environment, in order to improve the experiences and outcomes for patients and to make the workplace a more rewarding environment for the clinical team. To achieve this, medical and, in fact, all clinical leaders need to move out of their comfort zone of everyday patient care, learn new skills, and particularly understand their own strengths and weaknesses. Well-trained and enthusiastic clinical teams are constantly striving to deliver the very best care possible, but the system often fails them by lack of support, encouragement, and the resources to collect the necessary data, implement the improved processes, and teach the methods that help to deliver that care.

Effective leadership at all levels of the system is the essential extra ingredient that is necessary to achieve the resources, improve quality, address risk, and provide the safest and best possible care in the complex environment that is modern health care. Effective leadership in this complex environment is not easy and requires much more than the best intuitive efforts of even the most motivated hospital department or divisional head. There are always resistance and barriers to change that have not been overcome before. The generally accepted wisdom about the characteristics demonstrated by leaders is that they have optimism, energy, and enthusiasm; they put their team first; they are adaptable and able to refocus their goals quickly; they show a commitment to task; they are bold in vision but careful in planning: and they have a willingness to change, to seize new opportunities, and to learn new skills. All of these characteristics and how to apply them are dealt with in this book.

Bryce Taylor, an active academic surgeon and medical leader, brings a lifetime of hands-on leadership experience, acute observation, and a deep understanding of the leadership literature to the task of helping others achieve their own leadership potential through the advice, examples, and knowledge contained in this most readable of leadership guides. He clearly understands the clinicians', and particularly the medical clinicians', point of view, and the vignettes of situations requiring many different leadership skills will be recognized as possibly happening in any modern hospital. It is through the clear and realistic demonstration of effective leadership principles for clinical teams that this guide derives its authority.

Bryce Taylor's writing gives that sense of optimism, accountability, and understanding of his colleagues that is necessary for any leaders to achieve the vision they have set for themselves and their team. The vision of what needs to be done and how to do it is itself a prerequisite for effective leadership. People have been writing about vision and leadership for at least a couple of thousand years: as in Proverbs 29:18, 'Where there is no vision, the people perish,' or in an alternate translation that might be more applicable to the health system, 'Where there is no vision, the people are uncontrolled.'

Much can be learned, as in this book, from the experience of current and past leaders. Medical staff working in the current hospital environment often are in need of a morale boost, and in my mind the most important attribute of a medical leader is optimism, which can prove to be infectious even in the most trying of circumstances. As that great Antarctic explorer and leader from the early 1900s, Sir Ernest Shackleton, said, 'Optimism is true moral courage.'

This is a very practical primer for potential medical leaders, not only in North America but across the world.

Bruce Barraclough, AO, FRACS
Past President, International Society for Quality in Health Care
Chair, Clinical Excellence Commission, New South Wales, Australia

Acknowledgments

I am indebted to those who gave me opportunity, to those who led by example, and especially to those who tolerated me for the last twenty-five years. The leaders in my medical career have made tremendous contributions to whatever growth I can claim, and they frequently didn't even know it. They include Owen Gray, Bob Wilkinson, Bruce Tovee, Don Wilson, Bernie Langer, Bob Stone, John Wedge, Tom Closson, Alan Hudson, Bob Bell, Michael Baker, and Richard Reznick – all are exceptional leaders, all are different, and all are effective.

I am grateful to my editors Kate Baltais, whose reorganization was critical, and Angela Wingfield, whose copy-editing improved the readability significantly. Jennifer DiDomenico, Anne Laughlin, Andrea Wilson, and Jenna Germaine at Rotman/UTP Publishing have made the experience for a relatively untested author both efficient and exciting.

To those who read drafts and helped me gradually smooth the rough edges, I salute your time, your thoughtfulness, and your friendship – especially Brendan Calder, Jim Fisher, Betty Watt, Andy Szandtner, Bella Martin, Garth Warnock, Hartley Stern, Elijah Dixon, Mike Abecassis, and Derek Dubay.

IBM ViaVoice has been an unusual but efficient companion, as I was able to write this book without disturbing my valued assistants Annette Remmes and Mary Vogt; they had a few other things on their plate as I continued my day jobs! The tolerance and support of my family during this time was astronomic, too great to be measured, and appreciated more than they can know; the remote influence of Bernie still lingers and always will.

Finally, I need to recognize the way of life of the health care provider, a way of life that has given me and millions of others around the world a unique meaning in life as we care for others. When we started on our journey in health care, few of us ever imagined the benefits we would reap.

EFFECTIVE MEDICAL LEADERSHIP

Introduction

After over twenty-five years in a variety of medical leadership positions it dawned on me that the various jobs I had undertaken had enriched my life tremendously and had taught me a great deal about organizations, administration, operations, financial management, strategic planning, and, perhaps most of all, people – what people are about, what motivates us, what stimulates us to work in teams, and what in the long run leads to a better product (whether that be a marketable item or a better and more comprehensive service such as the delivery of health care).

Demands by patients, both in their expectations and in their numbers, are rising exponentially at a time when our ability to deliver the highly expensive, technologically sophisticated care that this entails is meeting repeated obstacles. With such a fundamental conflict facing us daily, leadership in the health care industry becomes ever more critical to the ultimate well-being of the profession and certainly to that of the patient. As health care policy expert Michael Porter asserts,[1] what we are trying to do is create *value* for our patients, and that requires effective leadership, effective management, and a lot of hard work.

It was with these thoughts in mind that I started to put to paper some of my experiences and impressions over the last quarter-century. One subject led to another, and I realized that this topic was in reality very complex. I found myself having to dig a little deeper to articulate exactly what I thought about a particular issue or event. I originally did this for myself, as I'm a firm believer in writing down ideas; those residing in the cerebral cortex are usually jumbled and disconnected, whereas committing thoughts to paper demands organization.

This exercise has been not a labour of love but a labour of reflection and distillation of the thoughts about leading – for the most part, by the seat of one's pants. I am forever grateful for the medical leadership opportunities and for my career in surgery; if anyone else in similar circumstances can learn a little from these words and bypass some of the errors I've committed, or straighten the circuitous routes I've often taken, I will be more than delighted.

By and large, doctors are intelligent, independent practitioners working in a respected profession. They are well-educated, well-paid professionals, who have been held in high esteem by patients and the public in general. Although the ratio of men and women enrolled in medical school is virtually fifty-fifty, the leadership in medical and surgical divisions remains male dominated, and this may take a generation to correct. Nurses are well-educated, accomplished individuals, who, like doctors, make a lifelong commitment to their profession and who, in many cases, juggle a number of simultaneous responsibilities. Hospitals are complex organizations that provide care in response to a dizzying array of inpatient and outpatient problems, employing not only professional practitioners but also workers in many trades and using highly sophisticated equipment and processes to meet their responsibilities.

On the front lines of patient care in the hospital are massive teams of doctors, nurses, students, technicians, pharmacists, and allied health care professionals. All of these people, and many others, are dedicated to the same single objective: *effective patient-centred care.*

Effective care means that as far as every step along the patient's hospital journey is concerned, the right thing must be done right; that is, the most modern medical management must be delivered in a safe, efficient way, while avoiding errors of people, processes, and machines.

So, how do we get to that ultimate objective of successfully managing hundreds of patients in a major facility? The trite answer would be 'one patient at a time.' The practical and more helpful answer would be to create a hospital workforce and infrastructure that boasts the following four components: (1) effective leadership, (2) an effective set of management policies and procedures, (3) effective managers, and (4) an effective front-line workforce. Working together, they have to be capable of carrying out the innumerable steps of patient care that can truly have life or death consequences.

As we will see, the organizational structure of a hospital's workforce is unique, and the interaction and relationships of the people within its walls complex; however, the processes around patient care, the steps that lead to the delivery of excellent service, and the management of these processes and people can be compared to any service industry. For care to be effective and for outcomes including patient satisfaction to be maximized, a *team approach* in which every member is responsible and accountable must be adopted and followed continuously. The management of the patient can be challenging; the management of the workforce and processes, even more so.

This book is written for you, the aspiring medical leader. Up to now, you may have been a successful clinician, educator, or researcher, or all of the above – a 'triple threat.' Now you want to stick your toe into the health management waters. These waters in the twenty-first century are often choppy with wildly fluctuating temperatures, but the challenges of staying afloat and even striking out on new and uncharted seas represent an opportunity you don't want to pass up. Being a hospital division or department head can be a real challenge for those who yearn for an element of control in their lives; it will not be a smooth ride, especially if you want to make a difference, because people and circumstances will be either your allies or your obstacles.

It is my hope that this manual will get at the essence of effective medical leadership provided by medical and surgical professionals in a hospital setting, and offer some ways in which clinician leaders can elevate their game to a more active, productive level. If that higher level can be achieved, then the opportunity to lead will prove very exciting indeed.

In chapter 1, I will try to set the stage by describing the rather complicated environment of the modern hospital. In chapter 2 we will take a look at what leadership means in this unusual setting. In chapter 3 the issue of *team* and *teamwork* is approached because, in the effective management of literally thousands of hospital employees, teamwork is a necessity. Chapter 4 will deal with the most important asset of any organization, the people, and chapter 5 will address some aspects of your daily routine as a medical leader. Chapters 6, 7, 8, and 9 cover a number of selected issues that will occupy most of your time as a leader and manager, and chapter 10 will offer you some unsolicited advice, as a kind of decanting of my reflections on my personal experience as a medical leader. Finally I'll try to offer some statements in the epilogue as a reminder of what I think adds value to the medical organization.

As you go along in your leadership commitment, it will be important to keep in mind how you are doing – a kind of leadership scorecard.

Twenty-Six Questions: The Metrics of Your Success as a Medical Leader

The following are some questions to ponder as you go through each position in your career as a medical leader and, indeed, as you go through this book. The answers to these and related questions will serve as a kind of leadership scorecard, whether you are about to take on a new position or you are a seasoned veteran of management. Good luck!

A Now that you have left [name your particular medical leadership position]:
  1 What does your department [division, hospital, or other institution] look like: better, worse, or about the same?
  2 How many internal candidates applied for your job when you left?
  3 How did you assist in the transition to a new leader?
  4 Did you participate in the choice of a new leader?
B During the period that you were [name your particular medical leadership position]:
  1 Was patient-centred care effectively promoted in every possible way?
  2 Did the standards of clinical care improve?
  3 Are you better able to measure the results of clinical activity in your area?
  4 Regarding recruitment and/or retention of personnel,
    a Who left and who arrived?
    b Did those who retired under your leadership feel valued and comfortable?
  5 Were your 360 degree evaluations consistent and always improving?
  6 What processes in the organization were you instrumental in developing?
  7 Were you able to set up a system of communication that effectively got all individuals and groups involved?
  8 Did you have a positive relationship with both your clinicians and management?
  9 Did you walk the tightrope of representing your constituents but supporting the organization?
  10 Regarding programs, how would you assess the changes, additions, and modifications that were made under your leadership?

11 What were the metrics of research and education under your leadership, and did you change them for the better?
12 Did your leadership promote the organization's vision and mission?
13 Did you change the culture of your department [division, hospital, or other institution] for the better?
14 Regarding decision making,
    a How many people would be engaged in decision making under your leadership?
    b If and when tough decisions were made, some of your colleagues were obviously not happy, but were the decisions fair?
15 How did you engage your staff in planning, especially strategic planning?
16 What happened to your area's share of the resource pie in the organization?
17 Were you able to participate in effective capital development and renewal in the hospital [or other institution in which you were employed]?
18 Was fund-raising successful to support the mission and vision of the hospital [or other institution in which you worked]?
19 Did you take advantage of your position to champion fund-raising efforts?
C Finally, of some, but less, importance:
    1 Did everyone like you?
    2 Did everyone agree with your decisions?
    3 Were all your decisions the right ones?

1 Medical Leadership Is Different

Leadership is based on inspiration, not domination; on cooperation, not intimidation.

– William Arthur Wood

The Hospital Setting

Some years ago Community Hospital A experienced a serious crisis at the highest levels of leadership.

SITUATION 1.1

LEADERSHIP CRISIS AT A LARGE NORTH AMERICAN COMMUNITY HOSPITAL: *Who's Running This Hospital Anyway?*

In mid 1996 a crisis loomed at one of the biggest hospitals in a large North American city.[2] Long regarded as a health care institution delivering high-quality care to a vast number of local residents, the hospital was facing a confrontation that was brewing between the medical staff and hospital management, headed by the president and chief executive officer. Mr X, a highly intelligent, strong-minded, hard-working executive and former health care provider, saw it as his mandate to gain better control of the hospital's activities and budgeting. One strategy that he considered was to adopt the concept of doctors becoming *salaried employees* in the organization, rather than continuing with the traditional fee-for-service model and doctor independence.

Mr X began discussing this innovation at the board of trustees level, and because of his strength and persuasive nature, his thoughts were beginning to gain traction with board members. The president and the vice-president of the hospital's medical staff association (MSA) were also members of the board, as stipulated under the jurisdiction's Public Hospital Act. Until that point, the mandate of the MSA had been rather mundane and, as at many hospitals, pretty much limited to the arrangement of intermittent staff parties and the reception of visiting dignitaries. At the time, Doctor A, a general vascular surgeon, was president of the association, and Doctor B, a cardiologist, was vice-president.

That year the MSA undertook more than the arrangement of the occasional staff party. However, the plan to change the payment structure at the hospital (which I'll call Community Hospital A) didn't materialize, because of emphatic resistance from the medical staff, led by Doctors A and B.

Mr X then decided to go in another direction. The position of chief of staff became open. As with MSA executive positions, chief of staff was not generally a sought-after post; it did, however, involve the important chair of the medical advisory committee and membership on the board of trustees. As events unfolded, Mr X evidently approached Doctor C, an otolaryngologist at another hospital, to apply for the position of chief of staff. This was an unusual move because the hospital's by-laws clearly stated that the chief of staff must be a member in good standing of the hospital's own faculty. Furthermore, the staff of the otolaryngology department at Community Hospital A had not even proposed a possible recruit themselves, an exception unheard of in modern medical appointments. Here was a professional being parachuted in by the CEO to a surprised department of 'independent' practitioners.

What was the motivation behind Mr X's action? As the medical staff saw it, presumably he thought that this new hire would help lead the charge towards his ultimate agenda of doctors' subjugation.

Doctors A and B investigated the situation a little further and reviewed the terms of reference of the MSA and the implications of board membership. They then called an urgent meeting of the MSA on the subject of this single proposed recruitment. The turnout was surprisingly healthy for an MSA meeting, and during this meeting it came to light that Mr X had reportedly been trying to make changes in a number of other areas as well in the restructuring of the hospital.

The MSA immediately hired legal counsel and voted to support a levy of $1,000 per active staff and $500 per courtesy staff, amassing a legal war chest of $500,000 in about thirty days.

The MSA was wise in retaining Ms Z, a bright, ambitious, and tenacious lawyer, to represent their interests. They also went to the jurisdiction's medical association (JMA) to tell their story and were immediately rewarded by an on-the-spot contribution of $50,000 by the JMA executive to the MSA legal fund of Community Hospital A. The ramifications of Mr X's proposal at a large reputable public hospital were clearly of concern to the stewards of the medical profession in the entire jurisdiction.

A subsequent meeting of the MSA enjoyed virtually full attendance, and it was evident that as a professional staff the members felt unified, strong, and eager to make their collective voice heard.

The proposed otolaryngologist, Doctor C, got to the interview stage for the chief of staff position, but he had to jump the hurdle of meeting his own future departmental members who were not familiar with him at all. That meeting did not go well. The department's otolaryngologists declared publicly that they did *not* support his appointment.

Since hospital by-laws stated that a member to be recruited had to be a collegial professional who worked well with colleagues, this declaration of non-support would have seemed like the end of the proposed appointment. But it wasn't. Mr X took steps to circumvent the lack of enthusiasm for his choice of the next chief of staff. As CEO of Community Hospital A, he ordered a revision of the hospital by-laws that would remove the language about collegiality and essentially extinguish the flames of protest.

For the medical staff, that move meant war! The medical staff association unanimously passed a motion of non-confidence in the CEO and the board of trustees, and its members attended public board meetings in droves as white-lab-coated objectors.

The board of trustees (which consisted of a variety of interested local people, in an era when boards had fewer teeth and responsibilities than they do now, more than a decade later) began to unravel; resignations piled up, and meetings became increasingly disorganized.

Prior to the annual general meeting, hundreds of local supporters were encouraged by members of the MSA to pay the ten-dollar fee and join up as voting members of the hospital corporation; during this campaign they become educated about the events of the previous several months at Community Hospital A.

At the open annual general meeting, held in early 1998, the members of the corporation voted to throw out the board and the CEO and replace them with a new board, a series of supervisors, and then a new president and CEO. Now, more than ten years later, the relationship between the medical staff and the current CEO is courteous, mutually respectful, and collaborative, and the doctors generally feel that they have reached a stage of meaningful collaboration and effectiveness in the daily functioning of a large active hospital in a big city.

Who was running this ship anyway? For years Community Hospital A had carried on serving its patients in an exemplary way in collaboration with the medical and surgical staff, who were well educated and accomplished and who also considered themselves truly independent of the hospital's organizational processes (other than the consumption of resources, of course). This independence was confirmed by their relative absence on the institutional organizational chart (the 'org chart'), with the exception of the chair of the medical advisory committee and the president and vice-president of the medical staff association, all of whom sat on the board of trustees.

The extent to which the doctors had significant influence on the affairs of Community Hospital A was clearly debatable; they played virtually no roles in operations, their divisional and departmental leaders were relegated to the preparation of call schedules, and their representatives on the board of trustees were obviously easily outnumbered in this democracy. In other words, the org chart of Community Hospital A appeared to pay only lip service to the medical staff, the independent clinicians who 'practised' in the institution. Who would want to be a medical leader in this culture?

The keys to the doctors having important influence on the fate of Community Hospital A in this situation were unanimity, a clear message, solid legal advice, and an ability to work within the rules stated in institutional by-laws and the Hospital Act.

Comment: The medical leaders at Community Hospital A changed the organization, but they needed a kind of mutiny to do it because their stated place in the organization was dubious, to say the least.

Simply put, the events at Community Hospital A demonstrate that an unusual non-unionized group of individuals, the medical staff, worked hard at managing patients' problems but, from an operational standpoint, spent most of their time hibernating. Once the angry bears were wakened by a crisis, however, they were inspired to action and changed the organization forever. Although the ultimate outcome was positive, was this confrontation the best tool to exact lasting change? I hope that, after digesting the following chapters, the reader will be able to devise an approach to this problem that would be equally successful but less confrontational.

It's interesting to note that while all this was transpiring and obviously consuming the time, effort, and emotions of many, the community hospital and its health care providers continued to provide capable management to thousands of sick patients.

So You Want to Be a Medical Leader? Medicine vs Business

Countless volumes are available to assist the aspiring business leader[3,4,5] (see also under 'Managers vs Leaders: Let Your Managers Manage' in chapter 5). Books, courses, seminars, crash courses, diplomas, and degrees all attest to the intense interest in leadership and its importance in business success. Styles of leadership have been examined, reviewed, and dissected and often have succeeded in pigeonholing individuals in leadership positions so that they fit nicely into a specific definition or style such as those described by Daniel Goleman.[6]

The conventional leader in business usually participates in a pyramidal structure of governance and management in which positions are defined in detail and a clear reporting structure is in place: the board of trustees or board of directors (or governors) is collectively responsible for the results reported by the organization, and the president and chief executive officer is responsible to that board. In fact, boards of directors assume more responsibility today than they did in the past, when directorships were frequently examples of cronyism and a licence to accept handsome fees for relatively little work. Modern boards are truly accountable.

The major role of the board is to choose the president and CEO and intermittently evaluate his or her performance; in few cases does the board become involved with management decisions, because the president should ordinarily be left to oversee the management of the organization. In the simplest terms, every meeting of the board decides if the president is to retain his or her job and then involves itself in substantive changes, new directions, and major financial commitments.

In business, only the board can oust the senior management, and that is good – unless the board is ill-informed and doesn't recognize the quality of a CEO who is in a difficult or new situation; then the wrong person may suffer. In medicine, especially in the hospital setting, it is different. The admitting physician, an 'independent operator' who is a private businessman and appointed to a hospital to have privileges to use hospital resources, is the 'director' of the patient care delivered, whether in an academic institution or in a community setting. On the other hand, the actual care delivered on the front lines to patients is totally dependent on salaried hospital employees, who are usually unionized.

Traditionally, doctors have restricted their activities to patient care issues, and seldom have they been involved in day-to-day management and hospital operations on a greater scale; therefore, a 'we-they' relationship with management has often evolved, that is, the doctors vs administration or management.

Administration is frequently a term of derision, with administrators being seen as the enemy by those whose sole altruistic purpose is to help their fellow human beings. This clinical activity, of course, uses significant hospital resources and earns significant income for the practitioner. Doctors tend to feel that the use of these hospital resources is their *right* rather than a privilege.

It is also noteworthy that independent doctors, who see themselves as private businessmen, are less likely to change their behaviour or to be enthusiastic participants in organizational processes, especially when those processes represent a change in long-standing traditional practices.

In a public or private system, with this adversarial relationship between practitioners and hospital management, doctors are often in the position of encouraging patients to advocate to senior administration (and to politicians in a public system) for more resources. This attitude has been encouraged in the past by the relatively exalted position that doctors have held in society.

In business, if a number of middle managers are unhappy with the direction that senior management has taken, they might object at their peril, given the pyramidal hierarchal structure – strenuous objection might lead to an accelerated pink slip. In medicine, the unusual position of the clinician in the core business of the organization (delivering care to patients) offers an opportunity for influence perhaps not seen in the business sector. In fact at Community Hospital A in 1996, as seen in situation 1.1, a discontented medical staff basically threw out the board and senior management, despite not having official line authority.

In the past, medical leadership has consisted of divisional heads, to whom division members report, and department heads, to whom the divisional heads and their constituents report. The department heads are directly accountable to the chairman of the board of trustees and the president and CEO of the hospital. Other positions such as vice-president of medical affairs, chair of the medical advisory committee, chief of staff, and the executives of the medical staff association have taken on variable definitions and relevance in different institutions; these posts have generally been assigned responsibilities that pertain to aspects of professional behaviour, recruitment, quality of care, and other issues described in the jurisdiction's Hospital Act.

The actual day-to-day operations of the hospital are usually run by health care professionals, who may have backgrounds in accounting, health administration, and especially nursing. These individual management roles have been designated director of operations, executive director, finance officer, and, of course, vice-presidents, president, and CEO.

Not surprisingly, therefore, a hospital usually requires two organizational charts to capture the two lines of responsibility, one for hospital operations and one for the medical staff. The first, depicted in figure 1.1, indicates clearly that nursing, paramedical personnel, and others such as housekeeping and facilities report ultimately to the CEO and the board in a fashion familiar to all typical businesses. Figure 1.2 reflects the leadership positions for the heads of the various medical divisions and departments. The position of the board of trustees at the top of figure 1.2 and at the bottom of figure 1.1 is meant to emphasize the varied ways in which the organizational chart may be depicted in different organizations. Whatever diagram is used, *everyone* reports ultimately to the board.

The only obvious connections between the two organizational charts are (1) at the CEO level, to whom the department heads are accountable, and (2) at the board level, with the three representatives mentioned, that is, the chief of staff, and the president and the vice-president of the medical staff association.

Is this beginning to look like the optimal organizational structure? Some say that if it can't be pictured on one page, it's unworkable. We are already at two pages and, get ready, are not finished yet.

The Programmatic Structure of the Hospital

We've agreed that the place of medical professionals in a hospital's administration is unique in that they often possess little or no line authority on day-to-day operations in the usual divisional or departmental structure. Yet, medical professionals certainly have influence because they play unequivocally necessary roles in the core business of the institution. The relationships thus forged are challenging, to be sure; however, to add to the complexity, and perhaps confuse matters even more, let me here introduce the programmatic structure of the hospital.

For the past twenty years or so, medical organizations have begun to adopt a patient-centred approach to all of their activities. Previously, hospitals were built and their functional processes designed with the health care provider in mind. To give the customers, clients, or patients the kind of service that they required, those in the medical field finally

Figure 1.1: Management structure of a virtual organization with three hospitals

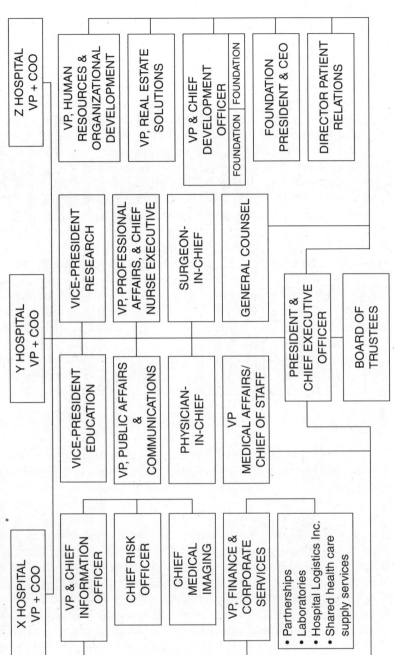

Figure 1.2: Medical structure in a virtual, academic hospital

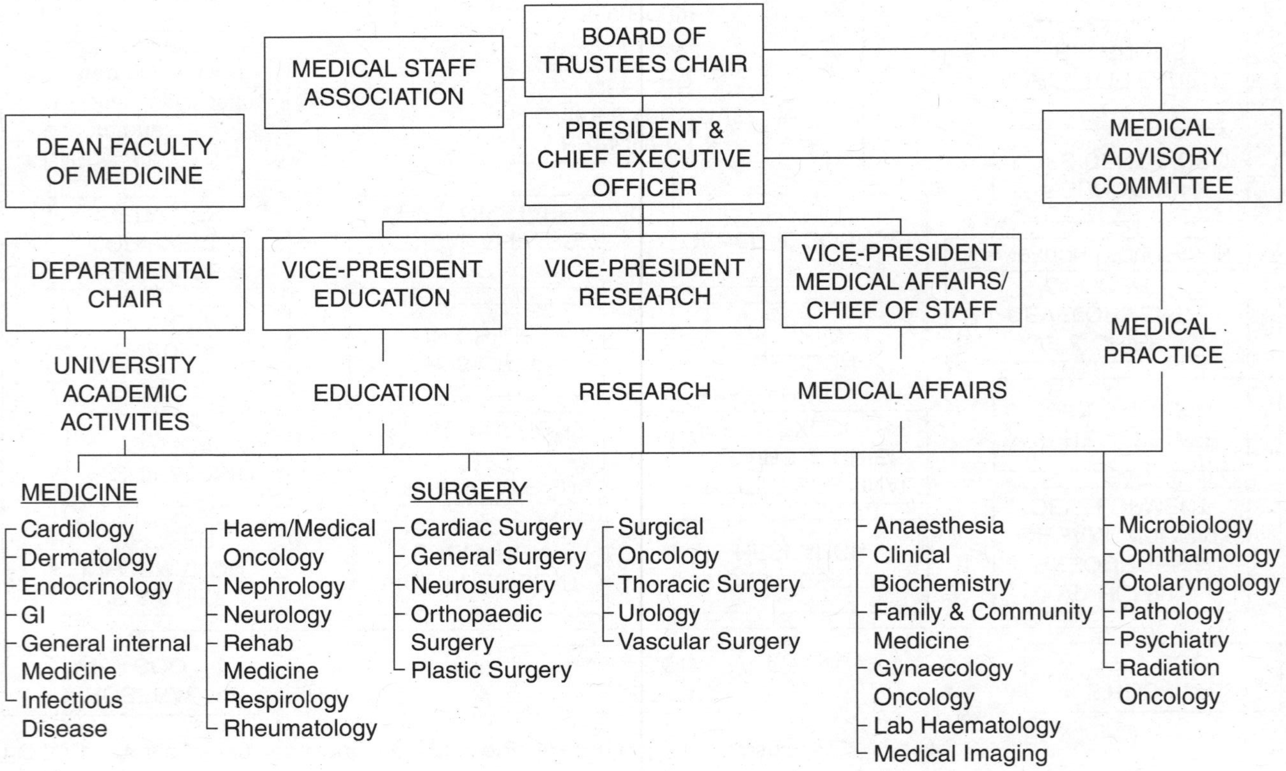

BOARD OF TRUSTEES CHAIR

DEAN FACULTY OF MEDICINE

MEDICAL STAFF ASSOCIATION

MEDICAL ADVISORY COMMITTEE

PRESIDENT & CHIEF EXECUTIVE OFFICER

DEPARTMENTAL CHAIR

VICE-PRESIDENT EDUCATION

VICE-PRESIDENT RESEARCH

VICE-PRESIDENT MEDICAL AFFAIRS/ CHIEF OF STAFF

UNIVERSITY ACADEMIC ACTIVITIES

EDUCATION

RESEARCH

MEDICAL AFFAIRS

MEDICAL PRACTICE

MEDICINE
- Cardiology
- Dermatology
- Endocrinology
- GI
- General internal Medicine
- Infectious Disease
- Haem/Medical Oncology
- Nephrology
- Neurology
- Rehab Medicine
- Respirology
- Rheumatology

SURGERY
- Cardiac Surgery
- General Surgery
- Neurosurgery
- Orthopaedic Surgery
- Plastic Surgery
- Surgical Oncology
- Thoracic Surgery
- Urology
- Vascular Surgery

- Anaesthesia
- Clinical Biochemistry
- Family & Community Medicine
- Gynaecology Oncology
- Lab Haematology
- Medical Imaging
- Microbiology
- Ophthalmology
- Otolaryngology
- Pathology
- Psychiatry
- Radiation Oncology

realized that everything surrounding patient care had to be reviewed and assessed through the patient's eyes, as was so clearly articulated in the book *Through the Patient's Eyes: Understanding and Promoting Patient-Centered Care* (1993), edited by Margaret Gerteis et al.[7] It emphasizes that better, safer, and more efficient patient care can be delivered if all the people and processes involved are engaged according to the needs of the patient, not just the provider.

As an aside, some prefer the old standby noun *patient* over the terms *customer* and *client*, which have become standard terminology, because the latter two seem to degrade a personal service to a commodity; this is today's reality, but it still may rankle.

When patients seek care, they usually have little idea what department or division may offer them the best diagnosis and treatment. However, they probably know what disease or disease category concerns them – ergo, the birth of *programmatic organization* within hospitals. Whereas patients used to be managed on a specific service in a specific department, they now enter the care continuum in a program such as Trauma/Critical Care, Oncology, Heart and Circulation, Gastrointestinal, or Neuroscience.

The programmatic structure implies that a patient will be managed by a professional team, which is better integrated than it was in the past and which has come together to offer more seamless and coordinated care. Therefore, a patient with neurological symptoms will presumably be managed by a team of neurologists, neurosurgeons, neuroradiologists, nurses with a special interest in neurological disease, and occupational and physical therapists. All of the practitioners on this team belong to the neuroscience program.

How this operates efficiently in real life and how the improved outcomes and more efficient patient care can be demonstrated may be a subject for debate, but the idea has been adequately seductive that it is now the norm rather than the exception in hospital organization. (This may be analogous to the transformation of medical student education, which has evolved into small-group education and problem-based learning [PBL] from the more traditional subject-based learning of the 1960s. By now PBL has been adopted in countless centres around the world without any convincing evidence that the product, that is, the competent doctor, has improved. But many seem to think it works. Unfortunately, in a variety of domains in medicine our measurement methods of straightforward stuff are lagging far behind other scientific advances in the field.)

The programs listed above have administrative structures within the organization, and medical professionals must play critical roles in the programs for obvious reasons. So, how do these leaders associate and interact with the leaders in the traditional divisional and departmental structure? The answer is, 'Very carefully.' Because the traditional medical leadership model is usually depicted as a chart on a two-dimensional sheet of paper, the additional dimension of the programmatic structure creates a so-called matrix that can be adequately captured in a 3-D diagram (see figure 1.3). Easy to show on paper, but how on earth can this work in real life, and how could this interact with the governance model of hospital operations in figure 1.1? At this point, let me further add to the confusion.

The programmatic leaders may also be the traditional divisional or departmental leaders, but often they are not. Therefore, it's not uncommon for a division head in neurosurgery, for example, to report to both the surgeon-in-chief and the neuroscience program head, and that same neuroscience program head may well be a neurosurgeon who, in fact, within his own division reports back to that neurosurgical division head. Or, how about the hospital surgeon-in-chief who reports academically to the relevant chair of the university department, who within the hospital reports to the surgeon-in-chief, while both of these leaders within their 'home' division of general surgery report to the general surgery division head, yet another surgeon. Dizzy yet? All of these currently exist at some universities.

A business leader might view this scheme and ask, 'Now let me get this straight. You have a complex leadership model of divisional and departmental heads who have little or no line authority in the organization but seem to have enough influence because of their function in the organization that they can help to effect change or, in some cases as we've seen, demand change. Right? Now you add another dimension of programmatic leadership that involves the same activity (patient care) and that interacts with the traditional leadership model with no defined relationship between the two, and it too carries no line authority. Are you trying to think of ways to complicate your life or do you just like to court indecision, conflict, and disaster?'

Those are legitimate questions, especially from business leaders who boast the sign on their desk 'The buck stops here.'

> **In hospital medical leadership the buck stops in a whole bunch of places in addition to the desk of the CEO (and/or the dean, in the academic setting).**

Figure 1.3: The medical service program matrix, representing the surgical divisions of departments only of X, Y, and Z hospitals

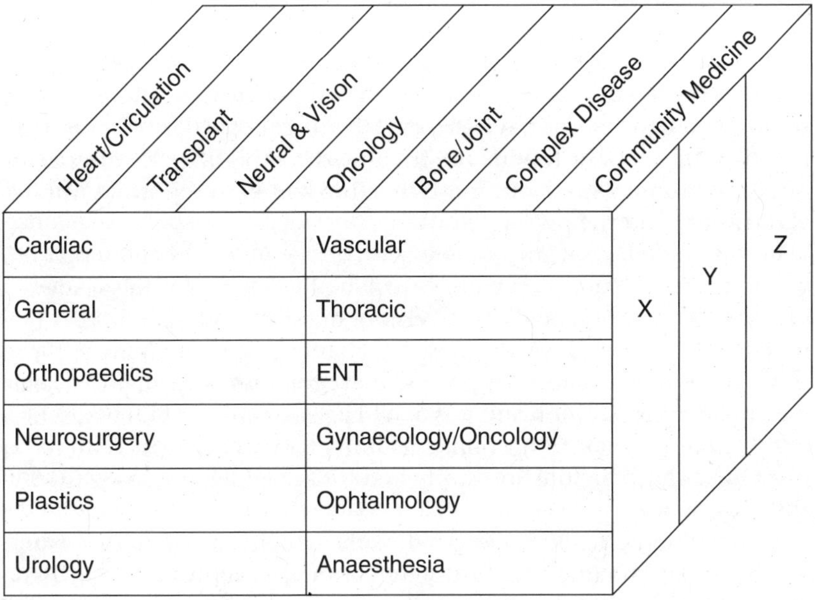

Heart/Circulation	Transplant	Neural & Vision	Oncology	Bone/Joint	Complex Disease	Community Medicine
Cardiac			Vascular			
General			Thoracic			
Orthopaedics			ENT			
Neurosurgery			Gynaecology/Oncology			
Plastics			Ophtalmology			
Urology			Anaesthesia			

The Place of the University in the Academic Setting

The first organizational charts focus on the complex hospital structure without reference to the academic domain in which the university obviously plays a critical role. In a sense, the dean of the medical faculty in some American centres may be the effective president and CEO of the organization in that he or she controls to a great extent the resource allocation to faculty members, and reports to the university president and the board of governors of the university. In other situations, that fiscal and academic influence may well be in the hands of individual specialty chairs, with or without some sort of tithing to the dean that recognizes their academic obligations. In the United States, therefore, your ultimate report in an academic hospital is usually to the specialty chair or to the dean of the faculty of medicine; in Canada your reporting responsibility represents a delicate balance between your hospital president and the dean of the faculty (and his or her chairs). The Canadian setting is complicated by affiliation agreements between the medical school and participating teaching hospitals; in some cases these agreements afford the dean significant influence on hospital direction and program development, and in others, the hospitals retain greater independence in their ability to develop programs and focuses of academic excellence. To complicate the setting further, some Canadian centres have adopted the so-called chair/chief model, in which the chair of the university department is also the physician- or surgeon-in-chief, creating a closer linkage between academic responsibility and the purse strings.

In the academic setting, or any setting that you are contemplating, you must ask the question who is working for whom. Do the academic physicians and surgeons set the vision, mission, and agenda and formulate plans, and does the hospital management implement those plans? Or is there some other process that promotes movement towards the organization's vision and mission? The clear answer to the question varies from hospital to hospital and university to university, and you must have clarity before you apply and/or accept the proposed leadership position.

The traditional academic leadership, the hospital medical leadership, and the programmatic structure of the hospital can only coexist if all the personalities and intellects involved are on the same page. That comes from a long-standing single focus on *patient welfare* as the ultimate objective for everyone, and also from leadership that can tie these apparently disparate groups together. One way to alleviate the potential conflict is to have the divisional or departmental leaders also act as program heads whenever possible. On the other hand, having the traditional leadership separate, as described above, might arguably produce more valuable debate when resource allocation is discussed.

A matrix structure in the hospital, then, depends on the compatibility of the players and the ability and influence of the major executive on the clinical side, which is usually the vice-president or medical director in charge of clinical programs for the whole organization.

The job description of the program medical director, regardless of the exact language used, will have many elements that overlap the responsibilities of the divisional and departmental chiefs. This is surely an invitation for confusion in the minds of business professors; however, the interests that are common to both may be the following:

• Planning

- Clinical priorities
- Systems improvements
- Performance measurement
- Education and research
- A mandate to represent the program and the organization externally

How these tasks are assigned and how individuals are made accountable is ultimately up to the individual who is in overall charge of clinical programs.

I'd love to know what sense the management consultant and author Peter Drucker might make of this apparent confusion and what kind of composite organizational chart might capture all aspects of the foregoing.

The Patient

At some point in our medical service industry came the revelation that the customer is the most important consideration when we speak of efficient cost-effective service. *Patient-centred care*[8] is the current and future buzzword of health care, as it should be, and patients have ever-increasing expectations that they will receive timely, high-level care provided by the best medical experts available in an error-free environment.

One simply has to read the daily media reports that indicate how powerful the patient has become in the design of the structures and processes fundamental to health care in this century – and that has to be a good thing. Why has this happened? First, patient-centredness is fitting because the customer or client has ultimate influence over his or her care, especially in a system where the patient is paying for the services through taxes and/or insurance. The three major issues of interest to patients and providers alike are *access to care, quality of care,* and *avoidance of medical error and liability.*

Patients in North America now realize that the health care system is far from perfect and that they, in fact, are in the driver's seat. As a result, some of the critical reasons for health care cost increases are the over-investigation of patients' problems, the so-called cover-your-ass (CYA) syndrome, and the retention of patients in hospital longer than usual or necessary to ensure good health and to avoid the unexpected. In addition, whereas doctors used to be held in the same high esteem as was any respected member of society, they are now seen more as agents who help provide the care that the patient demands and deserves – the doctors are, indeed, accountable for it – and that too is probably a good thing. So, we conclude that we have the following conundrum:

1 We have patients with high expectations of care and who want everything done regardless of cost (sometimes unreasonably).
2 We face increasingly higher costs of health care delivery with an absolute need for improved efficiency.
3 We need to address medical error and decrease untoward events.
4 We must do all this with the cooperation and the enthusiasm of a large group of well-educated, relatively wealthy, *independent* practitioners who are, in fact, dependent on hospital resources (especially with regard to surgeons) and who are professionals on whom the hospital is very dependent for (a) excellent care with good outcomes, (b) a strong reputation, and (c) attraction of donations from benefactors.

Let me say at the outset here that I will resolutely avoid the controversial issue of a two-tier system of payment – private and public; that's a separate, long, and winding road.

How do we organize and lead this group of difficult independent doctors? Leadership of such a group is often unwanted by the constituents because the doctors would like nothing better than to be left alone and to look after their clinical and academic responsibilities, make their living, and advance their careers without interruption from 'management.'

The Critical Step: Doctors Become Involved in Management

First, we must *change the model*. We must invite the professionals into the tent and reorganize the tent so that doctors have a significant role to play in the operations (processes) of the organization. This requires education on the part of the doctors, patience on the part of the administrative leaders, and time. In other words, the organizational charts have to be melded, at least in part, to engage doctors and nurses to play much more substantive roles in hospital operations and decision making.

In business, this devolution of power and influence from the top is referred to as *flattening the pyramid* and has proven effective in many manufacturing companies where workers and middle managers have been applauded for initiating important changes on the production lines. To date, this has occurred sporadically in the hospital setting, and in these instances health care providers have come to feel engaged and are contributing to the organization as a whole. In fact, currently at Community Hospital A (see situation 1.1) the CEO meets regularly with health care professionals, there are vehicles for information transfer and decision making, and the culture of collaboration seems to be pervasive, according to the senior clinicians working there.

Many of the following comments about leadership in a hospital setting relate to surgical processes as these are far more expensive than any other procedures; however, all clinical activities in a hospital and the resultant resource allocations remain under one roof.

The good news is that most clinicians are intelligent and can grasp the fundamentals of arithmetic, accounting, and human resource practices with relative ease. The bad news is that most clinicians think they inherently know more than they do know and that they don't have to be educated. There are various courses on offer at a number of North American schools, such as Harvard University, Kellogg School of Management, Rotman School of Management, and University of Toronto's Department of Health Policy, Management, and Evaluation (HPME), which focus on issues pertinent to the present or future leader. However, many feel that these courses simply represent a 'ticket to ride,' obligatory for those seriously interested in management.

The real preparation comes from on-the-job training, which requires putting in time, facing drudgery and paperwork, and making interminable small decisions before any big decisions can be made with confidence and authority. (For those who wish to be major health care leaders, there is no substitute for more formal and intensive courses in management, which can be pursued without the daily burdens of patient care and hospital matters.)

The average clinician already has a day job. So you simply won't have enough time to devote to management issues, at least early in your career. There are many intermediate steps and jobs that can be taken by the future medical leader in order to invest in administrative training, however, from the simple ones such as the scheduling and organization of rounds to the more challenging ones such as project leader, quality officer, associate head of a division or a department, or educational director.

The best leader in any organization is one who has a head start by knowing and understanding various aspects of that organization, while, of course, being able to extricate oneself from the details of past experiences when assuming the leadership position. You must *not* micromanage, and you must learn to delegate and to let your managers manage (see chapter 5, under 'Managers vs Leaders: Let Your Managers Manage'). So, what does the job involve?

2 The Medical Leader's Job

It seems natural that a job you apply for in any marketplace would come with a clearly articulated job description. Unfortunately, in the medical field this is not necessarily so. Even if there is a job description, it may be so bland and generic that you have no idea what you're getting into. On the other hand, that may be good news, in that a good medical leader who takes such a vaguely described position may have an opportunity to define the job according to his or her vision and aspirations.

Job Description

In many hospitals throughout North America the leadership jobs may be regarded as a penance in which a succession of respected clinicians have to take turns representing their constituents, often tolerating administration. This is especially true of many community hospitals in which a chief of division (or department) can't wait for the next in line to take over.

The culture in such a hospital obviously separates the clinical domain from the management domain, and in many institutions this works well, with profit margins and product lines consistently positive. In these hospitals the medical leader may sit on the medical advisory committee and be part of senior management, acting as an advocate for staff and as a participant in a two-way conduit for the information that clinicians and management need from each other.

The extent to which this medical leader becomes involved in the hospital's operations (processes) is often limited to running an operating room in the case of surgery and coordinating service activities in the case of medicine. A doctor may take a position as chief of staff and in some organizations may play a more substantive role in planning capital assignment and the like. A credentialling office often employs a physician as well, someone who may be the vice-president of medical affairs (or another flattering name) to represent the credentialling function of the hospital.

As these jobs vary significantly from hospital to hospital, it is imperative that the responsibilities be clarified for the applicant. The positions described, whose appointees aren't involved in major management activities, don't pay very much (hospital funds for salaries are always scarce), which is probably one of the reasons that doctors generally don't seek them out. For the outlay of time required, a doctor can earn much more by caring for patients than by pushing paper.

There is a current shift, however, to involve medical leaders in more meaningful roles in the hospital organization, and this is where a prospective leader has an opportunity to become seriously involved in hospital activities. In some institutions the medical leader may be an integral part of the running of the organization, a framework that may take years to evolve. And, as stated previously, a medical specialist may have to devote time and energy for further personal education in order to focus on becoming a true contributor in the field rather than a bystander or a peripheral player.

Job descriptions are traditionally stated in terms of the *activities* of the occupant of the position. But perhaps we should be thinking in terms of the *expected outputs* of those activities, in much the same way that the educational objectives of a lecture are phrased, 'At the end of the lecture the student will be able to ...' (see, for example, under 'Twenty-Six Questions: The Metrics of Your Success as a Medical Leader' in the introduction to this book). Perhaps using both approaches would be useful here in detailing the elements of a job description for a medical leader.

For the purposes of discussion, most of this book will be addressing the following medical leadership positions:

- Hospital division head
- Hospital department head
- Hospital program director
- University department chair
- University division chair
- Other major medical leadership positions

The first three positions constitute the 'traditional' framework of most hospital clinical departments. In essence, there is a four-pronged challenge facing you as a medical leader:

1 To represent your constituents (the clinicians) with vigour
2 To encourage your members to participate in hospital activities
3 To implement hospital policies, ensuring that in the end the patient is well served and that the quality of care is at or above an accepted standard
4 To ensure, in an academic setting, that the teaching and research mandates are embraced

Some of the responsibilities of a truly involved medical leader may include the following, and the most important among these will be addressed in more detail in subsequent chapters.

Responsibilities of the Medical Leader

Recruiting and Retaining Personnel

The most important activity of any medical leader involves recruiting and retaining staff (see 'Recruitment and Retention' in chapter 4). The medical leader will be responsible for selection and screening and, just as importantly, interviews, tours, and impact analyses, as well as for formulating offer sheets and ensuring that all aspects of recruitment (including real estate issues if the candidate is external) are being looked after.

As will be discussed, special retention strategies for an individual should be pursued only if the agreement struck does not compromise an already strong team (the Alex Rodriguez syndrome*). Resentment is not supportive of team building.

Your overall objective here will be to assemble a hard-working and effective, stable team whose members work well together and meet the organization's mandate.

---

* Alex Rodriguez is a superstar baseball player who was paid an exorbitant salary of $25 million over ten years by the Texas Rangers and then continued his career with the New York Yankees. In both settings he was successful, but he was resented by teammates who were 'mere mortals.' His former Yankees manager, Joe Torre, wrote in a memoir that his common nickname, 'A-Rod,' was bastardized by teammates to be 'A-fraud.'

Building Careers and Managing People

Once the medical leader has recruited the right individual, the process of building that individual's career begins. The leader is committed to helping to accomplish the following four objectives:

1 Provide resources for the new recruit
2 Protect time for the recruit's academic activities, if necessary
3 Render appropriate advice, as needed, regarding the best ways to succeed
4 Ensure that the clinician is aware of all hospital policies that must be followed

As a good medical leader you will spend the majority of your time managing people; this is the principal day-to-day activity of a leader in a complex organization, especially where professionals play important roles. (Note: some people don't agree with the term *managing people* because it may sound condescending. I appreciate that concern and propose that the term really means 'managing the events and processes that require people skills.')

The output of this activity, of course, is the personal success and effectiveness of each of the individuals recruited by the medical leader.

Ensuring Quality of Patient Care

The major focus of the medical leader in an institution, as far as the hospital's raison d'être is concerned, is quality of patient care. Quality and efficiency of processes and, more important, the *right care at the right time* with attention to the elimination of medical error have always been critical. Error has been especially recognized to be a huge flaw in medical care, ever since the Institute of Medicine's publication *To Err Is Human: Building a Safety Health System* (2000).[9] This will be covered in chapter 6, under 'Quality of Care and Risk in Medicine.'

The medical leader must be an outspoken advocate for patients and lead continuous quality-improvement and patient-safety initiatives. The best, safest, and most efficient patient care will be the result.

Involving the 'Troops' in Planning

Strategic long-range planning must be embraced by the whole hospital organization, but in the past it has tended to be not even a top-down process; it has been a top-up process between senior management and the board.

As a medical leader you have the major responsibility of ensuring that the 'troops' have adequate input into a consensus model, and you should even conduct separate planning exercises, if necessary, to ensure that all constituents have an opportunity to contribute. But get used to one fact: things are changing so quickly that if you want your organization to keep up, formal exercises will have to be frequent, probably as often as every three years (see 'Strategic Planning' in chapter 7).

The crucial outputs of effective strategic planning, in addition to meeting the hospital mandates of exemplary patient care (and academic objectives in teaching institutions), are progress, innovation, and an ability to change with the times.

Providing Input into Hospital Processes and Cost-Efficiency

As stated, medical leaders in some organizations are now becoming more involved with the actual running of the hospital, a welcome improvement that closes the gap between administration and clinical. In essence, the medical leader should actively participate in the planning *and execution* of the clinical and academic vision of the hospital.

The traditional tasks of the medical leader include the following:

1 Assigning hospital resources
2 Preparing schedules
3 Troubleshooting

Today's medical leader should also be contributing to the following undertakings:

4 Creating and implementing hospital processes and by-laws (see 'Strategic Planning' in chapter 7)
5 Reaching activity and volume targets
6 Monitoring performance, with the responsibility of continuously improving quality (see 'Quality of Care and Risk in Medicine' in chapter 6)
7 Meeting financial responsibilities, including capital planning, case-costing, and introducing innovative cost-saving strategies (see 'Hospital Finances and Capital Investment' in chapter 8)
8 Fund-raising (see 'Fund-Raising' below and in chapter 9)

In these functions the medical leader may chair or participate in a large number of committees, including those dealing with quality, operations, leadership, and operating-room activities. A truly collaborative approach to the business of medicine will be the result.

Academic Mandate

In the academic hospital, medical leaders must have a demonstrated commitment to education and research, and they must consistently support those aspects of the hospital's mission. That doesn't mean that the medical leader must be a successful basic researcher or an educational award winner; it does mean that as a medical leader you must have a *vision* about the academic success of your constituents, and you must be prepared to promote that vision with time protection, resource allocation, and an appropriate system of monitoring and recognition of performance.

Excellent measures of success with regard to your academic mandate will include proven innovation, scientific advances, manuscript publication, research grants, and a list of students who have been taught effectively and who report that consistently.

Representation

As a medical leader you will represent your team in a variety of settings. Depending on the position involved, you may sit on the hospital's medical advisory council, senior management, or board of trustees. These particular activities will be more time-consuming than desired, and you must regard them as necessities if you are going to keep informed and inform and take your constituents to a higher level of involvement.

Fund-Raising

Most modern hospitals face major shortfalls in research funding, educational funding, capital equipment, capital development, and building maintenance.

Clinicians have a huge advantage in nurturing relationships with grateful patients and in building projects around the subjects that can be referred to various particular disease processes. A wide variety of opportunities exist, often aided by foundations, and medical leaders have a distinct responsibility to be a critical factor in the promotion of these fund-raising initiatives.

As a medical leader you will have a chance to work in these monetary trenches to help implement important projects that could not otherwise be funded (see also 'Fund-Raising' in chapter 9).

Special Projects

Resulting from planning processes or occasionally from mandates coming from licensing bodies, professional societies, and accrediting or credentialling bodies, special projects may be embraced by the hospital. These projects can only go ahead and be successful if there is adoption and approval by leadership and enthusiastic buy-in by the general workforce.

In the hospital setting a *senior champion* is virtually always required for a special project, and if there are clinical connotations to the project the medical or surgical leader is usually the appropriate flag bearer.

The following are examples of outputs of special projects: successful conversion to an electronic patient-record-keeping system; adoption of a surgical checklist (see 'Implementation' in chapter 7); and completion of an electronic surgical-booking form.

External Relations and Media Contact

The senior medical leader must frequently assume responsibility for a number of external relationships. Collaboration with other regional facilities, if a regional approach has been adopted, is absolutely essential to the well-being of the organization.

Contact with the media may be an important feature of the job description (see 'Media Relations' in chapter 9). In addition, communication and association with licensing bodies, accrediting or credentialling bodies, and professional associations may be especially crucial for the medical leader at various times.

Personal Accomplishments

As a medical leader you will spend most of your time attending to other professionals and to the interests of the hospital; nevertheless, you must remain a credible clinician, researcher, educator, and fundraiser to the extent that these roles are valued in the organization.

To be a professional leader in medicine you must be respected in the domains that are recognized by those whom you lead, and, as stated, if you're not personally a quadruple threat, you must demonstrate at least an enthusiasm to support all four domains.

The major accomplishment of your effective leadership will be organizational success, not your personal success.

The Intangible, but Important

Last, but far from least, the medical leader has responsibilities that speak to something more than the mechanics of leadership mentioned previously. If you are to be effective, you will have many details to attend to, but if you want to leave an indelible mark, you will inspire, stimulate, and encourage your colleagues to succeed; you will do everything in your power to facilitate that success.

In the era of accountability the medical leader is accountable to the hospital through the senior clinical executive, the CEO, and the board of trustees and, in the academic setting, to the chair of the division, the chair of the university department, the dean, and the university president.

Most of all, in personal clinical activities the doctor is *always* accountable to individual patients.

The job description of a medical leader may be simply stated, but it is complex in reality, both in activities and in outputs. The tasks may be simple and few or convoluted and many, depending on the leader's aspirations, his or her ability and desire to expand the stated job description, his or her desire for involvement in operations, and the culture of management in the organization that allows or encourages that involvement.

These subjects will be covered, presuming that the medical leader will want to bite off as much as possible in contributing to the organization and its members.

The definition of a leader may be rather circular – that is, a leader is one who has followers – or it may be related to the features of leadership that may be considered important. A leader must be willing to accept responsibility for the various components of leadership. As a medical leader you must be able to promote consensus and cooperation from those you are leading, and you must be able to assess short- and long-term situations and make decisions to enhance the status and progress of your organization.

> The only important questions to ask about a medical leader's achievements are, 'What does the place look like, and what kind of leadership is present, after she or he has left?'

As a medical leader you must support the growth of the people you lead and their careers, and your performance must enhance the organization's performance.

Getting people to come together, getting information and making decisions, and supporting the growth and success of others in the organization are the routes to success for a medical leader at any level.

Leadership Styles: What Makes a Good Leader?

Plenty has been written about why certain people are effective leaders – mostly based on the characteristics of present-day leaders. Psychological analysis may also help in defining the character traits that precede effective leadership. One such psychological evaluation tool is the abbreviated Myers-Briggs test.[10] By answering seventy-two questions you will obtain your type formula according to Carl Jung and Isabel Myers-Briggs, along with your strengths and preferences.

Many leaders are ENTJ (extroverted, intuitive, thinking, judging), which may represent a combination of characteristics aligned to the classic larger-than-life so-called field marshal boss, seen more frequently in the movies than in real life. However, Jim Collins, a business authority and writer, has observed that frequently the effective leader in business is a quiet, self-effacing person whose main set of characteristics is not the outward persona of the typical field marshal but simply one that gets results and that others follow. As reported in his book *Good to Great*,[11] Collins found that often the most effective leaders were quiet, modest, data-driven individuals who were always thinking about the success of others in the organization. The notion of the unassuming organization man behind the scenes is much more common and compelling than the typical in-your-face, Lee Iacocca version.

Effective leaders come in all shapes, sizes, colours, and stripes, and their common trait is that they get results. The problem in medicine is, what results are we talking about? Which of the following outcomes are you concerned about as a medical leader: patient outcomes, patient mortality, medical error, financial solvency, innovation, successful research and educational programs, doctors toeing the line, and/or recruitment and retention of the best minds and hands?

The answers are yes, yes, and yes – perhaps all of the above – but the response is clouded by our inability (to date, anyway) to reliably and accurately measure many of these variables on an ongoing, consistent basis.

Leaders have personalities that may play well in the positions they hold, but in many cases there may be traits that actually hamper effectiveness. Personality traits are ingrained and might be analogous to the genotype. However, the public behaviour, or phenotype, of a person can be learned and modified, and this phenotype can create styles of leadership that are useful in getting results.

Many aspects of effective medical leadership can be learned.

Daniel Goleman, Richard Boyatzis, and Annie McKee, in *Primal Leadership* (2004),[12] describe six styles of leading, and these have varying effects on the target followers. The six leadership styles that they examined in a large number of business leaders are coercive (also known as commanding or directive), authoritative (visionary), affiliative, democratic, pace-setting, and coaching.

It's fun to categorize known leaders into an appropriate slot, but when you go through the exercise, you quickly realize that styles are assigned to individuals according to how their *images* seem to fit; how they actually operate on a daily basis may be quite different and certainly more complex than a single style would allow.

It's important to realize that what you see may well not be what you get when you assess behaviour from afar. One of the most effective leaders I have ever worked with had the outward appearance of employing a typical coercive style.

SITUATION 2.1
DOCTOR D'S APPARENTLY COERCIVE LEADERSHIP STYLE:
Don't Judge a Book by Its Cover

Doctor D was (and is) decisive, powerful, futuristic, action-oriented, fast-talking (and, with his Australian accent, almost unintelligible when excited). As chief executive of a major teaching hospital he demands much of his team members and deals quickly and decisively with important prospective issues as well as unexpected ones.

In a public town hall meeting, when faced with some difficult confrontational questions, he once declared, 'Well, if you don't like what we're doing, you don't have to work here; you have other choices!' What could be a more coercive approach than that?

However, Doctor D is the most democratic person with whom I've ever had the privilege of working. He has always sought out the opinions of others, achieved buy-in from his managers, and been very respectful of all sides of a problem presented to him – and not infrequently he has changed his mind without concern for how conciliation would appear. to others. Clearly, his outward appearance to many spoke to one image (coercive), but his real modus operandi indicated quite another (democratic).

One of my favourite illustrations of a leadership style was that of Cito Gaston, who was manager of the Toronto Blue Jays baseball team in the early and mid 1990s. This was memorable for me, a baseball enthusiast who has followed the Blue Jays since their inception in the American League in 1977 (the interest had been spawned many years prior to that, when I was a member of the 'knothole gang' watching the Toronto Maple Leafs of the International League in the 1950s).

SITUATION 2.2
CITO GASTON, AN AFFILIATIVE LEADER: *Let Your Players Play*

Cito Gaston was regarded as the quintessential 'players' manager' because he was a patient, hands-off *macro*manager, seldom intervening in his coaches' teaching, although he had previously been a hitting coach. He was supportive of his players, especially the more experienced leaders in the clubhouse. Gaston let players play and concentrated on positive relationships among members of the team. He was never negative in public with the media.

Cito Gaston and the Toronto Blue Jays were rewarded with world championships for three years (1992, 1993, and 1994, the latter being a default position during the famous strike year), and, of course, like most managers, Gaston was fired several years later.

Ironically in 2008, Cito was surprisingly rehired to inject a struggling underperforming team with at least change or at most a significant improvement in results.

The above description is typical of the *affiliative* leader who creates harmony, builds emotional bonds, and puts people, their values, and their emotions first.

Without going into details of the other leadership styles, I subscribe fully to the notion that each style has its value, and all situations may require varying styles. One writer likens this to club selection during a golf game – choosing the right attitude and methodology for the right moment, that is, a kind of *situational flexibility*. This might be seen by some as inconsistent or indicative of multiple personalities. I summarize this flexibility in the leadership talks I give by suggesting that *all* styles may be required in the same day: you're coercive or commanding in the operating room when the going gets tough; you're visionary when you're in the planning mode; you should be coaching much of the time with residents and students; you're affiliative with your divisional staff and your support staff; you're definitely democratic at home if you're smart; and you may be pace-setting when you're feeling your oats, but you should watch that!

> **As a medical leader you can be somewhat unpredictable in your handling of various situations, but you must be entirely predictable as far as principles and values are concerned.**

Does a Leader Need Intelligence? The Concept of Emotional Intelligence

Presumably, as a medical leader you do require an ability to think, an ability to express ideas in clearly articulated language, and an ability to frame those ideas in such a way that others with whom you work can make sense of the concepts and use them in everyday work. But is success in IQ tests and 'practical IQ' or 'street smarts' enough to make a successful medical leader?

SITUATION 2.3

CHRISTOPHER LANGAN, GENIUS: *Emotional Intelligence Trumps Traditional Intelligence*

In his recent book *Outliers*[13] Malcolm Gladwell profiles a genius named Christopher Langan, whose advanced IQ tests have shown him to possess an intelligence quotient somewhere between 195 and 210, surpassing Albert Einstein by twenty-five or thirty points. Apparently Mr. Langan has a mental capacity that far outdistances that of the vast majority of us, and he has demonstrated his monumental brainpower in interviews, national quiz shows, and documentaries.

If you have a chance, you should view the three parts of an interview with Mr Langan on YouTube[14] as he recounts a stormy upbringing and demonstrates his startling intellect. He never finished college and has no degrees, and the fact that he works as a bouncer is interesting: either he has chosen a job where the physical is paramount, allowing him to pursue his thought experiments (as Einstein used to do), or he is exerting an authority he has always resisted. He is a man with astonishing measured intelligence but with limited ability to work as a member of a team.

The subject of *emotional intelligence* or the *emotional quotient* (EQ) has received much attention in the past decade, to the point that to some it is the sine qua non of being a modern leader. The problem is that there seem to be as many definitions of this concept as there are 'authorities.' Daniel Goleman is recognized as an authority, and he identifies the following five domains of EQ:[15]

1 Knowing your emotions
2 Managing your own emotions
3 Motivating yourself
4 Recognizing and understanding other people's emotions
5 'Managing' the emotions of others

As he has stated, 'the most effective leaders are alike in one crucial way ... they all have a high degree of what has come to be known as emotional intelligence.' Even without clearly articulated definitions of EQ, measurements of this elusive entity do exist and include the emotional competency inventory (ECI), the emotional and social competency inventory (ESCI), and the emotional intelligence appraisal.

Without trying to enter a minefield of behavioural science about which I profess to know only a modest amount, I would simplify these notions: to be a successful medical leader you have to have some understanding of yourself and also of the individuals you lead. You must have insights into your own interpersonal strengths and weaknesses and how these traits, along with those of your colleagues, can be managed to produce optimal results.

> Basically, emotional intelligence leads to getting the best out of yourself and the people you work with – a kind of coping with the predictable adversities that we all face.

If you believe that concentration on personnel is important practice in an organization (see chapter 4), then emotional intelligence is the innate and learned tool that helps you lead on a daily basis and promote the most important concept in any organization – *teamwork*. And if you view Christopher Langan's interviews on You Tube, I think you will agree that his striking conventional intelligence is matched only by his apparent lack of emotional intelligence.

Be a Legitimate Clinician, Educator, and Researcher First

In general, at least in North America, the medical leader has to be recognized as a capable clinician. If as a doctor you are going to lead a group of independent academic or community clinicians and you are not recognized to be at least an adequate clinician (or, preferably, a superlative clinician), you simply won't survive in the job. In the academic setting, since teaching and research are valued, a focus on excellence in one domain or both is desirable. In other words, you will be in the challenging position of delivering on organizational effectiveness through your leadership and guidance and at the same time maintaining your own personal success.

As a medical leader you must have insights into your own strengths and weaknesses. If others are going to be led effectively, you must at least have a solid frame of reference. What no one wants is a medical leader who leads in what I would call the 'Alexander Haig style.'

SITUATION 2.4
ALEXANDER HAIG'S 1981 PRESS CONFERENCE:
What's the Look of a 'Typical' Leader?

I will forever remember how in 1981, after Ronald Reagan had been shot and was going into surgery, Alexander Haig held a press conference and, flushed and sweating profusely, declared nervously, 'I am in charge!'

Watching this, I remember turning to my wife and saying, 'Brother, now we're *really* in trouble.'

Above all, a leader must instil, ongoing confidence of his or her leadership. This comes not by making an Alexander Haig–like declaration or simply being appointed after a search, but by earning trust after repeated, continuing, and consistent good work.

There are a few other attributes that might come in handy during the tough times. Ideally, a medical leader should have a vision of where the division, department, hospital, faculty, and university are going. In many of these cases the new division head, for example, will have to buy into the existing vision of these various levels of the organization. A reminder of that vision, posted beside the computer screen or the office door, is a good way to keep things in perspective while the alligators in the swamp are becoming more aggressive! (See 'Strategic Planning' in chapter 7.)

It also helps to have some street smarts, flexibility, consistency, reliability, honesty, an ability to exercise discretion, an ability to simplify and summarize complex situations, a tendency to listen well, and an ability to communicate clearly and economically. Some of these attributes deserve special mention (see chapter 10, 'The Character of a Leader').

A fundamental problem with medical leadership is what I call the corollary of the Peter Principle.[16] The Peter Principle states that 'employees within an organization will advance to their highest level of competence, and then be promoted to and remain at a level at which they are incompetent.' The twist to this in medical administration might be as stated in the box.

> Those clinicians with reputable skills in the clinical and/or academic domains will be promoted to an administrative leadership position for which they have never been trained, for which they may have little inclination, and for which they may be entirely unsuited.

Titles

One of my pet peeves has always been the answer given by residents or medical students to the questions 'Where do you want to be in ten years, and what do you want to be doing?' If the answer is 'I want your job' or 'I want to be head of a hospital, directing the operations of a major academic teaching institution,' I worry that the priorities of that individual are contaminated by ego and a drive for the outward perception of personal success.

Let me assure all medical leadership aspirants of one thing: the glow, pride, lustre, and prestige of a title just won by virtue of a legitimate search process endure all of about two days, when the stark realization of the responsibility and work ahead becomes clear.

I remember only too well a piece I read a number of years ago that was written by a retiring academic. He stated that the average length of time a retiring doctor is held in the thoughts and memories of those working in the organization is, in fact, about two days! I've never forgotten that, not because of the nihilistic perception that none of this counts but as a constant reminder that we must execute every day in a consistent, deliberate manner to achieve our goals; our personal influence will dissipate very quickly after our departure, but we hope that a legacy of effectiveness will endure.

Why are you taking the job of a medical leader? Is it because it's your turn – which is the worst of reasons but unfortunately the reality in some settings? If that is the case, you should explore ways that the job can become more meaningful, and this may mean a reorganization within the hospital of the various roles. The job has to be more than making out call, clinic, and operating-room schedules and attending some obligatory committee meetings.

The following are the best reasons for taking the job of medical leader:

1 You have a vision of where your interest area should be.
2 You want to represent your colleagues with a strong voice, to improve their lots and those of patients.
3 In looking at the details of the job, you feel it might be fun.

Never take a job before you consult with the incumbent and go through the daily routine of that individual. In the examination of an hour-by-hour account of that position it will be possible to see

- what appeals to you and what does not,
- what can be delegated and what cannot,
- which elements can be changed or improved, and
- which elements are immutable.

There can't be any surprises in the various activities and responsibilities of any position that you consider.

In the academic setting don't be fooled into thinking that a hospital leadership job may enhance your academic career. Success and promotion are usually graded on a combination of factors, including scholarly activity in research, outstanding and consistent educational contributions, and unusual or unique activities that pertain to knowledge transfer, clinical virtuosity, and the like. It would be unusual to be promoted because you did a credible job as a division or department head. That promotion would more likely be based on the aforementioned academic factors, which may well have contributed to your being chosen as the head in the first place.

Applying for the Job

If you're seriously considering a significant leadership position, you will certainly have to submit to a formal process and present yourself to a search committee. There are a few rules that I would suggest you familiarize yourself with before you declare your interest:

1 Be honest. Be forthright with your current boss if you're looking at a job in another hospital and indicate that you're considering a move. Any disadvantage this might have is far outweighed by your boss inevitably hearing it from someone else.
2 Do your research. Find out what the job entails. Speak to the incumbent and, if possible, meet with enough members of your prospective group to conduct a kind of review of the division, department, or program. You will likely learn things you didn't know, meet interesting people, and be able to get a sense of the culture of this group whom you may or may not want to lead. I have seen too many reputable practitioners fly in for the day to apply for a prestigious leadership position without even having the courtesy to meet anyone in the organization. Those individuals must savour airline travel and food, because they're certainly not going to be eligible for a position in any organization with which I am familiar.

> **To apply for something important, you have to know what you're applying for.**

3 Talk it over with your family. Once you've learned about the position, discuss with your spouse and family the ramifications of this possible move and the effects it may have on your personal life. This may be an obvious step, or even an inconsequential one, but family resentment of a unilateral decision can be profound.
4 Prepare yourself for the search process. Learn who is on the search committee, what their positions are, and how they relate to the job in question. Learn something about them – their professional qualifications, achievements and the like – and be prepared to use that information if you are in a one-on-one situation.
5 Learn about the format of the search committee meeting. Will it be a formal presentation followed by random questioning, or will there be a specific structure in which each group member asks his or her own question?

6 Contemplate answers to a few specific questions that are common in today's search committees:
   a Why do you want this job?
   b What specific attributes do you have that are suitable for this position?
   c Give a specific example of how you handled a difficult management problem and had a good outcome.
   d Give an example of a failure that you were part of.
   e What are your major strengths? Your major weaknesses?
   f How would you handle the following scenario? A physician under your leadership berates a nurse publicly in the nursing station on a medical service, and the nurse registers a formal written complaint. What steps would you take?

7 Prepare your presentation. You have one opportunity to make committee members aware that you know what the job is and that you are the right person for it. So, be clear, concise, honest; confident, but self-effacing and modest; serious, but with a sense of humour; critical, but with a clear vision of the future and a desire to reach that vision – not easy in fifteen minutes.

8 At the outset and at the end, thank the members for their time and consideration of your application. Don't forget that everyone wants to know about your family and social situation, so tell them. (Incidentally, if you as a woman think that mentioning that you have a growing brood at home will compromise your chances in this male-dominated profession, I believe you are mistaken; the ability of women to multi-task and attend to their roles both at home and in the workplace is simply admired by search committees everywhere.)

9 You have to know enough about yourself to clarify your qualifications without undue bravado, but emphasize how this opportunity comes at an opportune time for both you and the target group. You have to know enough about the division, department, or program to applaud its achievements but also to register concerns about the shortcomings that you would pledge to correct.

10 Above all, don't be afraid to say 'I don't know' to a question. Usually that answer is qualified by either the time or the investigation that would allow you to answer the question comprehensively, but you must avoid a rambling and non-answer to any question. (Sleeping search committee members will likely not vote for you!)

11 Keep your thick skin and don't be discouraged by either a second
visit to the search committee or the fact that you are ultimately
appointed as a second choice. If this looks like a position that
would enrich your life, take it and set out to do a far better job
than the first choice could ever have done.

Decision Making

Of all the professionals in the world today, medical practitioners must
be regarded as decision makers above all. Decisions must be made
about the differential diagnosis of a patient's problem, the choice of
appropriate investigations, the selection of a number of treatment options, and the continued follow-up of a patient's progress, including
possible additional deviations in a planned course of action. In preparation for those responsibilities, medical faculties educate the future
doctor by teaching the fundamentals of basic science; anatomic,
physiologic, clinical, and pathologic states; and the advanced thera-
peutics of a vast array of clinical presentations. Some schools have
even addressed the issue by using a problem-based learning approach. This methodology offers frequent practice in the assessment
and solution of clinical problems from an early stage in medical education, but does it really promote understanding of the decision-
making process that we will use every day? How does the human
brain gather information in a standard history from a patient with
type 2 diabetes, process that information (along with banks of remote
and recently published evidence) in real time, recall years of personal
experience with similar but not identical patients with the same afflic-
tion, draw conclusions about possible diagnostic possibilities, and
then formulate a plan of action for the next steps? All of this may seem
like a kind of medical kindergarten, but surprisingly few, including
myself, have grappled with the understanding of our actual decision-
making process.

Conventional teaching may imply that decision making is a mathematical process – information in, information processed along with
other information, and then decision out – and some effective leaders
may well succeed by using that approach consistently. But is that really
the key to success? I guarantee you that most of the issues you will face
as a medical leader will be like reading a new book: the players will be
unique, the plot line will be interesting and convoluted, and the conclusion may well be in doubt until the very end. The only problem is that

you may be faced with helping to create that end with your decision-making ability, and you have neither read that book before nor even heard of such a problem.

A must-read is a book by Jonah Lehrer entitled *How We Decide*.[17] In great detail, Lehrer describes what neuroscientists know about the chemistry of brain function, where decisions seem to be made in the brain, and which of the many factors appear to be important in the process. He describes the fact that our thinking requires *emotional input*, that our otherwise mathematical approach to solving complex problems requires feeling; he also reminds us that as humans we inherently practice a 'negativity bias,' that is, our fear of failure is a powerful motivator when we are making the tough decisions. If this is true, it places the medical leader in a most unenviable position. Taking the safe route to avoid the possible mistake or misguided approach to a problem may well *not* be in the interests of progress; bold, while potentially risky, may be beautiful!

Just as in morbidity and mortality rounds (see chapter 6), mistakes in management and leadership must be regarded as opportunities for learning. I have often said to my residents that the main reason I am a reasonably good surgeon with acceptable outcomes is that over the last three decades I have made every mistake in the book and tried to learn from each one of them. So too in leadership.

The *feeling* issue described by Lehrer takes me back to the issue of emotional intelligence ('Involving the "Troops" in Planning,' in chapter 2) and also the personality profiles of leaders ('Ensuring Quality of Patient Care,' in chapter 2). If you think of the typical ENTJ leaders (the field marshals) in your past experience, were they ultimately more successful or less successful than the leaders who may have exhibited characteristics such as sensing instead of intuition, or feeling instead of thinking? Just a thought to ponder.

Being decisive does not necessarily mean that a quick forceful decision by a coercive (commanding) leader is your prime objective. A well-thought-out decision with careful assessment of all the factors involved, using the appropriate input from colleagues and mentors and taking whatever time is necessary (within reason) for a fair evaluation, is, in the end, a reasonable approach, and if those steps become part of your reputation as a decision maker or leader, mistakes will be forgiven. However, just as in the clinical domain, mistakes must be reviewed and analysed, reasons illuminated, and lessons learned, and then you carry on with greater knowledge and wisdom than before.

Lehrer makes a number of observations that may help us as medical leaders to address the apparently complex problem in a more focused way:

1 We make decisions using our rational thought, with the prefrontal cortex acting like an orchestra conductor and our amygdala providing a kind of intuition or a 'wisdom of emotions.' The key is not to have emotions take over or to have too much faith in a rational approach and be overwhelmed with detail. Balance is the key.

2 We must avoid the assumptions that lead us to discount obvious facts; in other words, we must consider all options, even if they appear to fly in the face of our previous tightly held beliefs. Embrace uncertainty.

3 We should consistently think about how we think, and continually study our own decision-making process.

4 We should have faith that in our final decisions on a difficult topic our experiences will impart certain abilities and intuitions of which we may not even be consciously aware. This notion is at the root of Malcolm Gladwell's book *Blink*,[18] which emphasizes our innate ability to make complex judgments by using our intellect, our intuition, and our past experiences, while not even realizing that we are assimilating vast inputs into a single decision.

5 We should accept the fact that our decision making may involve moral judgments and that we may be bound by a feeling of what is right and what is wrong.

6 We should welcome dissenting views that can be tested against our own attitudes.

7 We should try to avoid being afraid of failure. No one likes to fail, but, as stated, the outcome of a less than ideal decision is an opportunity to learn.

8 We should remember that positive and happy people make better problem solvers; the rational brain is therefore not distracted by the noise of discontent, anger, and chaos.

I have often shared with friends and residents my own simple method for making tough life decisions, such as the acceptance of a new demanding position or perhaps a move by me and my family to a totally new environment and a novel opportunity, both social and professional. This approach is not revolutionary but happens to address both the thinking and the feeling aspects of the decision. First, I take out a sheet of paper and divide the page into two major columns representing the two options, for instance, staying in my city or moving to another organization in another state. Then down the left side I list every possible factor that my family and I can possibly think of when trying to reach a decision, stressing the advantages or disadvantages of each. Then I write down thoughts and feelings on the growing chart, being as specific as possible about the pros and cons of each choice. I carefully assign a 'value assessment' to each of the factors; for instance, being close to in-laws may be a very strong pro factor for staying or may indeed be a very strong pro factor for leaving!

This process so far follows the mathematical tendency of our brain in making calculated judgments. So now my chart is complete: it has the two major options, it has all the factors that weigh in on the final decision, and it has the relative importance of each of those factors. Now we're ready to get the calculator out and decide where we will be next year, right? Wrong! What I do now is, for me, the most important step, which by now may well be the easiest: *I tear up the chart and make the decision.* I believe very strongly that in such tough life-changing situations we need to carefully use our prefrontal cortex to evaluate all the factors that must be considered, discuss with trusted friends, verbalize and record in writing our thoughts and feelings, and then trust ourselves to make the right choice. Whether this can be termed in the end *a gut feeling* or *a decision from the heart* may be a subject for debate, but I believe it will be generated from the marriage of thinking and feeling that Lehrer talks about and will be appropriate for the circumstance.

Such an imperfect science as decision making is brought to bear every day in the life of a medical leader. Decisions are to be made carefully, with all the values held dear, including honesty, integrity, and caring about how the decision will affect others.

Group Decisions

As a medical division or department head you have an apparently impossible task. Keep in mind that whether issues be related to patient care, quality of working conditions, or resource allocation, you must represent your constituents, being an advocate for these professionals. At the same time, you as a medical leader have to be a corporate citizen and uphold (and be *seen* to be upholding) the vision, mission, and processes of your hospital and university.

When there is conflict between these two solitudes, where does the medical leader stand? In the first place, you are in a management position such as division head because of an appointment by a department head; or, as a department head, you were appointed by the CEO of the hospital and/or the dean in the academic setting. Therefore, the ultimate responsibility and accountability in that leadership position is to the hospital CEO and/or the dean. Can there be a better example of walking a tightrope? Why would anyone want to subject themselves to that possible contradiction? Wouldn't the tightrope analogy be better considered a barbed-wire fence, with the danger of losing one's balance being only a little more calamitous?

The last thing a medical leader wants is to be seen as the sycophant of his or her leader, but nevertheless you are ultimately accountable to those individuals.

> The medical leader lives a schizophrenic existence, to be sure, in that the same person is both an advocate for his or her constituents and a company man for the 'suits.'

> If you are taking up an organizational position, your first responsibility as a leader is to support organizational effectiveness.

Conflict in decision making was crystallized in my mind when the hospital in which I was working faced the usual impossible task of radically cutting services to come in line with budget. This is an ongoing mandate in Canada where a single payer (the provincial Ministry of Health) dictates both the budget and the accountabilities.

Although there are periodic funding announcements coming from the ministries in every province, budgets are relatively fixed, and management takes the frequent quarterly overruns very seriously. Indeed, the CEO's job depends on fiscal responsibility.

SITUATION 2.5
THE MEDICAL LEADER AND FISCAL RESPONSIBILITY:
Everyone *Supports a Tough Decision*

Like many other hospitals in 2002, the University Health Network (UHN) in a major North American city was faced with the projection of a substantial deficit at year's end, as a result of the second-quarter results announced at the end of September. A vigorous debate ensued at the board of trustees' monthly meeting, with some financially motivated board members strongly supporting cuts. (These cuts could have far-reaching consequences, as they had about seven years earlier when similar tactics were advanced and adopted, and jobs lost.) Others took the stand that services should be continued even at the risk of remaining over budget and offending the ministry. The former group consisted of an impressive bunch of CEOs and financial officers in the city; the latter group was led by Doctor L, Dean of Medicine (and later president of the university), and by the former premier of the province.

Both men made eloquent and impassioned pleas, based on their extensive political experience, that the UHN should, indeed, risk the appearance of flaunting its deficit position in the ministry's face and do the right thing for patients. The board ultimately decided on the more fiscally responsible route. There was a lot of shaking of heads in exasperation, and the former premier was so moved that he resigned from the board.

The board's decision meant that I, in my position as surgeon-in-chief and director of surgical services for the three-hospital corporation, had to apportion reductions in operating time and numbers of inpatient beds that would lead to reductions in surgical expenditures. This was not to be an easy task, given the entitlement felt by all surgeons and the sense of ownership they had of hospital services, as well as the inevitable tightening of the hospital's compensation line, that is, salaried positions.

In a subsequent meeting with Mr Jack V, the CEO of UHN, I continued the arguments of Doctor L and the former premier. I told Jack yet again how difficult and indeed unfair it was for surgery to take the brunt of the proposed cuts. He said to me, 'Bryce, you have to realize that the board has made the decision that we are to go ahead with the reductions.'

I persisted with my passionate arguments, which I felt were certainly well-intentioned, logical, and persuasive. Jack said, 'I don't think your thinking is in line with the organization's decision.' It was at that point that this gentle but firm executive finally got through to my thick skull. What Mister V was really saying, always with a wry smile, was, 'Bryce, either you're with us or you're not – and if you're not, *you're out!*'

I learned a lot from that experience. I believe that I still continued to work hard at representing my constituents, but in the final analysis my management position required that I serve both the doctors and the hospital, and the hospital position came with very specific responsibilities.

I also learned that high-level meetings are for vigorous and sometimes contentious debate, but after a decision has been made, the debate is over, and managers have to unequivocally support the collective decision regardless of the difficulty in reaching it. The former premier reacted in a way that was appropriate for him as a volunteer board member, and I eventually saw the light and did my own job (because, behaving as a corporate citizen, I wanted to keep it). Finally, I learned that a strong personal relationship with my CEO was the basis for his patience and coaching despite my impertinence and was the principal reason I was not fired on the spot.

(I should emphasize that the focus of the CEO in this academic hospital was not only on cost containment and fiscal responsibility. Although immediate concerns often related to apparently insurmountable challenges of budget and service, the long-term objectives of this CEO involved a passionate commitment to academic imperatives.)

After a collective decision has been made, the debate is over, and the decision must be supported universally.

What we saw in the first chapter is that the administrative structure in the health care system, and in hospitals in particular, is indeed different and very complex. In chapter 2 you have seen that the continued presence of a medical leader on the front lines – of patient care (at least, intermittently) – in order to maintain credibility is an oddity peculiar to medicine. However, there are many similarities between the business world and health care delivery; the patient (or client or customer) as the object of the exercise continuously drives progress, change, and the deliberations of management, and the characteristics and styles of an effective leader are similar whatever the setting.

For all intents and purposes, therefore, the leaders in business, the leaders in medicine, and their behaviours are the same, but the atmosphere, administrative structure, and culture differ in many ways.

3 The Team and Teamwork

Capital renewal (such as the necessary renovation of operating rooms) has always been challenging in the practice of hospital medicine because the escalating costs of patient care frequently drown out the necessary repair and reconstruction of bricks and mortar.

An operating room (OR) and the processes involved in its functions are profoundly complex, and they require input from many different professions. The journey of a patient on the day of surgery through registration, preparation, preoperative testing and verification, transport, the procedure itself, and early post-operative recovery is a highly detailed one, and therefore perioperative suite design demands exhaustive attention to form and function. Furthermore, the execution of plans for such a facility must be carefully examined and, above all, inclusive. Every person working in the area should be consulted for input, and every step of the way (that is, the *patient's* way) has to be considered in detail during the functional planning.

Some years ago I was part of a team that helped put together the plans for a new suite of twenty-two operating rooms in a major hospital.

SITUATION 3.1
BUILDING NEW OPERATING ROOMS – A TEAM EFFORT:
The Tenants Plan Their House

In 1996 a creative proposal was submitted to the government of a large province in Canada to rebuild parts of two major hospitals in the province's capital, Community Hospital B and Community Hospital C. A public bond of $281 million, underwritten by one of Canada's major banks, was floated (the total amount of the proposed costs was to be $350 million when adjacent lands were sold) with the promise that when the massive reconstruction had been completed seven years later, the bond would be repaid over fifteen years out of the excess hospital revenues that would accrue from the savings produced by the more efficient buildings.

The real prize for surgery was a brand new suite of twenty-two operating rooms at Community Hospital B, to be built on an entirely new footprint (not a renovation of the old facility), which would accommodate advanced operations, including transplantation, cardiac surgery, and surgical oncology procedures of all types.

A large team with *co-leaders* of surgery, nursing, and anaesthesia was assembled. More than one leader in any endeavour is generally considered risky, but in the OR environment in which nurses and anaesthesiologists live and surgeons visit, it was felt that this departure from the advisable norm was justified. In fact, it worked very well, but mainly because the three leaders (Doctor E from Anaesthesia, Ms Y as nurse manager, and I, representing Surgery) worked so well together on a personal level.

Functional planning proceeded with a clear definition of all the steps taken by the surgical patient on the day of a procedure. All of the following were considered in the architectural and functional design of the new OR suite:

- Appropriate access to the hospital and the perioperative area
- Registration and processing
- Multiple steps of identification
- Undressing and hospital gowning
- The nursing assessment and appropriate repeated identification of the patient
- The preoperative visit by Anaesthesia and Surgery
- The incision-marking and confirmation of the intended operation
- The administration of preoperative medications
- Transport to the operating room

Input into these details was welcomed from surgeons, nurses in the various areas, anaesthesiologists, respiratory therapists, hospital assistants, and blood technicians. In fact, input was invited – and welcomed – from everyone who would be coming into contact with the patient during his or her experience of surgery.

Biweekly collaborative meetings of all stakeholders (up to twelve people) and other invited individuals resulted in a free interchange of ideas and an agreement on the best patient-centred processes that would satisfy the objectives of patients and caregivers alike. Decisions were always made by consensus.

The actual design of the operating rooms was more challenging because a wide spectrum of surgery is performed at this centre. Nevertheless, in the end every group was satisfied that we had produced the best environment that we could, and that, most importantly, no one could think of any improvements over the final product. In each of the twenty-two operating rooms we had paid attention to the following:

1 *Size.* Larger rooms would have to accommodate more anaesthetic space, lots of new equipment, an adequate place for a nursing station, an X-ray system, et cetera. In general, the usual 400–450 square foot room would have to become a 600–800 square foot room, depending on the type of surgery being performed.
2 *Ceiling-mounted equipment.* Whereas all new equipment in the past had to be trucked in with wires and cables dragging, ceiling-mounted hydraulic booms were installed with scores of electrical connections to accommodate a wide variety of machines. The floors were therefore liberated from countless wires and cables.
3 *Convertibility.* We recognized that the demands of this particular operating room suite were unusual in that a huge amount of open surgery such as transplantation, heart surgery, and cancer surgery had to be recognized, but at the same time minimally invasive surgery was becoming increasingly important. Therefore, the final design produced operating rooms that would accommodate a liver transplantation, including back-table work, and possibly a laparoscopic colon resection immediately thereafter.
   Although this flexibility was felt to be critical in the twenty-first century, it was not offered by a number of companies who were willing to produce cookie-cutter, minimally invasive (MIS) products in which only MIS surgeries could be performed, to the exclusion of 'open' procedures.
4 *Consistency.* Over the years, operating rooms in various specialties usually developed idiosyncrasies and peculiarities that made them different from other operating rooms, even those in the same suite. This created problems for nurses and anaesthesiologists who must move between rooms and still provide efficient care. In preparation for our new operating rooms we ensured a consistency that would make this movement seamless; in other words, all of the extras such as sutures, audio-visual equipment, X-ray machines, and tables were put in precisely the same spots in each room.
5 *Cupboard space.* There is never enough storage space. Seventeen-foot-wide sterile corridors were built between banks of operating rooms so that the ORs themselves harboured only essential equipment and such immediate necessities as sutures and life-saving instruments.

6 *Communication.* As each of the ORs became necessarily larger, and the footprint of the whole suite virtually Brobdingnagian (as Lemuel Gulliver might have said), communication issues obviously became critically important. These were solved by using a collaborative approach that involved several companies and ultimately consisted of video links, standard telephones, wireless telephones, intranet hook-up, and electronic emergency call buttons. The footprint is large, but the connections to the functional brain, that is, the management centre, are many, varied, and efficient.

7 *Capturing of images.* For the purposes of education and consultation, we needed to be able to capture images of both open and laparoscopic procedures. This requirement was satisfied by the installation in most ORs of standard digital cameras, as well as cameras with the ability to digitalize analogue images and send them to the next room, to conference rooms, or indeed around the world.

8 *Medical imaging and surgery.* A final major decision had to be made, about what we were going to build in our operating room area that recognized the current and future marriage of imaging and surgery. The various examples in North America and Europe involved computerized tomography (CT) scans, image intensifiers, and magnetic resonance imaging (MRI) machines, but the options available were rather dizzying, and we had no one champion who had enough knowledge for us to commit so many resources to a novel facility.

The group then made probably the best decision we could have made at the time. We decided to shell-in 4,000 square feet of space that would remain dormant until we were more confident about its eventual use. At the time of this writing, six years after the opening of the main ORs, we have completed the construction of half of the shelled-in space, a multi-purpose OR that houses minimally invasive cardiac and vascular procedures such as percutaneous valve replacements and endovascular aneurysm repairs. In the adjacent suite, the other half of the shelled-in space, a guided-therapeutics operating room will use cone-beam CT and MRI to close the gap between imaging and surgery. These particular decisions were made by expanding the already large team to involve the medical imaging and research physics groups at the hospital.

All of these choices were made as a result of the collaborative decision making of the members of a large team. The team was unusual in that it had three leaders and many more members than is generally recommended. The keys to the success of this team were a single goal of the *best functional operating rooms possible* and the excitement of building a replacement for a facility that had been active in its original format since 1955.

One example of this team-oriented approach was the organization of an OR equipment fair. The gymnasium of the adjacent nurses' residence was transformed into an international technology fair in which surgeons and nurses could attend and 'play' with operating room beds, light standards, hydraulic booms, and other machines and items that had been set in place by several of the leading companies in the industry.

Not all surgeons, nurses, and anaesthesiologists visited that fair, but none could say they didn't have the opportunity for input. Feedback was honest and straightforward and sometimes brutal. I have no doubt that any of the companies could have produced a fine collection of operating room 'furniture,' but in the end, input from the folks who would ultimately use the equipment on a daily basis was the deciding factor.

During this rather exhaustive series of exercises the minutiae that were considered were many and detailed, to say the least. Decisions on everything from the optimal positioning of all light standards on ceiling anchor points right down to the texture and colour of the OR floor and the height of scrub sinks were made by all members of the group in a consensus-driven fashion. If that hadn't worked out, that is, if there had been no agreement on an important decision, we would have had to find a less democratic solution, but that would have been lamentable. One memorable photo saw Ms Y on her hands and knees examining the colour and feeling the texture of several installed floor samples. We had but one chance, and we had to do it right.

In the end it's reasonable to say that the members of the large multidisciplinary team that conspired to put this surgical facility together during more than three years of intensive planning were all content that the final product reflected their respective concerns and requirements. Indeed, the only extras that caused problems were those that the builder had gone ahead and instituted without consultation (such as electronic operating room doors that were so sensitive they opened in response to any passer-by), but such 'innovations' were quickly dismantled.

There are always daily irritants with any facility that is by its very nature complicated, but the final product of the Community Hospital B operating rooms was a direct and comprehensive reflection of the input of the people who use the facility. There is authentic ownership that all OR personnel can feel every day as they walk through the automatic doors. However, this surgical suite is certainly not perfect, any more than are the health care providers who had a major hand in designing it.

Conventional wisdom might state that every effective team must have a single designated leader. In health care there are, indeed, situations in which leadership can be truly shared, as long as the ultimate objectives are agreed upon and the various participating leaders are able to park at least most of their egos at the door.

> This is the era of accountability; it's also the era of collaboration and cooperation. Whether in business, patient care, biomedical research, or education, groups of individuals working towards a common goal is the new effective norm.

Medical personnel spend their lives working in teams in their pursuit of better patient care, but in many cases we are not familiar with the modern use of the word *team*. The traditional medical model is very hierarchal in that the doctor resides at (or, shall I say, dictates orders from) the top of a management pyramid, with other caregivers carrying out those orders. This is becoming inconsistent with the concept of team in hospital management. In health care no one can do it alone.

Nature, whether human or animal, seems to gravitate towards collections or groups of beings with declared leaders who are nominated on the basis of domination or an arranged pyramidal structure. However, in the past few decades business research has suggested that although this structure can be effective in a simple organization, a more subtle, refined, and ultimately more productive approach to reach organizational effectiveness is required in a complex one.

Teamwork is defined in Webster's dictionary[19] as 'a joint action by a group of people, in which each person subordinates his or her individual interests and opinions to the unity and efficiency of the group.' Needless to say, a doctor barking orders at minions as he does on the television program *House* does not fit that description. Dr House is most assuredly *not* a team player. For those interested in scientific equations, teamwork might be represented by the input of a and b producing c, where c is greater than the sum of a and b acting separately (the potentiation effect).

When you enter into management activities in the hospital, you should overhaul your perception of *team* and think about a consensus model that respects and encourages input from every member of the group, something which is perhaps lacking occasionally on the inpatient service.

A wide variety of groups calling themselves teams exist simultaneously in the same institution. In the hospital setting these might include the inpatient service rounding team, the operating room team, the house staff team, program teams, project teams, the middle management team, and the senior management team. These are all legitimate examples of teams, but they are all constituted differently and certainly operate very differently from one another.

This section will focus on some of these team differences but then will direct attention to the modern organizational team that is constructed at the senior management level to serve the institution in its various mandates, which, of course, include patient care and many other hospital activities as well.

A team assembled to handle a specific project can be small and short-lived and can answer a limited number of questions. Consider tissue banking, as in the following situation.

SITUATION 3.2
SETTING UP A HOSPITAL'S TISSUE BANK: *Involving All the Owners*

A hospital's pathology department was looking to organize a formal institutional tissue-banking project. This is usually a rather incendiary and controversial subject that prompts questions about the following issues:

- Appropriate consent
- Confidentiality
- Ownership of tissue
- Expedient acceptance of the research proposal
- Methodology of tissue capture and preservation

Clinician-scientists may be conducting meaningful research; they are often the ones who actually collect the tissue in question, using their own methodology and resources. They, therefore, might feel a sense of entitlement to the ownership of the tissue, and they are concerned that any addition of 'bureaucratic' levels of administration might stifle the flexibility and responsiveness of their research. However, the jurisdiction's Hospital Act clearly stated that anything removed from a patient was the responsibility of the pathology department – a sticky issue to be sure.

In attempts to set the stage for resolution of a potential conflict, the clinician-scientists were asked to form a team with a strict mandate to come up with suggestions about how the tissue bank should be constructed, what governance model it should have, and what principles should guide its operational aspects, including the variety of preservation techniques to be used.

The two critical directives of the small team were to design an organizational model that would satisfy all stakeholders but would retain the flexibility and responsiveness that the clinician-scientists felt were necessary to support their research proposals in a timely fashion.

A passionate, intelligent, fair-minded, and effective leader was chosen from the group of clinicians to head this small team so that the research interests were appropriately represented. A strict timeline of six weeks was set for negotiation with pathologists and submission of recommendations to the hospital's senior vice-president, who would make the final decision.

This is one example of how a legitimate team can be set up to answer an important question. You might also call this type of ad hoc team a *task force,* a very useful tool that is employed by a medical leader as a democratic way of getting to the core of a difficult problem and that at the same time has the salutary effect of spreading the responsibility of leadership around and coaching potential future leaders.

You may be tempted to call a major committee a team, but, as will be discussed later in this book (see 'Meetings and Committees' in chapter 5), a large group that essentially meets for informational purposes on a monthly basis cannot be regarded in modern business lingo as a team.

What Is a Twenty-First-Century Senior Medical Leadership Team?

Senior Leadership Teams: What It Takes to Make Them Great (2008),[20] a book by the Harvard group of Ruth Wageman, Debra A. Nunes, James A. Burruss, and J. Richard Hackman (as one of the Leadership for the Common Good series), addresses this topic in detail. While these authors specifically refer to *senior* teams, many of the principles of idea generation, interpersonal relationships, and actions could be applied to any team in the organization. The Harvard group feels that the key to competent leadership of the senior team is to put in place three essential conditions:

1 The *real* team
2 A compelling direction
3 The right people

Furthermore, the team will require three enablers:

4 A solid structure
5 A supportive context
6 Team coaching

Attention to these six concepts together can increase team effectiveness.

Depending on the position you take up, you may have the opportunity of sitting on the senior medical leadership team. This group will be critical in developing major strategies to further the vision and mission of the hospital (or other institution). As the group becomes more senior, that is, closer to the board of trustees, the number of people and the number of issues dealt with on a regular basis must decrease. This is another expression on a big scale of *let your managers manage* (see 'Managers vs Leaders: Let Your Managers Manage' in chapter 5), because the major directions have to be formulated by the senior medical leaders, and they cannot be cluttered by issues that should be managed by reports (those individuals who report to them).

If you have an opportunity to be on the senior medical leadership team, don't pass it up, because the chance to make a long-term contribution to progress that will affect the health and lives of a local population is perhaps the most exciting thing you can be involved in.

Activities

In 1965 Bruce Tuckman, an American psychologist who is now widely considered to be an authority on group dynamics, published a short article entitled 'Developmental Sequence in Small Groups.'[21] In it he postulated that teams in general go through a life-cycle of the following five stages:

1 Forming
2 Storming
3 Norming
4 Performing
5 Adjourning

The gradual movement of a group of medical individuals from a leader-dominated model to a form in which all members participate and contribute to the overall objectives may occur in weeks or months. The same five stages might be applied to the group addressing the issue of tissue banking just described (situation 3.2) but in a much shorter time span.

The senior medical leadership team should represent an ongoing bridge between the board of trustees and the operations of the hospital, a bridge that constantly requires maintaining, refreshing, and rebuilding with new materials and new minds. Occasionally the bridge between the board of trustees and the senior medical leadership team must be replaced, using a completely novel set of architectural drawings and materials (see situation 1.1 at Community Hospital A).

Personal Relationships of Team Members

The more senior and strategic the medical team, the more the individual members should know one another as people. That might apply to any group in any organization, strategic or operational, but it is especially important in a senior medical leadership team in a hospital setting.

Some organizations go to great lengths to arrange team-building exercises so that participants can bond during non-working experiences such as social activities and mini-team competitions that require group planning and group-dynamic games. Some critics point to this type of contrived team building as placing too much peer pressure and stress on the participants, such that the outcome is negative rather than positive. (Proponents of the activity might assert that such a sensitive person should not be on the team in the first place.)

SITUATION 3.3
FOSTERING BONDING AMONG TEAM MEMBERS:
Getting to Know You

One such positive experience in which I was involved a few years ago demanded that pairings of the senior medical team spend thirty minutes together learning 'things about each other that others would find surprising.'

The resultant brief accounts of the profiles and life events of every person in the room were revealing, interesting, and frequently moving, and everyone in the room learned a lot about the people they thought they already knew.

Leader of the Team

In your role as leader of a medical team you must make sure that you communicate a clear instruction that teamwork is expected, and that you model teamwork yourself, encourage every member to support the concept, and reward group achievements.

Behaviour of Team Members

The emotional intelligence described under 'Be a Legitimate Clinician, Educator, Researcher First' in chapter 2, is at the root of the behaviour demonstrated by a team player. A good team player must live the principles of respect for others and of interest-based bargaining. As a medical leader, you must listen, have input, question, participate, appreciate, and, above all, park your ego at the door.

In building a true team, everyone must have input; there can be no wins or losses, just advances and improvement in plans, actions, and effectiveness.

In your position as a medical leader you will be a participant in teams of various sorts. Make the most of it; listen, respect, contribute, articulate your opinions as clearly as possible, ask questions, discuss, and, as a foundation for all interactions, try to get to know your colleagues as more than just working associates. The organization *and you* will be the beneficiaries. As usual, Peter Drucker nicely summarized your effective behaviour on any team when he instructed, 'Listen first; speak last.'

The Culture of Your Team

Every hospital seems to have a 'feel' or culture about it, and in most cases that culture remains consistent despite the comings and goings of countless health care professionals.

Culture has been variously defined as 'group personality' or, as Edgar Schein said, 'a pattern of shared basic assumptions that was learned by a group as it solved its problems of external adaptation and internal integration, that has worked well enough to be considered valid and, therefore, to be taught to new members as the correct way to perceive, think and feel in relation to those problems.'[22]

Simply put, the culture of the medical team really represents the shared values of the members and the way they work together to create stability. An intensive self-examination by a medical team is sometimes useful in improving the way the team operates. The improvements may be obvious steps such as running meetings more efficiently, or less measurable advances such as getting to know each other better on a personal basis.

Those team members who know and understand each other are obviously in a better position to work towards the common goals of the organization, thereby becoming more effective leaders themselves. Extensive literature exists on the subject of team culture, and additional reading is recommended for any medical leader who aspires to continuous improvement in his or her effectiveness.

4 The Personnel

In a large hospital that employs thousands of nurses, secretaries, house-keepers, technicians, information technology (IT) staff, and food handlers, and scores of other professionals and workers, human resources (HR) is a large and critical department. If you were to ask any CEO in any organization about the keys to the success of the core business, the answer would be 'the people.'

The first job (Job 1) of a medical leader is, of course, to ensure high-quality patient care every hour of the day, every day of the week, and every week of the year. Thus, the corollary of Job 1 is Job 1a: to develop capable and reliable staff who can deliver the excellence required of Job 1. However, as you recall from chapter 1, the task of working with independent practitioners may be somewhat more challenging than that of being the manager or leader of a group of employees.

As a medical leader you have the concurrent tasks of executing the management directives of the hospital (or other organization) and developing and supporting the professional careers of colleagues. Along the way, you must be able to assess the quality of care provided by the clinicians on the team, evaluate their current and ongoing competence, and eventually help them prepare for retirement.

In this chapter we deal with some of those issues and gradually move towards the nuts and bolts of the daily life of the medical leader.

Recruitment and Retention

Vince Lombardi said, 'Winning isn't everything; it's the only thing.' This great motivator was, of course, talking about winning football games, and the focus on winning (the core business of sport) produced results. The same can be said in medicine for recruitment, which many consider to be the core business of a medical leader, whereas patient care is the core business of the hospital.

In medical leadership, recruitment is the key to everything. It is *the* win.

SITUATION 4.1
RECRUITING DOCTOR F FOR A MEDICAL LEADERSHIP POSITION:
You Must Pay for Quality

Doctor F was, and continues to be, an accomplished surgeon-scientist and urologist who established himself as a leader in the field of urologic oncology, specifically interested in the critical area of prostate-cancer prevention. He had excellent surgical training, and in addition to becoming a superb clinical surgeon, he devoted considerable time and effort to a research career at Community Hospital D in a large North American city, exploring the effect of various factors such as selenium, vitamin E, lycopenes, and other substances on the incidence of prostate cancer.

His academic trajectory was notable, and in 2002 at a relatively early stage in his career Doctor F was looking for growth and possible leadership positions. So what was the problem? Doctor F's academic progress and stature had accelerated at such an early age that although he was ready for new challenges, there were still at least two urologic colleagues at Community Hospital D who occupied positions of leadership, that is, the division head at the hospital and the university professor of the division. Timing is everything.

At that same time, another leader in the city was coming to the end of his term, and the position of urologic division head at the University Health Network (a merger of three major hospitals in the city) was being searched.

Doctor F applied for the position of urologic division head at UHN with a presentation to a regularly constituted search committee. His past accomplishments, current profile, and future aspirations as a clinician-scientist and medical leader were clarified for the group. The search committee recommended that Doctor F be offered the job, and then without publicly declaring a choice, the senior management of UHN entered into negotiations with the possible new leadership recruit. (Since the decision of the search committee was only the first of many steps in the recruitment process, it was deemed wise to remain silent until a final deal was struck; an early announcement followed by a failure of negotiations can be, and has been, disastrous in the long run.)

Doctor F was relatively new to the game of negotiation. Nevertheless, he knew very well that he was in a strong bargaining position and that this opportunity to have access to such a variety of resources was one that came along only intermittently in the hospital setting. So he decided that it was better to make his demands now, because he knew from past experience that the requests for hospital resources based merely on good sense are often a recipe for frustration.

As a result of his expressed needs and the available resources of the hospital, Doctor F was promised the following when he was offered the position:

- Office space
- Secretarial assistance
- Specific operating times per week in the main operating room
- Cystoscopy time
- A stipend to recognize his new administrative position as division head
- A pledge that a new endoscopy suite for Urology would be completed at one of the hospitals
- Control of the designated inpatient area, with the beds to be shared with the sister specialty of gynaecologic oncology

To support his clinical research, space would be provided for research assistants, and he would become head of the Site Group, an important position at the cancer hospital in the UHN.

Doctor F was met by the CEO and others in the organization who had cheque-writing ability, and I believe that he was as impressed with their commitment as they were with him. A great recruit always costs time and resources but is worth every penny.

The situation above was a leadership position search, but many of your opportunities will come from the recruitment of freshly minted clinicians who will bring to your institution a particular skill or knowledge. Generally, a proposal for the recruitment of a young clinician comes from the division head, and it then must be approved by the division members, the department head, and the university if an academic position is under consideration.

Recruitment should entail a stepwise process that includes deliberate long- and medium-range planning, articulation of staffing requirements, and definition of new or modified programs that may dictate a change or enhancement in staffing. Then an attempt should be made at painting a picture of the ideal recruit that meets the description of the division's needs and also fits the organization's overall plan.

Unfortunately, although the first steps are invariably taken, the process is often interrupted by the appearance of a 'must-have' recruit who possesses many, but not all, of the characteristics of the ideal staff member. Then the plans may have to change to accommodate that excellent recruit. Such is the process of HR planning and the importance of progress and renewal.

Very seldom do journal or newspaper ads produce applications for viable candidates. The bedrock of discovery of new available medical talent lies in word of mouth and in interaction at medical meetings.

The motivation for recruitment can be varied. In the community hospital setting the factors that lead to the expansion of staff may include retirement, departures, introduction of a program requiring special expertise, or a clinical load that needs to be shouldered by more clinicians.

In the academic setting, all of the above may be present, but the existence and availability of an outstanding individual who has been spawned and has demonstrated excellence in a specific domain may be the most common deciding factor in selection.

Twenty-five years ago most clinicians recruited to a hospital were thankful to have a job, and they made very few demands on the hospital, university, or local group to which they were appointed. Medicine was extremely hierarchal, and leaders and teachers were viewed with the same reverence as doctors were by patients: 'Thanks so much for the invitation to be part of your staff!' Like everything else, things have certainly changed.

House staff, particularly interns and residents, are acutely aware of their value to the academic system, and whereas they previously worked as relatively underpaid 'slaves,' they now have controlled, policed, and better-paid work weeks. Similarly, the young professional medical recruit fresh out of training clearly understands his or her value to the medical system.

In the community setting, new clinicians are not given much assistance early in their career, and they build a busy clinical practice based on the three A's: availability, affability, and (least important) ability. New clinicians will have success if there is enough work and if they are on call for emergency work on a regular basis. The competition for practice can be a challenge at the outset, but the young clinician can usually do well by taking the calls and cases that others decline, such as the troublesome fistula patient who will predictably be in hospital for weeks. Referring doctors will eventually realize there's a new boy or girl in town.

In the academic realm, the medical professional is usually truly recruited, and too often a bidding war results in difficult negotiations and bad feelings between institutions. An academic candidate will often undergo extra training in a specific field of interest, and this may be regarded as a magnet by many organizations.

The recruitment package might very well include the following:

1 Time protection
2 Guaranteed salary as part of a practice plan (see 'Hospital Finances and Capital Investment' in chapter 8)
3 Secretarial support
4 Research operating funds
5 Further support such as tuition for ongoing study towards a masters' degree

The medical leader must scurry around, exacting commitments from the various individuals in the hospital or university who can make such commitments. Generally, the division or department heads don't have the discretionary resources to make assurances on their own; they must beg, borrow, or steal promises from the university chair and the hospital's CEO, the chief financial officer, and vice-presidents of research and education.

A confounding factor in recruitment currently in North America is the variable financial capability (especially in academic organizations) to recruit. In Alberta, an oil-rich province in Canada that was unique in its financial position of zero debt before the 2008 financial meltdown, medical leaders often were able to guarantee huge six-figure incomes for academic specialists, whereas in many other jurisdictions a similar specialist was offered far less than 50 per cent of that amount. It may surprise some to know that many medical professionals actually turn down that kind of excessive offer, preferring other motivations to stay at home.

Jim Collins indicated in his book *Good to Great and the Social Sectors: Why Business Thinking Is Not the Answer* (2005)[11] that as leaders we have to get the right people on the bus. He stated, 'The executives who ignited the transformations from good to great did not first figure out where to drive the bus and then get people to take it there. No, they first got the right people on the bus (and the wrong people off the bus) and then figured out where to drive it. They said, in essence, "Look, I don't really know where we should take the bus. But I know this much: if we get the right people on the bus, the right people in the right seats, and the wrong people off the bus, then we will figure out how to take it someplace great.'"

Any medical leader will have to agree that if one considers legacy to be important, you must not ask the question 'How productive is this division?' but rather the question 'What will the place look like after I leave?' If a group of medical professionals has achieved much but is lost when the leader departs or retires, then the leader has failed.

All leaders declare publicly that they try to bring into the fold professionals 'who are better than me.' There are enough egos in the business of leading that in many cases, I believe, some folks expressing that opinion really don't mean it, because their egos require them to be the best at everything. But it's a good line, and if it is followed fastidiously, it will undoubtedly result in an excellent staff. It is also said that we tend to recruit people who are clones of ourselves (the official term is *homophily*).This is exactly why there is a trend in academic circles now to engage in more formal search processes to select each and every new academic recruit. The trend will lead hopefully to a healthier, less in-bred collective, with varied backgrounds and varied futures.

What do we look for in new professional colleagues? Everyone is smart, everyone is talented and has completed an accredited training program, and everyone boasts a curriculum vitae that seems progressively more impressive because many, even as students, have worked in reputable research laboratories.

We are generally more comfortable with decisions made about individuals with whom we have worked intensively during our or their training. In that way, we can more easily predict how they will behave as a colleague and whether they will be compatible with the personalities already on staff. In fact, I have been impressed that, given the intelligence and talents of potential recruits, the following are the two questions most frequently asked by future hospital employers and colleagues: Does he (she) get along well with colleagues and other health care personnel? Does he (she) have a strong record of completing charts and complying with other hospital processes? The clinical and academic prowess almost seems to be considered a given. This is, of course, a very superficial approach but is the reality in many health care centres.

In the past, a new recruit's expectations were limited to the location of the office, the provision of OR time, and access to inpatient beds. Often hospitals selected a medical generalist to fit a pigeonhole perceived as a need by the organization, but now recruits often bring with them specific advanced skills and abilities that may be unique. As a result, they are now negotiating from a position of greater strength. In this case, how should recruitment be approached to ensure the best result possible for all concerned?

The key to good recruitment results, assuming that the right person has been selected to fill the right role, is the formal written agreement that articulates the commitments on both sides. We'll call this formal agreement a letter of understanding, a contract, or a written agreement (WA).

The Written Agreement

The written agreement must describe in detail the expectations of the individual clinician with respect to the provision of high-quality patient care and to adherence to all required hospital processes.

In the academic field similar measurable successes are expected for education and research activities, but if these are deemed important, the protection of time must also be clarified. Colleagues will cover for clinical responsibilities while the new clinician's academic mandates are being pursued. In addition, as a focus on education or research diverts attention away from more lucrative patient care, financial compensation is usually provided from other sources to support the academic (see, for example, situation 8.2, 'The Langer Practice Plan'). This may come from hospital operating funds or from colleagues who participate in practice plans that recognize the value of academic work. But how is such an agreement enforceable?

SITUATION 4.2
RECRUITING DOCTOR G AS A SURGEON-SCIENTIST:
Sometimes the Best-Laid Plans ...

In 2000, Doctor G was recruited as a surgeon-scientist with a special interest in endocrine surgery and in stem-cell oncologic research. He had trained in our postgraduate training program, so colleagues knew him as a friendly, collegial, hard-working surgeon who cared about his patients, and his clinical results were exemplary.

Upon his recruitment and arrival at our hospital, Doctor G enjoyed impressive support in every way:

1 His academic time was protected so that he could effectively start a laboratory.
2 His clinical practice was provided by referrals from colleagues who basically laid out a buffet table of interesting and sophisticated endocrine surgery from the start.
3 He was afforded substantial financial support, including augmented personal income, subsidized secretarial and office expenses, and generous research operating expenses.

In the first two years of his initial three-year commitment, Doctor G's recruitment cost the hospital and his colleagues approximately $600,000. From his standpoint, Doctor G lived up to his end of the bargain as far as activities were concerned:

1 He performed surgery competently.
2 He was a popular teacher with solid trainee-evaluation scores.
3 His research was progressing on schedule.

He presented his work at local, national, and international meetings and after about eighteen months was reaching a stature emulated by all academicians; he was marketable. As Doctor G's talents matched the needs of a prominent U.S. medical centre, he was aggressively recruited by that institution, and he departed after just twenty-seven months of his initial thirty-six-month commitment.

What happens to all that investment by the hospital and the surgical colleagues themselves? The usual written agreement stipulates a commitment of three years for all parties. The departure of a new recruit who has been successful is very unusual even after *five* years of appointment, although any time after three years complies with the language of the agreement. A twenty-seven-month appointment appeared to be in violation of the agreement, but this was simply unenforceable (and no one wants to work with a colleague who doesn't want to be there anyway).

This was a leadership lesson in that an academic's only obligation is to provide adequate clinical service and academic productivity if that is part of the agreement. The challenge for the medical leader is not to enforce the agreement per se but to help create fertile ground and an attractive atmosphere that will retain the recruits. When it comes down to it, however, they must practise where they feel they can be most productive, and they cannot be forced to remain in a setting in which they'd rather not be.

Since this event, the standard written agreement has been changed to include wording that commits the individual to a specific number of years with the organization and that if a unilateral decision to leave is made, there is a risk of financial penalty to the departing clinician to compensate for the support afforded by the organization. Whether that revised language is any more enforceable than the language of the previous agreement remains to be seen.

Tenure and Contract

The foregoing situation involved one hospital department's version of tenure, an achievement level in the academic setting that could lead to an indefinite appointment. Universities (medical schools) have other benchmarks, such as promotion to the next level in a specific length of time (for instance, promotion from assistant to associate professor within a seven-year period). That leaves the decision about prolongation of an appointment in the hands of a presumably objective body, using long-tested criteria, and in an odd way partially lifts the burden off the shoulders of the division or department head. If the criteria are not met as determined by objective assessors, the appointment is not continued.

In this type of culture the clinician who is clearly not making the grade when interim evaluations are carried out and who has ample opportunity and time to correct deficiencies in his performance will be able to forecast the inevitable and start looking for alternate employment. This process may seem draconian, but the usual length of time (seven years) should be adequate for both sides to determine whether or not an academic career will be successful.

In the community setting the contract agreements are usually less structured. Currently a newly recruited physician or surgeon must practice competently, be collegial (a team player), and abide by the hospital policies and rules and regulations as set out by the board of trustees and administered through the medical advisory committee.

As the measurement of outcomes, complications, patient satisfaction, and the like are so rudimentary, especially at the physician level, competence is measured approximately at best. When our hospitals improve IT systems enough that per-physician results in all domains are available on a monthly or quarterly basis, we will be in a position to link ongoing appointments to performance – the ultimate accountability, when an individual's results must equal or exceed accepted benchmarks. This is likely a decade off in universal terms because of the high cost of adequate IT systems, but it is already here in a few advanced organizations.

The issue of a doctor's right to make a living is a sensitive but important one. When hospital resources are provided to an individual to care for patients, and that doctor earns fees for services, it's not surprising that the 'right to practice,' in perpetuity, regardless of performance, becomes a standard in the doctor's mind. That thinking is quickly becoming replaced by an accountability model in which outcomes of practice are being monitored, and *good* outcomes are important in retaining your hospital appointment.

My own prediction, now that there is no mandatory retirement age (see 'Retirement' in chapter 4), is that in the relatively near future doctors connected to hospitals will have time-limited contracts with no mention of the age of the doctor, and renewal of that contract at intervals will be dependent on specific clearly articulated criteria. This is more like the situation in legal firms and may be a good way of achieving progress and renewal without the age factor being a driving force (as it has been for decades). Incidentally, if doctors were to be more competent with their own personal financial management than they have tended to be, the need to continue practising long after others have retired might not be so acute.

Recruit from within and nurture your recruit externally.

Stories abound regarding recruitment of famous people who are celebrated in national and international medical circles, who are recruited from elsewhere to a prestigious post, and then are found to have glaring weaknesses incompatible with success in their new environment. That speaks to the true meaning of due diligence (which may include actually engaging in clinical activity shoulder to shoulder with a potential recruit) and also to the advantages of recruiting an individual who has grown up with you. That said, to avoid cloning and intellectual boredom most departments and their new recruits will benefit from extra specialized training undertaken in a different setting in order to bring something unique back to the organization.

Once someone has joined an organization, it is the responsibility of a medical leader to ensure that promises are kept and that the individual clinician is progressing in the various domains described in the written agreement.

As a medical leader you have additional responsibilities regarding the new recruit. You will need to ensure that the person is welcomed by colleagues, perhaps offered aid in the finding of accommodation, and made aware of all necessary hospital processes, guidelines, and by-laws.

A *staff manual* is often an excellent adjunct for the new recruit to have as a reference and should be considered for each department.

To keep up with any concerns or insecurities, ensure that there are

- opportunities for appropriate coaching from mentors,
- repeated meetings with the division head,
- meetings with the research mentor, where appropriate,
- meetings with the hospital president, and
- meetings with the chairs of the university division and department.

Such frequent meetings are advisable in order to confirm the enthusiasm of everyone who has been a stakeholder in the recruitment process.

If the potential recruit is a more experienced professional, it's a good idea to actually spend some concentrated time with that doctor in professional settings, seeing at first hand the interaction with other human beings and the new recruit's clinical acumen, educational abilities, and so on. We are all vulnerable to the honeymoon syndrome, whereby a new recruit is lusted after because of obvious attributes, while weaknesses are ignored or overlooked.

A more mature doctor is usually recruited to a position of leadership or of an endowed chair. The named endowed chair is an effective tool, for reasons of finance and prestige, which provides flexibility for the chairholder, allowing him to pursue specific areas of personal interest (see 'Fund-Raising' in chapter 9). However, remember that a more experienced professional may be able to deliver a resounding presentation or perform magnificently in front of a search committee but may turn out to be an unanticipated dud in real life – therefore the importance of maximum due diligence.

> **Whenever possible, a meaningful prolonged exposure to a person in action is a great substitute for repeated glowing written reports from friends of the proposed recruit.**

SITUATION 4.3
JOE, THE MEDICAL STUDENT: *Lack of Due Diligence Will Bite You*

Perhaps the best example (or worst, depending on your point of view) of the importance of due diligence occurred about fifteen years ago with a university medical student. Joe was a fourth-year medical student (or clinical clerk) at the university in a large North American city. He was also a medical graduate from an eastern European country and had entered a special program that recognized students trained abroad as well as the shortage of doctors trained in this country, particularly family physicians.

The student was absolutely loved by patients because he spent time with them, got to know them and their families, was obviously moved by their trials and tribulations while they were in hospital, and was generally extremely compassionate to both patients and fellow health care providers. In fact, a number of patients went out of their way to compliment his exemplary care, supporting his status as a successful graduating doctor.

During daily rounds I asked questions of the various members of the team and began to realize that Joe's knowledge base was causing concern. Each incorrect, incomplete, or puzzling answer led to further questioning, and when I realized that his medical ignorance was profound, I eventually declared to a colleague, 'I'm not sure this guy has ever been to medical school.' Incidentally, Joe also mentioned that he had been on his country's Olympic track team, specializing in the 400 metre relay. No one had thought to question him further because he was a very nice fellow, sincere, cooperative, hard working, and apparently very athletic.

You know where this story is going. When Joe was given a dismal failing grade on our clinical service, very unusual in the past twenty years in our system, a recommendation was made that his documentation be reviewed. As it turned out, Joe (or whatever his real name was) had started but never finished medical school, had falsified his records, and of course had never been an accomplished athlete, let alone a member of an Olympic team.

Even though Joe was not applying to be a consultant surgeon, this experience emphasized our need to vigorously validate the past of every single individual regardless of apparent or stated status.

Retention begins the day after a prize candidate is signed on. A new recruit must have an appropriate road paved, as described in the written agreement, and the retention of that candidate can be more challenging (as illustrated in situation 4.2, featuring Doctor G) than the initial recruitment.

As evidenced above, we live a paradox every day as we encourage the building of successful careers and, in so doing, ensure that we will lose those professionals some day to apparently greener pastures.

The effective medical leader who truly nurtures individuals must regard new recruits as family members who are being given an effective start to life and development and who will predictably grow and move ahead. Ideally, that growth would involve new positions in the same environment, but predictably many will leave the nest.

If a medical leader can point to colleagues who have gone on to bigger and better things, especially major clinical or academic positions, then the job of career cultivation is being done effectively. If, however, the move is made out of frustration and an inability to meet the needs of the academic or community physician, that responsibility for failure must also be borne by the leader.

You will be responsible for *caring*, as you are with patients, and you should meet regularly with the new clinicians. You must probe to see if they are achieving an appropriate work-life balance, that they are devoting adequate time to family, that they are receiving the resources necessary to meet their objectives, that they are developing a relationship with their mentor, that they feel comfortable with the clinical backup that young practitioners always need, and that the financial compensation is as stated in the written agreement. If any one of these issues is of concern, it is your responsibility to act quickly and positively. The first few years are critical to the feeling of support experienced by the new recruit.

Many literature references are made to the accomplished, upwardly mobile individual as a 'thoroughbred,' obviously recognizing the form and function of a successful stakes racehorse. I appreciate that analogy and would add that some of my major responsibilities are to support those thoroughbreds, to tape their ankles when there are problems, and to ensure that the track is as dry and safe as possible for them to excel.

Some Additional Advice

The following are some additional issues about recruiting and retaining the best and brightest.

If, for example, a successful clinician comes to your office threatening to leave unless provided with more resources and a better deal than that of his colleagues, formulate your next response carefully. On the one hand, if the individual has delusions of grandeur, this may be an opportunity to be the first to offer him a pen to sign the letter of resignation. On the other hand, if this is a truly outstanding must-keep doctor, you have a problem. You may have to find a creative way to retain that star, for instance by providing resources in an area in which he or she has unique strengths, and colleagues will be less likely to complain that they are being disadvantaged. Professionals are difficult enough to manage fairly, and if one is able to negotiate a sweet deal in this ad hoc way, the integrity of the group and the process may be eroded. Remember that the news will travel by the speed of light, and chaos will be the result if undue favouritism is perceived.

You may be tempted to offer enhanced compensation, more resources, sophisticated equipment, or more time protection for specialized activities. Some or all of these may be necessary to retain an outstanding professional, but as the number of side deals increases, the effect on finances and on the team culture may be devastating; there are other human beings in your organization who will feel cheated.

My general rule is that any ad hoc deal made with a potentially departing doctor must explicitly support the hospital mission: if it does not, sayonara and good luck to the doctor.

SITUATION 4.4
RETAINING DOCTOR H, A WORLD-CLASS NEUROSURGEON:
Be Careful with the Ad Hoc Deal

When Doctor H, a world-class neurosurgeon, was on the verge of accepting a very lucrative offer from another academic centre, a number of steps were taken to improve not only his own personal professional situation but also the programmatic advancement in his area of cerebrovascular interventions in order to advance the hospital's mission and the mission of a substantial number of colleagues in his division and program.

The collaborative proposal had been made by Doctor H himself. If his interest had been restricted to his own welfare, he likely would have departed with little resistance from anyone.

SITUATION 4.5
DOCTOR T'S RECRUITMENT FROM AFAR: *Know the Motives*

Doctor T is an accomplished mid-career plastic and reconstructive surgeon specializing in microvascular breast reconstruction, and a leader in European cancer surgery. He was faced with the same predicament as scores of other outstanding surgeons in Germany, that is, the hierarchy in which the senior 'Herr Professor' rules the roost and chooses all plum operations, and everyone else remains at a plebeian level. This disgruntled but talented surgeon would have jumped at the chance of a North American academic post because it would promise a much better income, research opportunities, and potentially a new and exciting life for him and his family. His work was well known to many North American leaders because of his connections made at international conferences, and one such division head regarded this potential recruit as a real find.

Two trips to New York followed, and a very positive impression was made by this German practitioner through oral presentations, participation in rounds, and interviews where he was forthright, articulate, sincere, and collegial. Further discussions led to a declaration on Doctor T's part that, given the right circumstances, he would be willing to uproot his family, sell its home in Germany, and emigrate to North America.

This set in place a series of complex processes necessary to recruit from abroad, including those involving a formal university search, immigration applications, and consideration for special academic licensure in the state. A two-million-dollar endowed chair was made available as an unusually attractive perk, and a transatlantic video conference was held to interview this valuable candidate; the chair was subsequently awarded and confirmed by the hospital's CEO and the university's dean of medicine. All pieces of this complex puzzle appeared to be in place.

A type of memorandum of understanding was then sent to Doctor T, outlining all the written promises, and the document was promptly signed by him and returned as a commitment to close the deal. Several weeks went by, and nothing was heard from Doctor T, despite a number of emails asking him if there was anything he and his family needed to help facilitate their preparations for the big move.

The local licensing body was then contacted, and it was discovered that no official application had been made personally by Doctor T, a requirement of the licensing authority.

Realizing that something was amiss, the recruiting leaders sent a registered letter giving Doctor T one week to respond to their concerns regarding the licensure application; after all, his signed commitment had been in hand for three months by that time.

You know where this story is going. Doctor T sheepishly wrote back and admitted that he had received two other major job offers in Germany, and he was in the process of evaluating them despite his signed agreement to come to New York.

Have a nice day, Doctor T.

The senior leaders learned two things that day: (1) medical and surgical life in other jurisdictions can be as different as night and day from that in our own experience, and (2) you must put yourself in the place of the applicant, truly understanding his or her motives. Also, when you get burned, rather than react or become frustrated, treat the experience as another learning opportunity; you are wiser than you were yesterday.

> **Beware the experienced external academician or clinician who is applying for a medical leadership position. If the recruitment of this applicant seems too good to be true, it probably is. It may be that he or she is using you as a lever to get an enhanced deal back home, and you can use your time more wisely.**

The business of recruitment of leaders, and the assembling of packages with which a number of colleagues have to agree, can be an incredibly time-consuming process, and you don't need to spend your time helping someone get a better contract somewhere else.

Managing Medical Professionals

The well-celebrated video advertisement conjured up by Electronic Data Systems (a business and technology services industry, incidentally founded by Ross Perot in 1962) and showing images of horsemen herding cats in a wild west setting[23] may come to mind when the concept of managing medical professionals is considered. The presumed lack of control and the antiquated insufficient resources to do the job may be apt in some groups of individuals. However, with regard to the advertisement mentioned, we should remember that cats are wayward and perhaps adventuresome, but relatively harmless.

In the case of medical professionals, the image of a pride of larger cats or a sloth of bears may be more appropriate: these animals may be attracted by pleasures such as raw meat or honey, but the chance of angry retaliation is always present and threatens the zookeeper at all times. Rather than using this predatory image, I prefer to think of my surgical colleagues in a way expressed in one of my yearly 'state of the union' addresses, using a flock of migrating birds as a backdrop. These particular geese had different appearances from one another because their wings were in various distinct configurations. As I said then, 'This stylized image captures in my mind our surgical family at UHN. Its members all have the capacity to fly, and indeed soar above most others, and in their make-up and behaviour they are free-spirited, independent, and, as you can see, certainly exalt in being different from one another. But at the same time *they fly in formation*, knowing that by sticking together and acknowledging the power of team in sometimes unpredictable conditions, their performance (and the recognition of that performance) is the best it can be.' At this point, you might want to review chapter 3, 'The Team and Teamwork.'

> **Individuality and personal achievements are supported and encouraged but only in the context of being part of a team that must play by a set of well-described rules.**

One of the major features of the professional behaviour of physicians and surgeons is that there is invariably a sense of entitlement. This feeling is pervasive and, on the surgical side, was given even greater impetus by a recent pseudoscientific, published article from Barcelona. From a recent report in the *British Medical Journal*, researchers at the University of Barcelona found, in a small study, that male surgeons are more attractive to women than are other doctors. The researchers pointed out (and I kid you not) that 'surgeons spend a lot of time in operating rooms which are cleaner, cooler and have a higher oxygen content than the average medical ward where physicians spend most of their time, which could help surgeons keep their looks.'[24]

Is there any wonder how over decades a sense of entitlement, especially on the part of surgeons, might evolve?

Professionalism

The old definition of professionals in days gone by was in direct relation to what they were paid for their services; for example, an amateur athlete received compensation only for expenses, and a professional made his or her living from the activity. That sports analogy, of course, has been blown up long ago in both amateur and professional domains, and a much more detailed look at professionalism has occupied especially the medical profession in recent years. Being a professional in the twenty-first century implies the following:

- Becoming an expert in a specialized field
- Acquiring knowledge and skills that are used to serve patients
- Improving those tools on an ongoing basis, as knowledge in the field expands

- Having academic qualifications that satisfy standards of the certify-
  ing and licensing bodies that are ultimately responsible for the
  quality of care offered to patients
- Evidencing a high quality of work in a specific area
- Working to a high standard of integrity and ethical behaviour in the
  service of patients

The appropriate behaviours expected of us as professionals include
the following:

- Respect for all individuals with whom we come in contact, includ-
  ing patients, family members, colleagues, and other health care
  workers
- A personal appearance befitting our privilege of caring for patients
- Reliability and punctuality in our daily activities
- Effective communication with others
- Respect of confidentiality with regard to both patient and administrative issues
- Honesty, integrity, and empathy in our actions with everyone in
  the organization
- Acceptance of responsibility for our activities in our various roles,
  including the official transference of that responsibility to others
  when we are absent
- Knowledge of our own limitations, and the ability to seek help as
  required with decision making, whether patient or management
  related.

It will be your responsibility as a medical leader to first and foremost
be a role model for others in your own personal consistent demonstration of the elements of professionalism. Your patient management must
embody all the dimensions of patient-centered care, and your comport-
ment and behaviour must reflect the principles cited above as well as
the values held by your organization. Your tougher job will be to uphold those principles if they appear to be violated by your friends and
colleagues. That subject will be addressed now.

Treat Everyone the Same but Differently

The confusing subheading may suggest that I have finally given way to
the pressures of my job and that contradiction rules. But there is method in my madness. The one critical characteristic of the behaviour of

any leader who lives his or her values on a day-to-day basis is *consistency* – consistency in the demonstration of those inherent values, consistency in availability for discussing issues, and consistency in punctuality and conduct of meetings, and so on.

Unfortunately, medical leaders are in the precarious position of what I might call perpetual impending suicide. Years of building a strong leadership image can be wasted by a simple error in judgment, a wayward act of impropriety, or an apparently inconsequential act of petulance. It's not that people are ready to knock anyone off the pedestal; it's that the sense of betrayal and disillusionment that enters the minds of workers when a leader falters changes the leadership dynamic. One has to look no further than daily newspapers and situation-room television on CNN to confirm that fact; the Bill Clintons, Larry Craigs, and Eliot Spitzers of the world are acutely aware of the far-ranging consequences of inappropriate behaviour.

Consistency of behaviour is a hallmark of anyone who wishes to set an example and walk the talk. Everyone, including management at all levels, has to play by the same rules in an organization and observe the mandate of accountability in all facets of their professional life. However, every individual is different with regard to background, needs, strengths, weaknesses, the ability to execute, and the ability to absorb victory and failure with equal determination for the future.

Many people who are reading this book may have the intimate experience of bringing up two or more children and realize how similar their kids are in some ways and how startlingly different they are in others. My wife and I often wonder how all these varied characteristics could emerge from the same gene pool and produce such distinct individuals as our children appear to be. Doctors are exactly the same; that is, they vary tremendously in their behaviour, especially in the crucible of the medical or surgical hospital environment. However, as with our children, we hope, expect, and anticipate that despite varying personalities the ability to adapt will produce excellent and consistent results.

I believe that the first task, or series of tasks, for a new medical leader is to get to know your colleagues better than leaders did in the past. If you are a new medical leader recruited from another city, that will be a formidable undertaking because you likely won't know all the personalities well; even if you're an internal candidate, getting to know your colleagues *better* is a necessary pursuit.

My recommendation for the first few months of any responsible position is that a medical leader should try to avoid making any big decisions (unless of course they are absolutely required). The first quarter should be devoted to meeting all members of the group *individually* to learn about their particular career goals, their personal lives, and their relationships in the organization.

Perhaps most important: solicit their opinions about where the enterprise should be going and how the enterprise should get from here to there. Everyone has an opinion; some opinions come from the most unexpected places and are surprisingly helpful.

In those first few months it will be possible for the new medical leader to make an assessment of the culture of the division or department by asking the following questions:

- Is it 'every man for himself'?
- Is there a spirit of cooperation and mutual respect?
- Is there a commitment to a meaningful team approach to patient care?

When you have answers to those questions, it will be possible for you to analyse what the next priorities should be and where your energies ought to be directed.

A small point: go to *their* offices to meet. Those of us from a more senior generation will always remember the days when we were called to the principal's or vice-principal's office in elementary school. At the very best it was, 'Oh-oh, what have I done now?' and at the very worst, 'I'm going to get the strap!' (or some other form of punishment). That statement about fear of corporal punishment undoubtedly dates me to a veritable Neanderthal time, but suffice it to say that a meeting for a clinician in a superior's office has certain connotations of power. It is a very simple thing for you, as a medical leader, to go to a colleague's office – and a more important gesture than you might think. Remember, you are going to a colleague's office to ask for information, for trust, and for cooperation and collaboration.

The personal relationships that a new leader establishes with colleagues are incredibly important, and the initial meetings often set the stage for them to be long and trusting. However, if no meetings occur and the only interaction is one of authority, an unhealthy or no personal relationship may be the result.

Politics in hospitals is a notoriously volatile game. The competition among professionals can be stiff and sometimes nasty, whether success be measured in number and/or kinds of patient cases done, amount of money earned, educational prizes won, grants held, or manuscripts published. As a medical leader you have a role to play in this potentially explosive atmosphere in figuring out how all the contributions of every member in a particular division can be valued and recognized. That, of course, captures the ideal situation in which every single professional is contributing positively in some way. If, however, someone is not making contributions and is consistently a negative influence on the team, then other steps must be taken. (This is not as easy in the medical field as it is in business, although firing, with cause or without cause, is challenging in both instances; see the 'Competence' section later in this chapter.)

The challenge occurs when a valued professional member transgresses normal behaviour and clearly needs to change that behaviour. Sterling accomplishments and achievements may far outweigh the negative act, but a less than appropriate response by the leader to that behaviour may erode the very foundation of the unique culture that has developed in a division or department in a hospital (or other medical institution). News travels at the speed of light, and bad behaviour left untreated, ignored, or even rewarded will be remembered. Surgeons especially are dependent on hospital resources, and the knee-jerk response is to deprive the delinquent surgeon of those resources as punishment, as an encouragement to change behaviour. However, this could be construed as consequently penalizing the wrong person, that is, the patient who may be on a waiting list for surgery and who perhaps cannot and should not wait for a later date.

The rearing of children is frequently reminiscent of the handling of behavioural problems with adults decades later in life. Rudolph Dreikurs made the observation in the 1960s that one has to be careful to separate the behaviour from the child.[25] The child is inherently a good person and, as a developing person, must learn the behaviours that are consistent with acceptable norms of society. It's incredibly important not to make children feel that they're bad people, but to enlighten them as to what behaviour is acceptable and what isn't. It may be discouraging and even dismaying for you as a medical leader to find that some grown men and women don't seem to have learned much during their childhood in that regard, but you'd better get used to reality.

You'll be surprised at the occasional selfishness, pettiness, and downright childishness of some adults. It will be up to you as a medical leader to mitigate disruption caused by such behaviour and to take steps to move your colleagues to a more stable norm. But how can you change behaviour? Although the easy response may be to temporarily deprive a professional of the ability to practise, that should be a last resort.

Can mature adults in their thirties, forties, or fifties actually change their behaviour and treat people and processes in a consistently more respectful way? Although I respect the beliefs of those who say that all our interpersonal relationships are indelibly imprinted on our limbic system somewhere between the ages of three and five years and are consistent with our mother's values, it is my belief that adults can indeed change their behaviour.

SITUATION 4.6
DOCTOR R CHANGED HER WAYS: *Play to the Strengths of Your Colleagues*

I used to have a colleague who frequently harassed nurses, belittling them in the operating room, in the intensive care unit, and on the inpatient service. In a rather perverse way, Doctor R was always consistent in her behaviour! After repeated formal complaints by nurses and discussions with her, followed by mandatory behaviour-modification courses, Doctor R did, in fact, change. Although the standard rehabilitation tool of a behaviour-modification course may have helped in her transformation, I think the major factor was the ascendance of this intelligent, driven woman to a more responsible position of leadership.

With her accomplishments recognized, Doctor R did become a new person, interacting in a very positive and respectful way consistently enough that nurses, in fact, came to prefer working with her. This is not to say that bad behaviour should be in any way rewarded, but playing to the strengths of an individual may create successes that do, in fact, improve behaviour.

At one point I was moved to make a short list of surgeons who, believe it or not, shared one characteristic: when especially young nurses saw that they would be working the next day with one of these surgeons, there was a statistically significant increase in sick time recorded. One fortunate fact about clinicians relates to their egos, and so a discreet discussion about this finding with the specific surgeons thus identified led to immediate improvement.

Ego can be disruptive, but it can also be a good thing and a motivating factor.

As a medical leader you always have to remember one simple but important fact. It frequently happens that an individual doctor's character traits that are leading to problems in the workplace are exactly the characteristics that have made that individual very successful in his professional career. For example, the following characteristics may contribute to clinical success and other accomplishments in education and research:

- A self-centred drive for perfection
- A single-mindedness that sometimes forgets that others are necessary for the completion of a task
- A selfishness that would be inexcusable in a caring relationship

As a medical leader you must try to understand the differing motivations of each of your colleagues.

Although the previous situation was what I would consider a success story, some situations are not always remediable.

SITUATION 4.7
DOCTOR J, AN IRREMEDIABLE SITUATION: *Sometimes Surgery Is the Only Solution*

About a year after I had taken on a new position I was faced with a problem created by Doctor J, a surgeon who operated in our institution and other hospitals on a 'part-time' basis. This designation was unusual in our organization since we no longer recruited surgeons who were not full-time academics. However, there were some practitioners in certain divisions who had been grandfathered from past associations and so continued to provide service in a number of hospitals.

During one particular surgical procedure Doctor J decided that he would fashion a new instrument that could serve to cauterize tissue in a novel way. Unbeknownst to the anaesthesiologists and nurses in the OR, Doctor J had brought into the room a length of sterile wire that he proceeded to fix into a loop configuration to the hand-held cautery instrument.

Knowing that all devices had to be formally approved nationally, as well as locally at the hospital level, the OR nurses immediately reported this to the surgeon who was covering for me in my absence, and indicated to Doctor J that he was using an unapproved and potentially unsafe instrument. He ignored them, continuing on with this modified hand piece.

Let me be clear that no harm had come to the patient, but concerns were expressed that this new instrument had not passed the necessary biomedical engineering tests and that it therefore should not be used under any circumstances. The acting surgeon-in-chief went into the OR to advise Doctor J to cease and desist. At that point, after Doctor J repeatedly refused to stop what he was doing, the acting surgeon-in-chief was forced to disconnect the cautery machine from the power source so that it simply could not be used.

The story was recounted in some detail on a standard incident report and confirmed by the nurses, the anaesthesiologists, and the acting surgeon-in-chief. I met with Doctor J, who admitted that all of the accusations were true. He was entirely unrepentant, and when I asked him what sort of punishment or action he felt should be taken, he became rather threatening in his behaviour.

Ordinarily in such a situation a prescribed series of steps might be useful to handle a particular behavioural problem; however, nothing like this had been described, and certainly this incident did not fit any 'crime' that anyone had ever faced previously in our organization. Owing to the perceived danger to patients, I considered this to be a particularly dangerous and offensive act. As any suspension from clinical practice would involve a mandatory notification to the licensing authority in the jurisdiction, I gave this usually competent surgeon the opportunity to resign his privileges for a six-month period. Doctor J did just that and elected subsequently to conduct his practice at hospitals other than ours. (Lest you feel that this surgeon was evicted from our house simply to wreak havoc in another unsuspecting environment, I must emphasize that he was, and is, a competent clinician who now works for a leader who is fully aware of past indiscretions.)

Sometimes significant disease requires surgical excision. In a rather perverse way, I welcome such opportunities to act decisively because the message sent to other surgeons, and especially to nurses, anaesthesiologists, and other health care providers, is thus clear and particularly supportive of every team member, their jobs, and accepted hospital standards.

The Disruptive Physician

Thinking about the potential advantage of having an incident that, when acted upon, demonstrates and confirms the values of the organization reminds me of *The No Asshole Rule: Building a Civilized Workplace and*

Surviving One That Isn't (2007).[26] By Bob Sutton, this erudite tome with the less than erudite name describes *the disruptive colleague phenomenon*.

The Ontario Medical Association, for example, has a service module devoted to the disruptive physician as part of its physician-health program. In addition, the College of Physicians and Surgeons of Ontario together with the Ontario Hospital Association have published a *Guidebook for Managing Disruptive Physician Behaviour* (2008).[27] The introduction to the guidebook opens with the sentence 'Disruptive behaviour occurs when the use of inappropriate words, actions or inactions by a physician interferes with his or her ability to function well with others to the extent that the behaviour interferes with, or is likely to interfere with, quality health care delivery' (p. 4). In addition, your hospital and university will doubtless have easily accessible written policies to guide you in your management of a difficult situation.

In his book *The No Asshole Rule*, Sutton argues that by having one disruptive individual ('an asshole') in an organization and handling the situation appropriately on a continuing basis, dividends are produced – others see regularly how *not* to behave. This presupposes that the bad behaviour is not rewarded. Sutton contends that it's better to have one or two assholes than none at all. (In Britain, the term *bully* is used interchangeably in this context, which is perhaps a more genteel moniker.)

There may be other clues that an individual professional has ongoing problems with relationships. The first place to look is the secretarial team. Some physicians will have changed secretaries (or administrative assistants) a number of times in any five-year period, with explanations such as 'incompetence' or 'inability to handle my difficult and busy practice.' This type of pattern usually speaks to a broader problem of people interaction.

Hospitals are like small cities with a variety of cultures in the various areas, including patient floors, research areas, operating rooms, and intensive care units. Each area harbours a cadre of professionals who work together, are reasonably stable in terms of their numbers and how long they hold their appointments, and are knowledgeable about one another's abilities, work habits, trustworthiness, and sense of humour.

A definable culture seems to evolve that identifies each service, and when one enters the area, this culture is palpable in terms of how people address each other, react to stress, solve problems, and interact socially. It only takes one or two individuals with disruptive behaviour to poison such an environment, and this type of behaviour may be overt or insidious. Disruptive behaviour may involve any or all of the following:

- Personal insults
- Sarcasm
- Rude interruptions
- Snide email messages
- Failure to collaborate
- Public derision of others
- Dirty looks

The absolutely worst kind of disruptive behaviour is perpetrated by an individual who is in a position of power over another and who at the same time is perfectly respectful to superiors – the 'kiss up, kick down' sort of person.

What should you do about this person, especially a medical professional who has proven accomplishments in a field that is valued by your organization? In business, the advice is simply to fire the offender, and when that person has gone from the organization, often people say, 'We should have done this years ago,' and productivity is enhanced. In medicine, replete as it is with independent practitioners, the best way to deal with disruptive professionals, of course, is not to hire them in the first place. The due diligence on recruitment therefore is critical.

In many cases your confidence in hiring someone is heightened because the individual is a surgical or medical resident who worked in the organization previously for extended periods during training. But beware of the judgment on a trainee who has worked with you. Before committing to hiring anyone, be sure that you know how that former resident or surgical fellow works with peers, students, secretaries and administrative staff, nurses, and other health care personnel.

> **The least reliable person to judge true behaviour may well be you as the former boss of the potential recruit – he or she always behaved well around you.**

Some Guidelines and an Exercise for Dealing with the Disruptive Physician

Let's say you *have* hired an academic and/or clinical star, Dr Comet, and now you realize you are dealing with a disruptive physician. Here are a few general guidelines for the times that there are difficulties concerning the behaviour of a medical professional in your division or department:

1 *Specific charge.* If there is a specific charge, you must go through the hospital process that is aimed at resolving issues between individuals, and take appropriate steps as per hospital by-laws and guidelines.
2 *Written complaint.* You should always encourage formal complaints to be put in writing; complaints that are not in writing cannot be taken forward.
3 *Informal meeting.* If there are ongoing concerns expressed about the insidious behaviour of a professional, but no specific charges in writing, the individual must know that you know, and an informal meeting should be arranged to discuss general issues.

Here are some recommendations for the meeting:

- You must always hear the individual's side of the story; however, if there have been recurrent concerns expressed by a number of different people in your organization, then there's obviously a problem.
- Dr Comet must be reminded that his contract states that he will act in a collegial manner with all health care personnel in the organization. The language will vary according to the hospital involved, but this statement regarding behaviour is always present. He should also be reminded that continued privileges for each individual working in your institution depend on appropriate behaviour.
- He must recognize that bad behaviour, although sometimes effective in getting what one wants on an ad hoc basis, will not be rewarded. As stated previously, the most common unhelpful act of a medical leader is to reward bad behaviour.
- He should be informed that repeated episodes and reports will lead to specific measures such as decreased access to resources, alteration in resident coverage (if yours is an academic centre), behaviour-modification courses, and possibly suspension of privileges.
- Dr Comet must know that possible suspension of privileges usually mandates first reporting the concerns to the medical advisory committee (the body that actually determines the ultimate punishment), the vice-president of medical affairs (chief of staff or other

individuals in your organization), and the local licensing body; the latter is a huge deterrent because such a report may lead to a formal review by that body, independent of the hospital.

- Dr Comet should be reminded that behaviour and ability to collaborate with colleagues are at the top of the list of considerations when hospitals are considering the recruitment of professionals and reappointment on a yearly basis.
- Dr Comet must understand the next steps that would be taken if there were to be recurrence of the behaviour.
- The meeting must be documented, and this documentation must be sent to the individual in a confirmatory letter. (Document, document, document.)
- It is important that you as a medical leader be serious, controlled, and impassive, and in discussing the issues and consideration of the next action, you must act as though there is no choice. You are following the guidelines of your organization. This is definitely *not* a case of vindictiveness; it is just a matter of process.

In this situation you as a medical leader may be in a particularly difficult position if you have known the offender for a long time, are younger than the offender, and/or personally like the individual as a friend. These reasons make it all the more important that the interaction be serious and businesslike.

One last thing about this issue: do not become disillusioned or dismayed. Just do the right thing, shake your head in disbelief, share the story with your spouse (if he or she is discreet), smile – and go on to the next challenge. And that, in fact, is more serious advice than it sounds.

Once an event or a situation involving disruptive behaviour has been dealt with, it must become part of an individual's record in the event of repeated offences, but it must not surface repeatedly as a subject that will compromise your future association with that individual.

In many situations, selective amnesia is appropriate!

Performance Evaluations: The 360°

Evaluations of performance are dicey undertakings. Current trends and appreciation of human behaviour have transformed the way human resources departments operate in organizations. It is assumed that everyone who works in an organization desires feedback and that all human beings wish to learn, to advance in their lives, and to improve their skills and options in the world. While that may not be true for everyone, it is a safe assumption that in the professional world, people care, and people do want to grow.

Periodic evaluations of performance are critical to personal growth, advancement in the job market, and financial gain.

Be careful of making evaluations of your co-workers. Giving performance feedback may be one of the most sensitive practices you will ever engage in as a medical leader. Few people are able to take constructive criticism even in the positive spirit with which it is intended; negative feedback is really tough to swallow.

SITUATION 4.8
MS W AND THE CLINICIAN'S EVALUATION: *The Tightrope of Performance Evaluation*

Ms W was a medical secretary who was loyal, courteous, relatively efficient, and a credit to her employer, Doctor K (a clinician), the hospital, and herself.

When a formal performance-review process was introduced in the hospital for the first time, Doctor K completed an evaluation form as required and answered the questions honestly: Ms W was an honest, hard-working, devoted secretary whose work habits were generally excellent and whose skills at word-processing were just average. The result of his honesty, that is, rating her as 'above average' to 'excellent' in most categories, and 'average' in some basic secretarial skills, was that Ms W became offended, saddened, and eventually quite distraught. The crisis abated, she continued on as a fine secretary, and Doctor K was then faced with the completion of the same evaluation form a year later.

Priding himself on being an intelligent individual and capable of learning from his mistakes, Doctor K decided that he was not going to be beaten a second time by what he considered a somewhat silly process in the first place. The next evaluation was simply superlative, Doctor K was pleased, Ms W was pleased, and she received a well-deserved raise. All proceeded happily ever after, or for a short time anyway.

About three weeks later Doctor K received a call from the hospital's CEO, who was inquiring about Ms W and asking if she was a capable and effective worker. Doctor K, of course, answered in the affirmative, after which the CEO indicated that Ms W had applied for a job in her office, and she was just making a final check with Ms W's supervising clinician. It had become obvious to Doctor K that the CEO had scanned the best evaluations of the executive secretaries, cherry-picked the outstanding one based on the evaluations, and approached the clinician's secretary, who had then made a formal application to work in the CEO's office.

Doctor K and Ms W had a very good relationship. He thanked her for all her service, and she transferred to work with the CEO.

Did Doctor K do the right thing by trying to beat the process of evaluation and being less than fully truthful on the evaluation form? Did he do his medical secretary and the organization any service by doing so? In fact, Ms W left the CEO's office three weeks later to pursue other opportunities, having found the work uninspiring and menial. Since then Doctor K has still been generous but entirely truthful, as he hopes his supervisors have been with him.

This same problem is illustrated daily in the ongoing assessments of the performance of students and residents in the medical and surgical training setting, which essentially constitutes a master-apprentice relationship. How is it possible that each and every trainee is above average or outstanding in cognitive and practical skills? Of course, there is the occasional resident who is either borderline or truly in need of remediation, but the vast majority are judged to be simply better than is statistically possible.

I'm reminded of the 'Sounding Board' piece in the *New England Journal of Medicine* in 1983,[28] which commented on the unreliability of the dean's letter of reference as a factor in making an evaluation of a candidate for a position. For dark effect and to make his point, the author posited that Adolf Hitler might be described in the following way: 'A natural leader ... good communication skills ... assisted in the development of a number of new technical advancements ... did independent work with minority groups ... likes to find solutions to problems ... special interest in mental health.' So we all need a strong dose of honesty and, along with that, a little coaching on how to give helpful, constructive feedback, which may vary in style according to our assessment of the individual's ability to handle that feedback.

The notion of a 360° evaluation also stimulates consideration of an important ongoing issue: the interpersonal relationships that as a medical leader you promote with your colleagues. What kind of personal connections and interactions lead to the best results, that is, medical leaders doing their jobs and their constituents feeling well served by the leaders? This is an extension of the section on leadership styles ('Involving the "Troops" in Planning' in chapter 2) but pertains more to how personalities interact. My own feeling is that this area is extremely important. Some might claim, 'Larry was not well liked, but he was respected,' and that this is why he was effective. I contend that if Larry were well liked, he might well have been even *more* effective. (However, you might remind me of the trap – we had Joe, the medical student who had never been an Olympic athlete and who was very well liked.)

There are innumerable instances when a medical leader says or does something – sends a directive, chairs a meeting, or stands in line waiting for coffee – and that same action will be interpreted one way or another. Since leaders generally are high-profile individuals, it's not surprising that colleagues will usually have an opinion about anything the medical leader says or does.

Many actions or expressions accredited to individuals are complex and therefore can be interpreted in any number of ways. If you, the leader, are liked as a person, an action you undertake may be interpreted in a positive light, but if you are not liked, the assumption about that same action will be that some draconian measure is afoot. That is not to say that being 'Mr Nice Guy' is the goal, but if someone is pleasant and stimulating to be around, good things happen, and interpretations of events tend to the positive.

How are you seen by your colleagues? It is said that there are three versions of each one of us: how we are seen by others, how we see ourselves, and the *real* truth.

Many individuals get along very well with superiors but have problems with colleagues. Others have no problems with colleagues but do not interact in a consistently positive way with reports.

SITUATION 4.9
MS S DOES NOT BECOME COO: *Examining the Hemispheres of the 360°*

Ms S is a successful financial manager who works hard, is resourceful, presents financial summaries well, and is applauded by her vice-president and senior managers. She gradually climbed the corporate ladder within a major hospital and became its director of finance, always producing solid work in support of the organization.

The position of chief operating officer became available. Ms S applied with the hope that her lack of clinical knowledge and experience would be superseded by her long-standing reputation in the financial field, an absolute mainstay of modern hospitals' success.

During the course of the search process a number of issues came to light. Over the years, Ms S had had increasing numbers of people working under her in her department, and the stories from these individuals were consistently unfavourable. As she assumed more and more responsibility, Ms S was recognized by those who reported to her to be rather abrupt, unfriendly, and sometimes tyrannical. It was said that she took little time to get to know her co-workers.

This profile came as a shock to those on the search committee who knew her to be an affable, pleasant, and socially friendly individual. It was almost as though Ms S presented two different images of herself, depending on with whom she was interacting.

What many potential leaders don't realize is that the relationships with those 'under' them are critical to their personal and their organization's success. The higher you climb on the organizational ladder, the more numerous and important these relationships become. Ms S didn't get the job, and she continues her work as an effective director of finance.

This same framework exists in relationships that medical and surgical residents develop. It may be surprising to some (but it shouldn't be) that a resident who is apparently very likable in the consultant's mind is regarded as a pariah by nurses and especially by more junior trainees.

When I want an evaluation of an individual medical resident in terms of ability to interact in the clinical realm, I always go to nurses, hospital assistants, and other professionals *outside* their own tight circles. The world outside the individual's own personal domain will provide truth in assessing that resident. As a medical leader you must always realize, regrettably, that the way people treat you may well not be the way they treat other people in the workplace.

The formality of relationships varies according to the situation. In the presence of committees or groups that involve individuals outside the organization, or in the presence of patients, I certainly advocate formality and a level of decorum that is friendly and businesslike. For all other interactions, such as internal meetings and discussions, I always advocate and stress that communicating on a first-name basis is the rule. In a hospital setting, everyone must realize that for excellent, seamless patient care and all other activities in a large organization every link in the health care delivery chain is crucial, and I believe simple gestures like the ability to call a senior medical or administrative officer by first name is an easy step to take, and a step in the right direction.

Competence

Of all the topics that concern independent professionals competence may be the most sensitive and arguably the most difficult one to address. The subject of an individual doctor's quality of care and the implications of untoward clinical events that incite a medical leader's response will be discussed in a subsequent section on quality of care. Indeed, if such events are repeated, they may prompt a question of competence. The subject of retirement age and the changing laws of most lands is the one that has led to a somewhat more scientific approach to the issue of competence.

Virtually all jurisdictions have now eliminated any reference to retirement age, and medical organizations have followed suit, striking the subject from hospital by-laws (see the next section, 'Retirement'). The first consideration after the issue of competence in an *aging* clinician is mentioned is that of the competence of *every* professional working in an organization, regardless of age or specialty. Following are questions to be considered:

• How is competence defined?
• How is competence measured?
• What steps are taken if an individual clinician's activities are in question?

The subject of measurements of performance is poorly understood and managed, whether it be in patient care, education, research, or management. In the domain of clinical competence, the measurement of performance is crucial.

Professional bodies in North America have scratched the surface of this vexing problem by demanding proof of ongoing continuing medical education (CME), also known as continuing professional development (CPD). This requires confirmation of yearly attendance at professional meetings and, in the case of maintenance of certification (MAINCERT),[29] which is outlined in Canada by the Royal College of Physicians and Surgeons of Canada, other forms of reading, self-study, and learning projects. Random audits are performed to confirm the number of hours claimed, and the threat of cancellation of specialty certification with the major body is a compelling impetus to comply with the regulations. But is this a reliable measure of competence? Probably not, but it's a start.

In the United States, periodic re-certification and the accumulation of academic points for regular attendance at meetings are seen as reasonable methods to maintain standards.

One very rough yardstick of competence is the lawsuit. Good doctors are sued, and bad doctors may never see the inside of a lawyer's office. The reasons for legal action vary tremendously; however, if a doctor is sued, competence may be brought into question, and a more comprehensive review of a particular practice may be in order (see 'Quality of Care and Risk in Medicine' in chapter 6). The majority of lawsuits involve not only bad patient outcomes, with which every doctor has some experience, but almost always *communication* problems. The doctor has been deemed by the patient and the family to be absent, unresponsive, unrepentant, uncaring, and unsupportive of the patient and his family. The personal relationship is thought to lack caring, and so an element of vindictiveness enters the picture.

I don't feel that the fact of a lawsuit points technically towards clinical incompetence, but repetition may bring to light a tendency that is dangerous for the doctor and an ongoing risk to the organization.

Jonathan D. Beard, a British expert on surgical competence, has extensively studied manual dexterity in aging surgeons and found a diminution in technical skills as time advances. [30] Whether this fine movement compromise, presumably accompanied by judgment that may be actually *enhanced* by experience, results in poor outcomes remains debatable.

Clinical competence involves appropriate selection of patients; judicious testing via, for example, radiology, blood work, and/or biopsy; introduction of treatment; and assessment of the outcomes and complications of that treatment. To date, no universal measurements have been developed for assessing these aspects of clinical competence, but this situation is likely to change soon as funding for hospital information technology and sophistication catch up to the level enjoyed by most businesses. When data are available, it will become possible to stratify all patients with respect to acuity and risk. It will also become possible to judge the appropriateness and quality of diagnosis and treatment, specific for the diagnoses, division, and consulting doctor.

In addition to the outcomes and quality of care, the hospital will be just as interested in the metrics of *efficiency*, with cost-per-case analysis, length of stay, complications, et cetera, for each practising physician or surgeon. Undoubtedly, in the relatively near future the conditions of granting privileges at a hospital will include the necessity of a doctor meeting certain 'corridors' of efficiency in patient care. As stated in the sections on recruitment and retention, for the present time anyway, fairly blunt instruments will have to be employed to get at the truth.

One such blunt instrument, but one that is very interesting, is the Alberta physician assessment review (PAR) project.[31] Each year, in cooperation with the College of Physicians and Surgeons of Alberta, the licensing body, an independent firm sends out separate questionnaires to patients, colleagues, and co-workers in organizations, asking questions about specific physicians. The questions posed are very probing, asking about such things as the amount of time spent with the patient and so on. At the moment, this exercise is not designed to be punitive but simply to give the individual clinician feedback on this unusual 360° evaluation. If it becomes validated with other metrics in future, however, it is easy to see how satisfactory assessments on the PAR might become a condition of maintaining licensure in the province of Alberta and being awarded privileges in a particular hospital. As with all metrics, if validation occurs, patients may demand that this comparative information be available for their scrutiny.

Other proof-of-concept projects are being carried out in the kind of format that airlines employ to assess their pilots on an ongoing basis. In addition to routine simulator activity, which tests reactions to unexpected events during a flight, other processes are used to examine pilot performance.

Mark Auerman, an experienced Air Canada pilot, has spent almost twenty years in the cockpit, flying A320 airbuses and other aircraft for Canada's national airline.[32] In addition to his day job, Auerman has other responsibilities during which he's termed a *check pilot*. A check pilot sits in the cockpit jump seat just behind the co-pilot or, in some cases, acts as the co-pilot during a normal flight. His objective is to grade the overall performance of the flight crew, seeking to document those little slips or irregularities in a flight which, if multiplied and joined by other such imperfections, might create the perfect storm of circumstances or the 'Swiss cheese' model of events described by James Reason.[33]

In this model a number of events may all coincide to produce a disastrous result (the holes in a number of slices of Swiss cheese line up to create one continuous hole, that is, the disaster). At the end of the flight the job of the check pilot is to document all aspects of the experience, summarize any major concerns, and record and discuss the implications with the flight crew. This exercise has proven very useful in illuminating small details for a flight crew who may not have realized the potential consequences of an apparently innocent series of occurrences.

The same sort of process is currently being studied in the operating room at Community Hospital B. A visiting surgeon observes a surgical procedure with a list of descriptors in hand, which will be applied to his or her observations. The 'check surgeon,' of course, knows the operating surgeon, and since the majority of indicators speak to the conduct of the operation rather than the specific technical manoeuvres required, the check surgeon can be a specialist in another field of surgery. The observations are recorded and then discussed with the operating surgeon after the procedure. Importantly, the results of the check surgeon's deliberations do *not* become part of the surgeon's record and are simply used as feedback. These deliberations might include the following:

• Was there a healthy atmosphere during the operation?
• Were decisions made with all available information?
• Was communication adequate among all team members?
• Were there appropriate responses to urgent situations?
• Was there opportunity to learn for all members of the team?

Similar to the Alberta PAR tool, assessments such as these initially serve to provide objective feedback on performance; if and when there is future study to confirm validation, they may be used as more forceful instruments in continuous quality improvement.

This kind of consistent peer review is possible in every medical and surgical domain, but active participation in such a program is dependent on the practitioner's willingness to participate and the organization's commitment to mandate such processes as a condition of privileges in the hospital. In the end, patients demand improved quality of care, and hospitals and clinicians comply as a condition of funding and continued employment.

Retirement

At the other end of our academic life, issues concerning retirement have received significant press in the past few years. Peter Drucker, the management guru, died in 2005 at the age of 95, having just completed his thirty-fourth book. He clearly was old *and* wise and had really never stopped working. Hospital by-laws in the past have often stated that clinicians will become 'honorary staff' on achieving their sixty-fifth birthday.

We have always recognized the notable contributions of our academic surgeons and appreciated that they have made significant financial and other sacrifices over their career in an academic centre as compared with colleagues who may have chosen a community-based practice.

Approaching the retirement issue with appreciation and respect has promoted the idea of collaboration and mutual understanding that addresses in each case the needs of the organization and those of the individual doctor and is a declaration of how we should treat each other yesterday, today, and tomorrow. After all, our achievements are usually directly dependent on those achievements that have come before; we really do stand on the shoulders of our teachers and predecessors in that regard.

Medical leaders tend to be somewhat more experienced than their colleagues on the team, and therefore they are usually closer to retirement. Is there any subject with which a leader deals that is a better example of the ethics of reciprocity? (Christians call it the Golden Rule, that is, 'Do unto others as you would have them do unto you,' and most other religions express a similar sentiment. As the Dalai Lama is quoted as saying, 'Every religion emphasizes human improvement, love, respect for others, sharing other people's suffering. On these lines, every religion has more or less the same viewpoint and the same goal.') It makes good organizational and personal sense to treat the subject of retirement with appropriate care and respect because you might not be all that far away from retirement yourself.

Medical professionals are unusual in that when they assume a position, and especially if they achieve tenure in an academic setting (the definition varies significantly from university to university), the position is essentially open ended; in other words, there may be many details articulated about the initial appointment and expectations of all parties for the first few years, but there is also an assumption that thereafter the world will unfold as it should. This rather loose arrangement apparently has survived for many years because of two factors. First, hospitals, universities, and political jurisdictions (through labour laws) have articulated specific retirement ages, usually sixty-five, which have prompted clinicians to prepare far in advance for their retirement. This is especially important for medical professionals who have been notoriously questionable in their investment-portfolio decision making! Second, hospital budgets and spending weren't monitored and scrutinized as they are currently. The resources provided to doctors to conduct their clinical practices within an institution were determined by the patients coming in the door who needed whatever investigations and treatments were required and available. In Canada, in the first decades of Medicare the hospital bills were simply paid at the end of the year, the budgets expanded, and the provincial ministries of health picked up the overruns. However, things have changed: laws within organizations, universities, and countries have fundamentally eliminated the notion of a specific retirement age, and all medical institutions are counting pennies as they never have before.

The right of an individual to make a living never stops, but *someone* has to make decisions on how the resources are assigned, and that someone is the medical leader. These decisions are more critical in the surgical specialties because surgical activity is far more resource dependent than are the services provided by physicians (with the exception of procedure-based specialties such as cardiology).

As stated previously, many professionals such as lawyers actually sign binding contracts that are time related, rather than linked to the age of the employee, but virtually the whole population of medical professionals has the open-ended arrangements described above. So how do you as a medical leader grapple with this challenge when dealing in a personal way with colleagues?

Since the decision concerning retirement has to be unrelated to any factor that could be construed to be discriminatory, it clearly has to be bilateral in nature, that is, with input from the individual and from the hospital (or other organization, such as the medical school). The decision concerning retirement obviously is an example of interest-based bargaining, and the negotiation must be initiated at an early date, be respectful, and be based on principles and values held dear by both parties.

The issue of competence is critical at any age, but it may be of special interest and a contributing factor in retirement discussions. The business of clinical competence was approached in the previous section of this chapter, but for the purposes of discussion here, we will assume that a clinician who is potentially retiring has no issues of questionable competence.

At what age do we start having discussions about retirement? The answer is at *any* age. Any meeting about career development, even with a forty-year-old professional, should include speaking about a twenty-five- to thirty-year plan, and this emphasizes the importance of having regular fireside chats about career and whether the individual and the organization are meeting their respective expectations. If that sort of meeting occurs on a regular basis (at least once every year or two), then a specific meeting called at the age of sixty-four years and six months would not be necessary.

As death is a part of life, so too is retirement a part of one's career.

The foundation of any discussion concerning retirement is respect – respect for the contributions of an individual to the organization and respect for the clinician's right to have a major role in the decision making about his or her future. During the course of previous years, it is hoped, a relationship of mutual respect has been nurtured. In that way, the issue of retirement is one that is approached together, with the medical leader actually caring about the feelings and the situation faced by the clinician who is soon to retire. The most important qualities of a health care professional in the patient's eyes are *caring and effectiveness*. Those sentiments can also be applied liberally to leaders in their relationships to colleagues. If as an effective medical leader you care, you will be aware of other doctors' motivations, personal needs, and family issues, and the degree to which they have pursued outside interests in addition to the practice of medicine.

On an ongoing basis, as a medical leader you have to discuss with all division or department members the unit's overall plans for the future, the most crucial component of which is recruitment. From observing the development of young stars, the introduction of some programs, and the strengthening or elimination of other programs, it will have become clear to you that gradual changes will be necessary and that the collective work of the division members will have to move ahead. *Renewal* is an absolute sine qua non of progress.

There must be a full understanding by members of all ages of the assignment of resources available to clinicians and, in addition, whether that assignment is dependent on specific criteria. In the past, surgical operating time was frequently distributed according to the size of an individual's practice, and therefore, as the years went by, operating-time assignment often became historical and a tough tradition to break. At our particular academic institution for the past twenty years many factors have been taken into account when resources are assigned to particular surgeons and physicians, including the following:

- Historical pattern of resource allocation
- Busyness of practice

- Uniqueness of practice
- Length of particular operations
- Inpatient-bed requirements and utilization
- Academic productivity

Those doctors who are very academically productive, as measured by research activity, grants held, manuscripts published, and educational performance, may be rewarded with better access to resources; however, this criterion may be irrelevant in the community setting. Other considerations more recently evident are the published wait lists for various operations, which should necessitate a pooling of resources such as operating-room time among surgeons of like interests so that affected patients receive timely care.

Generally, as clinicians age, their practices predictably drop off because their referring doctors dwindle in numbers and younger referring doctors tend to refer to *their* contemporaries. The practice activity begins to naturally decrease, and the profit gap between billings and expenses decreases – a kind of natural selection process; unfortunately, expenses may remain fixed unless the less busy doctor can team up with another and split some secretarial and other costs.

During the course of discussions about retirement a number of options may emerge. Physicians have the advantage of not being expensive in terms of hospital resources, because medical doctors can consult and run successful and lucrative offices outside an institution. Surgeons present a more vexing reality because they incur significant hospital costs of operating time and inpatient beds during their practice; however, after retirement they can still consult and 'feed' patients to their colleagues for interventions. It may be possible for a more mature surgeon who wishes to practise part-time to share expenses and a secretary with another in the same situation or with another professional who is just starting out; in some unusual circumstances, former partners or the hospital itself may partially support the office costs of a surgeon who has made long-standing contributions to a division and a hospital.

There is another option for a surgeon, in particular for one who may have a specific skill that is valuable to a division and to an institution. A surgeon may continue to work, assisting in the hospital's operating room, providing an important service to other staff, and perhaps even teaching young staff members certain techniques that they might need to develop further. In this way, the hospital does not incur any additional costs, and the semi-retired surgeon can earn a decent living charging assistant's fees. For some, this is an unacceptable insult compared with the previous stature as a full-time surgeon; to others, it's simply a shift to a different mode of activity at a different stage of life.

The most common strategy is to provide a retiring surgeon with a soft landing, that is, a gradual diminution over several years of the resources provided, inexorably decreasing operating time, availability of inpatient beds, and endoscopic time. This gradual decrease is easier to swallow and should be part of an individual retiree's plan to fill the gaps with other activities. Some of those activities may be medically related such as consulting with insurance companies and legal firms, or they may simply involve growing a non-interventional practice in which surgical patients are sent on to full-time practitioners (therefore, a kind of rainmaker role).

These discussions about retirement must take place over a number of years, and at the same time plans must be put in place to recruit new staff who, it is hoped, will have novel skills and abilities that signal progress. The renewal process will be functioning, and if a healthy approach is followed consistently, you yourself as the aging medical leader will be a beneficiary in the not too distant future.

Be careful about setting precedents. If an individual is kept on for an inordinate length of time, and resources in an institution continue to be a problem, it is imperative that the specific reasons for prolongation of activity be identified, known, and recorded. There may be a specific clinical niche being occupied by a practitioner until a new recruit can fill a void, or perhaps an unusual academic need is being fulfilled temporarily. If care is not taken in this regard, an average or replaceable individual might have a legitimate argument to practise indefinitely.

We've seen in this chapter that the close associations with peers can be a sensitive issue for the medical leader, requiring empathy and sometimes finesse. You will often realize that you are engaging in the eighty-twenty rule; that is, you're spending an inordinate amount of time on relatively few issues or, quite frequently, on a few specific people and personalities.

> **Never forget this one point: the *people* are the reason you will succeed or fail, and they're well worth the time and effort you spend trying to solve your and their problems and promoting *their* success.**

5 A Typical Day

Now that I've tried to create an impression of the unusual and indeed unique hospital setting (chapter 1) and the medical leader's role (chapter 2) and established that having the best people working in teams (chapters 3 and 4) is generally the best way to achieve organizational effectiveness, let's get down to some of the nitty-gritty of the daily life of a medical leader. The following is not prescriptive at all; in fact, whatever works for an individual is probably good for the organization as long as the overall success of that organization is kept front and centre at all times.

I like to think that when I get up in the morning, a successful day is one in which I live my values unerringly; work closely with my assistants in a respectful, efficient, and productive way; interact with all my reports (those who report to me) and colleagues, using clear communication and with a constructive exchange of ideas; and always keep my eye on the long-term vision and mission of the organization. Perhaps most important, I hope I ensure that the people I work with know what their responsibilities and accountabilities are – and then I let them do their jobs. In other words, *pave the way and then get out of the way.*

Living Your Values

For the first forty years of my life I didn't give one thought to defining my value system, even though it surely must have existed and presumably guided me. I suspect many others are in the same boat. When our lives are devoted to building our own careers and families without much reflection on the fundamentals of our existence, it's not surprising that contemplation of this sort is placed on the back burner – and may not even be in the kitchen.

A good exercise for any medical leader is to submit to a personality evaluation, as described previously, and also to think about the values that you hold to be important and the standards by which to live your life. Interesting tests and exercises in this regard can be found on the Internet, such as the one offered at SelfCounseling.com,[34] in which the reader is challenged to choose ten important values from a list of approximately seventy-five and then to whittle them down by priority to five, then four, then three, then two, then one. In the medical domain most people, I think, would choose honesty, integrity, caring, and other such altruistic concepts for the top of their list.

Just as important as the constellation of personal values is the stated set of values that guide organizations such as health services centres. For example, in a 2001 strategic planning exercise my own organization declared its values:

1 Caring
2 Excellence
3 Teamwork
4 Integrity
5 Leadership
6 Innovation

The latter was seen to be particularly appropriate for an academic institution. We have since added the following:

7 Respect

We thereby recognized respect as one of the important features in the era of patient-centred health care delivery, especially with our diverse patient and workforce populations.

It is imperative that the personal values of an organization's leaders, and ideally all its employees, are aligned consistently with those of the organization. It is equally imperative that the medical leader lives those values every day and is *seen* to live them as the bedrock, the foundation of a life and of an organization. If medical leaders aren't capable of adhering to this consistent value system, and if Jim Collins (author of *Good to Great: Why Some Companies Make the Leap and Others Don't)*[11] were in charge, he would let them off the bus at the next stop.

SITUATION 5.1
REVIEW OF A MEDICAL SCHOOL DEPARTMENT: *The Medical Leader Is Just 'One of the Group'*

Some years ago I was asked to review a department in a prominent Canadian medical school. In examining details of the day-to-day work in a certain hospital division, I discovered that Doctor M, the division head, routinely assigned twice the operating time to himself and his own clinical interests, while some of the other surgeons were relegated to operating every other week. Doctor M also operated in an outside private clinic, which further upset any sense of there being a fair distribution of hospital resources.

This was an extreme example of a medical leader who placed his personal effectiveness above the effectiveness of the organization and who disadvantaged others while favouring his own hands and pockets. After my review, Doctor M continued his career as an accomplished academic surgeon, and another individual was appointed to head the division.

A good leader must live the values but also live the *processes* of the organization.

SITUATION 5.2
NURSE BETTY: *The Importance of Process*

For more than twenty years Betty was an operating-room nurse manager at Community Hospital B in a large North American city. She had been recruited from another large North American city as a young, very accomplished, and very outspoken nurse. Community Hospital B didn't know what they were getting into at the time. Nurse Betty, as she was known in a subsequent article that appeared years later in the *Globe and Mail*, was a larger-than-life figure whose commitment to excellent patient care and modern exacting standards was legendary.

Nurse Betty also knew and was truly interested in all her reports personally, including details of their private lives away from the hospital, their strengths, weaknesses, hopes, and dreams. She was entirely and passionately supportive of everyone in her bailiwick, but if you strayed from the standard of care or an accepted behavioural norm, you'd better watch out because you would be placing yourself squarely in the cross hairs of Betty's formidable weapon – a memorable dressing down.

I once found myself in those cross hairs. The operating suite at Community Hospital B is usually an efficient facility, which unfortunately suffers – like many of its type – from a lack of flexibility. Surgical procedures are long, averaging four hours, and they involve major programs including cardiac surgery, complex cancer procedures, and transplantation. To deal with unexpected emergencies, a *surgeon-of-the-month system* had been put in place whereby any contentious emergent surgical booking that would necessitate bumping an elective case had to be adjudicated by a team consisting of the surgeon of the month (a volunteer practising surgeon), a nurse communication team leader, and the anaesthesiologist on call.

On this particular day a decision was made by the team to hold off on an emergency vascular surgery until after another case had been finished, rather than bump a third case that was about to start. The vascular surgeon came to me, in my role as acting vice-president of surgical services, specifically to plead his case. I listened to the story and was convinced that the vascular surgeon had effectively made his point. I overrode the decision of the team, letting vascular surgery go ahead with the emergency case. This was a bad mistake.

It was a bad mistake not only because as an interim leader I had made a decision that flew in the face of an accepted and proven process but because I then suffered the wrath of Nurse Betty, who in no uncertain terms indicated, among other things, that I ought to grow up.

Comment: I learned a lot that day, and since that event I have never once overridden the decision of someone to whom I had entrusted a job or authority. The lesson of delegated authority has stayed with me these many years later. I learned more from Nurse Betty that day, and subsequently, than perhaps from any other professional with whom I've had the privilege of working.

Nurse Betty lives her values every day, but she also lives the guidelines, rules, regulations, and processes of the organization.

Your Executive Assistant or Secretary

The importance of a loyal, competent, knowledgeable, effective, and independent executive assistant cannot be overestimated.

SITUATION 5.3
MS U, EXECUTIVE ASSISTANT: *What Are the Person's Core Values?*

Now a middle-aged executive assistant, Ms U started working in the hospital setting at the age of eighteen, when she was right out of secretarial school. Ms U had had a challenging start to life in her first fifteen years: she had suffered the divorce of her parents, the loss of an older brother to a motor vehicle accident, and the trauma of another brother who at the age of five sustained major injuries that spared his life but claimed much of his ability to function normally. He then required continued support from his younger sister who, in addition to organizing institutional and halfway house care, remained available at all times for recurring problems.

Throughout these continuing trials Ms U remained dedicated to her job, her family, her husband, and her cats. The interruptions to a smooth daily routine were frequent, but she continued to handle these personal issues with an enthusiasm and equanimity that characterized her work with patients at the hospital. Ms U's ability to multitask amid a variety of pressures was recognized early, and she was asked to take on a major administrative role subsequently when a senior position became available. Being tested even more, Ms U and her husband took in his mother to live with them because the mother needed periodic surveillance and company.

Ms U proved to be heroic in many ways, but she always offered respectful, helpful, direct, and friendly assistance to any colleagues, managers, or executives at work, and when the current mandate has been completed for her executive position, she will undoubtedly be one of the most sought-after associates in the organization.

Comment: This vignette, which may sound dangerously like a soap opera, is absolutely true and is related for one reason: the characteristics and values of hard work, fairness, commitment, loyalty, and leadership demonstrated by any individual are often most evident in his or her private life. The chances are that if a person's value system is rock solid, and particularly if it coincides with your own and that of your organization, you'll have a long association with that person that is efficient and productive and stimulates mutual growth. If you hear of such personal courage and commitment in an applicant to a position in your organization, and the basic requirements of the job are fulfilled, sign that person up.

Your executive assistant has to be appropriately deferential when you are meeting with others, and appropriately forward and provocative in private if he or she is trying to help you, correct you, or remind you of what you have to be doing. He or she must be cognizant of the processes, by-laws, guidelines, and policies of the organization and be intimately familiar with the rules and regulations around the specific sources where all these elements can be found (books, manuals, web sites, intranets). Your executive assistant must be courteous at all times and treat people with respect, but be tough when needed – exactly the same characteristics of interacting with you, the boss.

A very good barometer of your potential as a medical leader is the length of time you have spent working with close associates such as secretaries, nurses, nurse practitioners, and executive assistants. If a potential recruit or a potential leader goes through secretaries as though they were on an assembly line, beware the interpersonal relationships; due diligence demands that you take a closer look and do more interviews with previous employees and colleagues.

When was the last time you contacted a business and your whole impression of that business was born of the quality and friendliness of the greeting? The communication skills of your executive assistant will be a reflection of him or her and of you and your administration. They are the outward face of the department or division. So pick wisely and don't hesitate to prescribe exactly how you would like your assistant to answer the phone and deal with people.

I personally encourage a dualistic relationship in that I expect formality when others are in the room, and I insist on first names in private. If I call someone by his or her first name, by definition that person calls me by my first name as well.

SITUATION 5.4

CLINICAL SECRETARY MS Q: *True Caring Is What We're About*

Ms Q is a legendary clinical secretary. She is the epitome of patient-centred care in that she gets to know patients and their whole constellation of friends and family personally, and she seems to feel what they're going through. When patients are investigated, Ms Q keeps them up to date at all times about the next appointments; greets them when they're having tests, X-rays, and biopsies; visits them during their hospital stay, armed with popsicles (at the appropriate time), as well as post-operatively; and ensures that they have contact coordinates should they have any problems after discharge. The patients' responses to this kind of personal caring are at first disbelief but thereafter gratitude and appreciation.

Ms Q constantly receives thanks and mementos of patients' appreciation, and she emphasizes that this is the beginning of a long relationship. Patients frequently seem to be happy enough to see their surgeon, but they're delighted to meet Ms Q again. What does Ms Q have that many people don't have? Ms Q has the ability to care about people and to place herself in the shoes of patients and families facing crisis, and she to some extent lives their crises along with them.

I believe that in Ms Q's story there is a kernel of truth for every medical leader in every endeavour, whether patient-related or not. To be able to make appropriate decisions and to be effective, every medical leader must place himself or herself in the shoes of the colleague, the boss, or the front-line worker. Most decisions are complex and multi-factorial; the perspective of each of the players involved must be appreciated before the best decision can be made.

The other barometer of the quality of your executive assistant is the number of people lined up to hire him or her. If he is approaching his job in the way described, he will undoubtedly be an attractive recruit to countless offices in your organization. You must therefore have ongoing retention strategies that are as aggressive as those you use for your prize medical professionals. Your assistant needs what we all need: challenges, an ability to complete tasks, recognition for a job well done, tangible appreciation of excellence in general (such as financial remuneration, gifts, birthday presents, Christmas bonuses), and interest in her and her family as people *outside* an organization.

Don't be afraid to share some of your life with your executive assistant. If you are open enough to admit some personal sensitivities, you will nurture a friend in addition to an employee. The key word, as always, is *caring*. If you care about your assistant as a person, and he or she feels the same way about you, a bond is established that enriches your life and, as a by-product, is very good for business as well. This may sound somewhat contrived, and perhaps it is; however, I am convinced that what may start out as a contrived motivation will end with a genuinely nurturing relationship.

What makes a good executive assistant? A good executive assistant is someone who is connected with all her counterparts in the organization, knows about processes or where to access information about them, is courteous with a healthy sense of humour, is unafraid to speak up when you need it, and is organized with regard to her time and yours. Last, and least important, a good executive assistant possesses good technical skills. Good technical skills are nice to have, but in my opinion they aren't nearly as important as the other characteristics.

One final piece of advice with respect to your executive assistant: be the boss, be generous, be appreciative, give bonuses and praise, but take advantage of the usual three-month probation at the outset. If there are *any* concerns that this recruit may not work out for any reason, cut bait when you don't have to justify your decision. Your relationship with your executive assistant is too important to take a chance on if you're not absolutely confident in your choice. The choice of executive assistant ranks very high on the impact scale, behind the choices of your life partner and your job application. If you err in your choice of executive assistant and you come to realize your mistake after the probation period, you are not going to enjoy writing that severance cheque.

Communication

Speak Plain English (or Spanish or French in North America)

Since health administration has entered the business world as a major force and, in particular, a major consumer of resources (Canada spends about 10 per cent of its gross domestic product on health care, and in the United States the proportion is closer to 15 per cent), it seems natural that a more scientific approach has been taken in the past three decades to providing health care services that are more efficient and safe, with concomitant attention to the spiralling costs of compensation and supplies.

Medical and surgical care is a business and must be treated as such. Whereas in the past hospital administrators in Canada simply informed their provincial governments of their cost overruns, expecting a cheque to be issued the following day, strict budgets are now enforced with the threat of 'supervisors' and 'reviews' as formal audits of performance. As we have become part of the business world, our language of communication has gradually changed; we now speak in *administratese*, a dialect full of neologisms that has infiltrated plain English to the extent that complete sentences can be uttered with only a smattering of familiar words. As I said in my first 'state of the union' address about ten years ago, referring to my first obligatory management course:

> Basically, I learned about a lot of *things*. I learned about commonalities, time frames, bundling, initiatives, synergies, compliance, granularity, drivers, clarity, hooks, clients, stakeholders, frameworks, benchmarks, aliquots, alignments, disconnects, priorities, strategic alliances, meaningful inroads, and many other creative nouns in the lexicon.
>
> In terms of *actions*, I learned how to box in, go forward, cluster, drill down, validate, operationalize, harmonize, legitimize, articulate, blend, focus, resonate, incent, commingle, empower, and to make meaningful inroads.

And I will do all that in the hopes that I might use, as frequently as possible, the following *descriptors:* discordant, congruent, robust, client-focused, paramount, illusory, contextual, granular, counter-intuitive, nimble, blended, lockstep, and strategic.

Earphones for translation are available at the back of the hall, and if you wish, you can play this new game called bullshit bingo that I recently received, which allows you to follow along the neologisms, and when you score horizontally, vertically, or diagonally, you jump up and yell the word at the top of this sheet (the first word in the name of the game). Please resist playing the game until the next lecture you attend.

> **I can't stand it! Please resurrect the English language to a beautiful, descriptive, plain level that *everyone* can understand.**

Having denigrated those who have adopted the neologisms above, I must stress that the medical leader who is becoming familiar with hospital operations must become comfortable with many standard financial and operational terms in the business world, from fixed and variable costs to positive variances to cost allocation to profit sharing. *This* language you must learn.

Email

Email is yet another good news–bad news story. There has never been a more efficient tool to use to answer simple questions, deliver and forward pertinent information, transfer images that can speak a thousand words, schedule meetings, and keep a whole organization in touch with its members, and its members in touch with one another.

On the other hand, email has many regrettable sides. Most people receive so much information every day that they frequently forward messages for printing (and later reading) to their secretaries, completely defeating the objective of paperless communication. (I am guilty as charged on this one.) To avoid the spam reality, most of us have two or three email addresses in order to protect our main business server, thus complicating our lives further and increasing exponentially the time spent in responding. (This is certainly counter-productive if timely response is a value you hold dear.) But in my mind, the most offensive aspect of electronic communication is the threat to face-to-face meetings.

Email can not and should not replace meetings at which facial expressions, immediate interaction, body language, and contemporaneous exchange of ideas can make the dialogue more meaningful and informative.

GUIDELINES FOR EMAILS

I have a few personal rules about emails. I try to answer the whole day's email activity on that day, and as often as possible I call on the phone for a personal interaction if that is convenient for both parties. I don't agree with the people who have their secretaries screen emails, supposedly to save time. This is disrespectful of the people who are trying to contact you, and it is unnecessary, especially if you have taken care to protect your email address against spam, public access, and advertising. Furthermore, any confidential message obviously should not be read by the wrong person. In fact, if that is an outcome –not sending anything confidential in an email – I'm all for that.

Never sit in front of the computer screen answering emails as they come through. Try to answer your phone personally for a few minutes, and you will see how much time is simply wasted in that activity. Emails must be answered in batches, and the responses must be made in agreement with *your* schedule.

An outgoing email that is full of spelling mistakes and grammatical errors is another disrespectful expression. Make sure that you screen every outgoing email or response for mistakes before it goes out. Every message is a reflection of you as a medical leader, and leaders should not send messy notes with grammatical or spelling mistakes.

Many people will express an emotion in an email that speaks to their feelings about a subject or action. This frequently results in a stream of volleys over the net that accelerates in both intensity and the number of people copied. If I am copied on such an exchange of messages, I immediately call one of the 'combatants' and encourage another, more constructive way of communicating. Some use the twenty-four-hour rule to express anger, in which they give themselves some time to think about the issue before sending an electronic emotion. My modification of that concept is certainly to sleep on the message, and if it should be delivered the next day, do it *in person*, not via the printed word.

I never send a blind copy of a message to a third party. That action has a secretive connotation that is always counterproductive and is simply wrong. It is also an invitation to disaster when the recipient of the blind copy then forwards the message without realizing that it was blind. The results can be a sense of betrayal felt by the original recipient that will be long lasting; emotional reactions are easy to acquire and sometimes impossible to eliminate. To clear my conscience, if a third party must see a message, I will take the time to send it separately along with a note that explains why the message is being sent.

There is an adage that goes something like this: 'Never write anything in an email that can't stand the test of the front page of the national newspaper.' With the wonder of the Internet, ill-chosen words can be read instantly by countless unintended recipients – ergo, the need to express ideas clearly, succinctly, and hopefully in a way that will not be subject to misinterpretation.

So, in summary, you have several options from which to choose when you receive an email, according to the acronym FADE:

1 Forward it (to a capable colleague who can handle it)
2 Act on it immediately
3 Delete it
4 Enter it into a to-do list with a deadline by which to deal with it.

You cannot leave an email suspended in the ether.

Having drawn attention to the many negative features of email, I need to stress that communication is the key to running any business, and email has been, and will continue to be, a critically positive and helpful tool if managed appropriately.

Meetings and Committees

Every medical leader who assumes a new position vows to minimize the number of meetings that everyone is obligated to attend and promises succinct, purpose-driven, and economical meetings that will respect the most valuable asset of health care providers, that is, their time. Then unfortunately that leader will want to establish a high profile and an interest in many domains and will end up calling at least the same number or even more meetings than before. Why does this happen?

Meetings and committees are critical parts of any communication strategy, but they are also time consuming, sometimes wasteful, often contentious, and virtually always inconvenient for at least some of the attendees. Remember that everyone in the organization wants to be fully informed about the most relevant issues, and more and more people feel entitled to have input into all decisions. Another interesting fact is that those individuals who are most vocal and passionate about being a part of all decision-making processes are often the same ones who don't show up to meetings.

The following are a few observations and guidelines that reflect these conflicts, as well as some suggestions that may render meetings more palatable.

The most effective meetings are those that involve two or three people who have similar objectives and values, understand one another, and have a very brief agenda and a deadline to meet. Major businesses have a significant amount of expansive thinking and strategizing among the members of a very small group, often called a committee. However, the core aspects of further organization-wide development and implementation of ideas must involve the whole corporation. Committees and communication, then, are a reality of modern medical practice, but they must be used judiciously.

First, with regard to forming a committee, you must determine the following:

1 The purpose of the committee
2 Its terms of reference
3 Its chair and other officers
4 Its accountability and reporting structure (for example, if decisions are made, to whom are they reported?)

Most important, decide whether the committee is representative of specific constituents (for example, with decisions made in a democratic fashion) or advisory to the chair. If committee members assume that they are representing specific constituents and then during a heated discussion discover that they are simply acting in an advisory capacity to the chair of the committee, resentment will be the likely result. Search committees for leadership positions, chairs, and the like are good examples of the second scenario; that is, committee members offer advice to the chair of the committee, and therefore the chair must stipulate the ground rules and reporting structure at the first meeting of the committee.

Meetings generally can be held for the purposes of receiving and/or giving information, discussing, and/or decision making.

One might argue that if a meeting is just for receiving or giving information, then that can be transferred more easily by the written or spoken word. However, there may be virtues in personal meetings in which facial expression, vocal inflection, and body language are important factors. Emphasis on specific issues is more effective if it comes from a mouth rather than from a page.

For obvious reasons, meetings with a large attendance are best suited for the dissemination of information, and decision-making meetings are more effective if only small numbers are present.

The conduct of a meeting often varies according to the nature of the subject discussed. If an important meeting is to take place with a specific decision anticipated, observation of *Robert's Rules of Order* is advised,[35] with an appropriately constituted quorum present. However, a casual and friendly atmosphere is usually necessary to attract the attendees on a regular basis.

Never try to make a major decision on a contentious issue with a large number of people in the room. Never try to wordsmith a document with input from many people; you will be wasting your time, and you will jeopardize friendships along the way. Leave those arguments to politicians in the House of Commons or the House of Representatives.

Agenda and Conduct of the Meeting

The ideal meeting is one that is convenient, attended by people who know each other and who have similar values, is time limited, and at its conclusion gives all members a sense of participation and accomplishment.

In my opinion, the best time for a meeting is between seven and eight o'clock in the morning. For some people, this is an ungodly hour; however, surgeons are present at 7:00, have to leave at 7:55 in order to start operating at 8:00, and have to be awake and refreshed at that time. By the end of the day, most are beginning to unwind, while anticipating that glass of wine with family. Midday meetings of large numbers of people are precarious, suffering from overruns of the previous commitment and the need to leave for the next.

No meeting should last more than one hour, and every meeting should have a fixed conclusion time. Chairpersons will enhance their standing if they periodically break early to give their colleagues the gift of time.

If you have a difficult issue to be discussed and it requires consensus, you should discuss it with every member of the group or committee *before* the meeting. This does not have to appear as a manipulative strategy, but it is simply designed to ensure that all members understand the issues and have time to weigh their various options prior to a meeting when they will be asked for opinions. This approach is less contrived than it is respectful of members' thought processes; it takes time, but the time is well spent.

In my opinion, it is preferable *not* to hold votes on issues. If there is not a meeting of the minds on an issue that requires resolution, it's better to strive for a best alternative to a negotiated agreement (BATNA),[36] with some facile interest-based bargaining, than it is to hold a vote on a specific stance that will have the predictable consequences of winners and losers. A consensus decision is always preferable.

When the meeting ends, any decision made is then a collective decision and must be supported by all members regardless of their stances expressed in the meeting. If a member strays from that resolution and speaks outside the meeting about how he or she disagreed with the conclusion, that member should be relieved of committee duties.

During a meeting the responsibilities of the chair are as follows:

• Stick to the agenda
• Maintain decorum
• Ensure that the discussion keeps moving
• Inject some fun into the proceedings
• Call on as many people as possible for their opinions

The more the chair can advise individuals beforehand that they will be called upon, the better their responses will be. In medicine and surgery the more serious and grave the discussion, the more necessary the humour that should be added as a condiment.

A particularly odious practice is the use of cellphones and smartphones during meetings. This shows tremendous disrespect for the process, the subjects discussed, and the chair and should not be tolerated. I have even seen rather loud, animated conversations take place, using cellphones, right in the middle of important meetings. Although we all recognize that some medical emergencies take precedence, the reaction to those events can be subtle and focused. All speakers at a meeting deserve the respect of every attendee, and such frequent 'side meetings' are to be abhorred. Some committee chairs prohibit cellphones and smartphones, but in a medical environment this is not practical, given that life-threatening situations do occur in our hospital setting.

During one meeting a few years ago a colleague was busy answering emails on his smartphone during an important discussion, and I went around the conference table, apparently eager to see the new contraption, as I had not yet 'blessed' myself with a smartphone. I asked him if I could see this fascinating new device and then proceeded to put it in my pocket and continue the meeting. That was an example of childish behaviour on my part (not recommended), and it may have embarrassed him temporarily, but it emphasizes how strongly I feel about the subject.

Regular attendees of committees should be rewarded by a committee-member stipend (if feasible), recognition, public appreciation, and formal commendation in newsletters and the like. Delinquents should find something else to do at seven o'clock in the morning.

Confidentiality is paramount in some situations. If the discussion at a meeting is deemed confidential, as in a particularly sensitive search process involving both internal and external candidates, the chair must declare confidentiality at the outset of the meeting, indicating that any and all content of the meeting must not leave the room. If that code of conduct is breached, the loquacious member must leave the committee and be educated about the importance of confidentiality if he or she ever wants to participate again.

Inviting outside members to present specific topics is an excellent method to keep meetings interesting, well attended, and informative. That said, it is imperative that presenters be given a specific length of time for presentation and discussion, with the assurance that they will be cut off after a specific number of minutes. It is always preferable to have someone speak either without notes or with a visual computer presentation, but not with handouts. Computer presentations are bad enough for retention purposes, but listeners who are scanning a handout hear virtually nothing. I prefer to have presentations made without notes but with the assurance that handouts will be available at the end of the meeting.

A communication tool that is in growing use is the telephone conference, even with a video hook-up. This is a very effective way of conquering geography and sometimes extremely busy schedules as long as the chair realizes the shortcomings of this kind of process. It is certainly better for either information meetings or meetings where a single subject is raised for serious decision making. Don't forget that many on the line will be attending to a variety of subjects and tasks, especially those innumerable emails that can be answered by the time the phone meeting wraps up.

> **The most important element of any meeting, especially meetings where decisions are made or policies are approved, is the clear understanding by all those present of what has transpired.**

Policies that will be enforced as a result of the meeting must be understood by the committee members *during* the meeting, and there must be a clear plan set in place for the next steps, along with timelines and the identification of those individuals responsible for implementation. This will close the gap between the contents of the discussion and the subsequent minutes, which are sometimes fraught with conflict because of lack of understanding and untimely articulation of minutes.

Minutes

Preparing minutes after a meeting is an ironic practice. There are specific rules by which minutes should be constructed, and the importance of accurate minutes cannot be overestimated, especially if the motions, discussions, and decisions are substantive. However, be assured that few members will actually read the minutes in detail, unless they're needed for verification of an issue at a later date. Recognizing that fact, it is imperative to prepare minutes in such a way that committee members can quickly review the salient points. The descriptions of the discussion should be as detailed as is necessary, depending on the importance of the topic. The most important aspects of minutes are the action items, each of which should be specifically identified and assigned to a responsible and accountable individual, with a designated timeline for task completion. Attachments discussed or presented by visitors at the meeting should accompany the minutes.

The One-on-One Meeting

The one-on-one meeting may be the most useful form of communication for a medical leader. Whether it be an encounter with someone who reports to you, or with a peer leader or a boss, the opportunities to get to the point, make decisions quickly, and put strategies in place are plentiful in the one-on-one meeting. The sessions can be invariably more efficient and businesslike than an 'open' meeting at which multiple personalities must be satisfied. That said, this does not imply that unilateral (or bilateral) decisions should be made in any organization, because the best decisions are the ones to which many individuals contribute.

The considerate medical leader prepares for these intimate sessions with a carefully laid-out agenda, just as for a more formal meeting. This is advisable for most sessions but mandatory when you are meeting superiors. Just as in patient-centred care where we are now looking at our actions from the patient's perspective, you must make a presentation with the listener in mind. If you go to your CEO with a proposal to expand a clinical service by adopting an expensive new operation, for example, you must have a plan. You must present according to the *listener's* train of thought. To be effective in a one-on-one meeting with a superior, say, your CEO, you should state the following:

1 The subject in terms of the CEO's or the organization's goal
2 The need that the organization has for this additional procedure
3 Your recommendation of exactly what should be adopted
4 The benefits to the hospital, the CEO, the board, and the patients
5 Any evidence that the proposal has been, and likely will be, successful
6 Your conclusion and summary
7 Your recommendation of the next step

Obviously these steps would apply to any formal business case, but if the process is followed for even routine matters, you will become known for your organized approach.

If important issues are discussed, and especially if a verbal decision appears to be made, a confirmatory letter describing any issues or decisions should follow.

The Unscheduled Drop-In Meeting

The concept of team is essential to the well-being and growth of any medical organization, and therefore committee meetings are regarded as the bedrock of a team effort and as the best way to make decisions and communicate them effectively and quickly to appropriate staff. However, those who live in a fast-paced environment, where decisions sometimes dictate a more rapid response, know that there are other valuable interactions. A good medical leader, just like a good father or mother, always has time for a respected employee or colleague who thinks the subject is important enough for him or her to drop in and discuss it.

There are obvious limitations to this openness, and in some cases the leader must simply cut off the individuals who take unreasonable advantage. Along the same line, any individual who is engaging in an end run by accessing an executive over the head of an immediate superior must be politely heard and then referred to the appropriate manager for further discussion.

In real life, the spur-of-the-moment, drop-in meeting is often the way that timely responses to events are best achieved. The culture that supports this type of interchange is incredibly important because it is reliant on the personal relationships of the executives and, in fact, further nurtures those relationships.

Unscheduled meetings are usually less prepared and may be more focused on a particular topic than are meetings that involve a number of formal presentations on organized subjects. In fact, even if talk drifts towards family life and how the kids are doing in school, the long-term benefits to the relationship, and the generation of trust, are inestimable.

Such impromptu encounters may last only a few minutes, but they can be a critical part of an ongoing dialogue and trust between professionals.

Managers vs Leaders: Let Your Managers Manage

When you are a manager, you manage people, processes, and commodities; when you are a leader, you lead and leave managing to others. This is a subject that, in my opinion, has stimulated more discussion than it deserves. In one sense, we all manage and all lead in the various domains of our lives each and every day, and the separation of the two activities – leading and managing –may for the most part be artificial. Having said that, some acknowledgment of the differences may be useful in planning the roles in any particular process design.

Mark Sanborn has written extensively about a number of subjects and has tried to examine the differences between managing and leading.[37] According to Sanborn, on the one hand, *leaders* are those people who

- are creative,
- are supportive of others,
- strategically use time and energy to grow people and their careers,
- have a vision of where to go in the long term, and
- have a notion of how to get there.

On the other hand, according to Sanborn, *managers* are those people who

- are detail oriented,
- are disciplinary,
- monitor and supervise performance, and
- concentrate on what has to be done today to arrive at an immediate destination.

Sanborn also posits that good managers tend to be good leaders, but good leaders are not always good managers.

When I talk about these concepts to groups of aspiring medical leaders, I show columns under each of the 'Leader' and 'Manager' headings but then apply a large intersecting Venn diagram, clearly indicating that there is substantial overlap in the components of these two concepts.

Role clarity is critical. The effective medical leader must know and appreciate the details of a manager's job description but must let the manager manage. If this is supported, the manager will be more accomplished, will grow as a manager and a human being, and will be appreciated for the work; if micromanagement by the leader occurs, disillusionment, resentment, and apathy will quickly ensue. For individuals who have had significant experience in middle management, delegation of authority and activity can sometimes be the most daunting challenge of becoming a more senior administrator.

Micromanagement is the enemy of any senior executive, even though that executive must understand and be aware of the importance of attention to detail at every level. Both leaders and managers lead and manage, and they should not be worried about differentiating these activities; as the titular leader, just ensure that your reports have an opportunity to do both.

Time Management

Discussing time management with an experienced, likely overworked doctor is potentially insulting, and you no doubt have developed many strategies over your career to deal with time, the ultimate non-renewable resource. Our tendency as physicians has been to take on new responsibilities without enough careful analysis of their effects on the rest of our lives; such is one of the major pitfalls of medical life, especially when we are slaves to unscheduled emergent commitments that interrupt any carefully laid plans.

When you take on an additional responsibility, you must ask yourself if you have either the time for this commitment or the tools for adjusting your time-management strategies.

A number of random bits of advice on time management will be seen throughout the book, but a short list here may be of some use.

1 Have a planner, which is an obvious necessity, in the form of a paper appointment book or an electronic computer program. These are necessary for appointments and recurring obligations but are usually only useful in the office setting. In particular, it's wise to place warnings of upcoming deadlines so that you will have time to prepare.

2 Prepare a daily list. A busy manager often starts the day with recurring, daily A and B lists of things to do (don't ever let the B list grow).

3 Hire the best, most organized assistant you can and keep him or her happy.

4 Plan daily 'open' time to ensure your ability to deal with the unexpected.

5 Never get caught up in answering emails and phone calls as they come in. When you deal with multiple messages, apply the FADE rule.

6 Multitask and get used to the feeling of having some projects unfinished at the end of the day – but set deadlines for completion of projects along the way.

7 Keep a desk that's right for you. I have seen desks of very accomplished professionals that have ranged from the ultraclean to the incomparable mess, even though each individual was very successful. Just don't let the physical mess get in the way of your effectiveness.

8 Apply Pareto's principle. Each activity must be assessed according to priority and to the amount of time and energy that may be wasted. The eighty-twenty rule may apply more frequently than you imagine.

9 Develop an ability to be available for your colleagues, promoting an open-door policy, but with a finesse that allows you to say yes in creative ways (for example, 'Sure, I'm available. Can we agree on a time I can get right back to you?')

10 Delegate responsibility and tasks. This will lighten your load and also promote the abilities of others under your leadership.

The foregoing in a sense, I hope, describes a typical day. Please don't think that emphasizing these principles in my own leadership has paved a smooth road, any more than my surgical operations all proceed without complications or unexpected adverse events. It's not coincidental, however, that the success or failure of a day, month, or year is dependent on the activities of the people and the teams and on the communication issues emphasized in chapters 3, 4, and 5.

6 Quality of Care and Risk in Medicine

Now that you have an idea of the lay of the land, your office is organized, your various teams are in place, and communication has been optimized, what are the hot topics you'll be dealing with, in addition to all the personal issues and their accompanying eighty-twenty rule?

As a medical leader you'll be attending to countless subjects day to day, but you'll have the greatest satisfaction at the end of your mandate if you can actually see that the big ship has moved in a different (and hopefully better) direction. Your focus on quality of care and risk with respect to measuring and improving patient outcomes will be at the heart of any of your team's success.

The Quality Issue

In the 1990s the Ford Motor Company used the tag line 'Quality is Job 1.' That line is perfect for our commitment to quality of patient care. The stepwise conduct of assessment, diagnosis, and treatment of the disease that demonstrates an orderly, efficient, and cost-effective approach to a patient's problem is what effective and timely health care is all about.

Carl Yastrzemski is regarded by many as the best living Boston Red Sox baseball player. His experience at Massachusetts General Hospital emphasizes much about the timely, standardized care in that institution.

SITUATION 6.1

CARL YASTRZEMSKI AT MASSACHUSETTS GENERAL:
A Hero Receives a Hero's Care

On 19 August 2008, sixty-nine-year-old Hall of Fame baseball player Carl Yastrzemski suffered mild chest pain and tightness, was seen by his family physician, and was immediately referred to Massachusetts General Hospital, accompanied by his wife, Nancy. Carl was seen within fifteen minutes by a triage nurse, then reviewed within minutes by the shift emergency physician, who determined a likely myocardial ischaemic event. An emergency cardiogram confirmed ST changes, the results of a serum troponin test were confirmatory, and a clinical diagnosis of myocardial ischaemia was made.

Oxygen by face mask was applied, two large-bore IVs were started, and within thirty minutes a coronary angiogram revealed a significant block in three coronary vessels, including the left anterior descending (LAD), one of the 'widow makers' – lesions that can be silent until a massive infarction leads to congestive failure and often death.

Carl was fortunate, and within three hours he was in the operating room undergoing a standard triple coronary artery bypass graft (CABG), from which he recovered quickly after a six-hour procedure. He left hospital about a week later and was back active and ambulatory within several weeks, to be followed by his cardiologist and physiotherapist.*

Comment: Yastrzemski obviously benefited from high quality, seamless medical care; the processes of care were implemented in an exemplary fashion.

Another dimension of quality in medical care has to do with the *correct approach.* Did the health care providers (in any given case) act appropriately, given the evidence presented to them? As stated previously, both aspects of quality could be captured in the single question, Was the right thing done right? Furthermore, did the professionals carry out their responsibilities according to standard care, and did they do so in a timely and efficient way?

Do all patients receive the kind of quality care that Carl Yastrzemski was afforded? Unfortunately they do not. A second story emphasizes the right-care issue.

SITUATION 6.2
THE QUAID TWINS IN LOS ANGELES, AND PREEMIES IN INDIANA:
Adverse Events Can Happen to Anyone

Zoe and Boone Quaid are twins who were born in November 2007 to a surrogate mother engaged by the future parents, actor Dennis Quaid and his wife, Kimberly. The twins showed signs of a staph infection in their first week at

---

* Associated Press, 20 August 2008

home, and they were readmitted to Cedars-Sinai Medical Center in Los Angeles on 18 November for routine intravenous administration of antibiotics.

Two days later, instead of receiving intermittent IV heparin to ensure IV-line patency, the lines of the twins were mistakenly flushed with heparin 10,000 units/mL instead of 10 units/mL, which is 1,000 times the recommended strength. The event was recognized soon after, when it was observed that blood puncture sites were oozing liberally, necessitating a short stay in the neonatal intensive care unit. The administration of protamine sulphate reversed the effects of the heparin.

A year earlier, three premature infants had died in Indiana, reportedly from complications of mistakenly receiving the stronger heparin. A further three suffered overdoses but survived.*

The Quaid story was broadcast on *60 Minutes*,** with all the accompanying obligatory drama, and litigation led to a financial settlement. Despite the happy ending, in which the twins were declared 'just fine,' the saga is a poignant and very public reminder that apparently minor slips can have profound consequences.

The possibility of mistakes, whether they be stocking a pharmacy with the wrong concentration of a drug, the faulty mixing of a concentrated base medication, the incorrect administration by a nurse or a technician, or the production of varying concentrations of a medication by a pharmaceutical company, is ever present. Even the most apparently straightforward process consists of a series of steps, any one of which could lead to disaster if performed inappropriately.

At virtually every institution in North America the processes that make up hospital care are fraught with problems. Emergency departments are clogged with patients who don't have a family doctor or who can't access a walk-in clinic because there are restricted hours of operations in many such facilities. These emergency departments are understaffed by doctors because of shortages, especially in smaller centres, as many emergency physicians have left for the big city; many are understaffed by nurses because of budgetary problems, as health care costs continue to spiral out of control and hospital leaders have long since realized that approximately 67 per cent of the hospital's expenses are compensation or people related. Today, the waiting times in emergency

---

* Reuters, 22 November 2007
** *60 Minutes*, 15 March 2008

departments before one sees a triage nurse can be measured too often in hours, not just minutes.

Many departments have not been physically constructed using appropriate functional planning, so that patient flow is suboptimal, and duplication of effort on the part of both the caregiver and the patient is rampant. Once the patient has been attended to, the concepts of human error and instrument and/or mechanical failure take over. Mistakes of *commission* in misinterpretation of results, administration of the wrong drug or dose, and a myriad of other problems and those of *omission* such as failure to follow up test results combine to create an unsafe atmosphere.

Medicine is more than ever committed to improving the processes of care and patient outcomes and safety. The medical leader must commit to finding short- and long-term answers to the access issues mentioned above and also participate in ways to enhance the right care, that is, the elimination of mistakes in diagnosis and treatment. How did this commitment come about?

The wake-up call for continuous quality improvement in the medical field did not come from watching successes in the Japanese car industry or reviewing the phenomenal steps taken by the airline industry to reduce fatal accidents. As usual, the stimulus for change came from something far more personal. The medical profession was fundamentally undressed in *To Err Is Human: Building a Safer Health System*.[9] Published by the U.S. Institute of Medicine in 2000, this is a report of the results of an audit done in New York State fifteen years earlier, in 1984.

The delay between the audit and the publication was significant, but not nearly as momentous as the reaction and subsequent impact on the medical profession. Essentially, this report declares that as many as 50,000 to 99,000 people die in the United States each year as a direct result of medical error – mistakes committed by health care providers or resulting from a malfunction of the equipment they used to provide care. By extrapolation, Canada could similarly plead guilty to approximately 10 per cent of that number, as confirmed in ongoing studies by Ross Baker at the University of Toronto and his colleagues (see, for example, 'The Canadian Adverse Events Study: The Incidence of Adverse Events among Hospital Patients in Canada').[38]

This field of study has become perhaps as active as the drive for innovation and advancement in the discovery of mechanisms of physiology, pathology, and diagnosis and the treatment of disease. Judging from media coverage of the incidents and high-profile disasters, more and more people in the public are becoming engaged by the subject.

The right to be offered exceptional care at any age has been intensified in the United States by the upfront personal cost of health care, and in Canada by the high taxes that are justified in major part by the concept of universal health care; in other words, 'this is costing us a bundle, and we want proof that we're getting our money's worth!'

Recognizing and Correcting Problems in Our Hospitals

The traditional 'blunt instrument' to grapple with the concept of unexpected or adverse events is the morbidity and mortality conference ('M&M rounds'), now known in most jurisdictions as quality-of-care conferences.

The medical leader must ensure that quality-of-care conferences are meaningful. They must involve the whole team of caregivers, including all those dotted around the previous pyramidal structure (figure 1.2). The conferences must be well organized and prepared, with all the facts about contentious cases reported and available. After all, if decisions are to be made as to the appropriateness of care, the corroborating or disputing evidence must be on the table.

The traditional quality-of-care conferences have usually suspended the concept of a blameless atmosphere. The common cut-throat conferences have had an appearance more like television's *House* than *Dr. Kildare* (for those who can remember that 1970s series starring Richard Chamberlain). Especially in the surgical domain, students, interns, residents, clinical fellows, and consultant staff have frequently dreaded the exposure of their well-intentioned but imperfect patient care.

In the current era of supportive adult education and political and social correctness the usual electric atmosphere of these conferences may have become dampened somewhat, but nevertheless a learning environment must prevail. If every person attending such a conference is aware of the ultimate objective, that is, improved patient care, then *any* approach, however draconian, is probably reasonable, especially if the rounds are protected from legal discovery.

The important end point is not to criticize and not to embarrass, but to document a specific problem and solution for any or all of the following four purposes:

1 Changing practice
2 Teaching

3 Preventing future adverse events
4 Improving patient care

Closure of the loop in all these discussions is the most important and precarious aspect. The standards by which improvements are possible and sustainable include processes of care, communication and implementation of those processes of care, and continual audits of those processes of care.

> **Concentrate not on the human mistake that an individual may be accused of but rather on *the process* that might be put in place to prevent the mistake from happening again.**

The field of elective surgery is perhaps the easiest field to evaluate in terms of quality of care: a diagnosis is made, a plan set in place, an intervention applied, post-operative care provided, and the results are evident at a relatively early stage.

Surgery has the advantage over medicine in this regard. Patients who are admitted on medical services often have multisystem disease with a number of diagnoses, and whatever intervention is applied may take much longer to assess in terms of efficacy. Responsibility for the quality of patient care rests with the individual clinician, of course, but from an organizational standpoint, responsibility rests with the division head, the department head, the medical advisory committee, and ultimately the board of trustees.

Therefore, how does one handle, for instance, the situation of a clinician's poor judgment that is suspected by a nurse who then reports the questionable event to his or her manager and subsequently to the clinician's division head? As in all such cases, it depends.

If the patient suffers a complication or what appears to be an unnecessary intervention, current culture demands that an incident report should be completed. Even though we always espouse blameless reporting, there still may be an element of intimidation. Unfortunately nurses are frequently put in the unenviable position of reporting or 'tattling' on the physician. If the quality-of-care conferences (aka M&M rounds) are appropriately constituted and frank discussion ensues, as it should, an irregularity should be brought to light, and the division head can then have discussions with the clinician involved.

If there is a recurrent problem, it is perfectly legitimate to audit a practice and review similar cases, for instance, with a view to assessing decision making and outcomes. If the event is clearly an egregious one, a medical leader must take more definite steps such as temporary suspension of privileges while the situation is being investigated. Although this heavy-handed approach may seem risky and violate the rights of the clinician, concerns about patient safety trump all other considerations. Nevertheless, the temporary suspension has to be private rather than one that involves licensing bodies, because irreparable (and unfair) damage can be done to a practitioner's career if precipitous and public decisions are made before all the facts are known.

Ideally, an apparent departure from the norm of medical management should be handled in a *generic* way, rather than be directed at a specific physician or surgeon. For example, if an unusual clinical decision has been made and concerns subsequently expressed, a medical leader can legitimately ask that the case be reviewed for the purpose of a divisional review and the institution of a protocol that can be applied to all such cases in future regardless of the individual clinician involved. In that way, consensus can be built with input from a number of colleagues, and this will not single out the clinician who incited the review; this is a constructive way to approach a difficult topic.

SITUATION 6.3

LAPAROSCOPIC SURGERY: *What Did You Know, and When Did You Know It? The Responsibility Issue, Part 1*

In 1993, in a large North American city, enthusiasm for laparoscopic surgery was exploding, as it was in every other centre on the planet. Training of surgeons varied across the continent, but it usually consisted of a fully trained 'open' surgeon submitting to a two- to three-day crash course on laparoscopic cholecystectomy somewhere in North America, which very likely did not involve any human patients.

Lectures and pig labs prepared surgeons for a life of procedures, most of which would therefore entail on-the-job training (correction, on-the-job *practice*). Not surprisingly, there were stories of horrible complications produced by this new technique, from life-threatening trocar injuries to laser injuries of the common bile duct (laser was the rage as a cutting tool initially but was replaced by an old-fashioned instrument called scissors).

Word got around very quickly that one city hospital had experienced three injuries of a major nature in a very short period of time, both bile duct and trocar injuries. In one case, the aorta was punctured by a trocar, and the patient almost succumbed with massive intra-abdominal bleeding.

Nothing was being done to correct the situation at the hospital, and my jurisdiction in quality of patient care was limited in my role at that time as chair of the division of general surgery for the university. That role is devoted to teaching and research in the various academic hospitals of the city, rather than specifically to quality of patient care.

Since the local division head and surgeon-in-chief were not acting, someone had to take responsibility. As division chair and surgical program director I had control of resident rotations in every general surgery division in the city. I therefore indicated to the surgeon-in-chief that a moratorium on laparoscopic procedures had to be instituted at the hospital until such time as surgeons could have adequate hands-on training. The lever was that if this did not happen, I would not be able to assign residents to that service, a threat to which all surgeons would listen.

Residents could not train on a service that had a concerning clinical record of patient safety.

The moratorium was applied, surgeons sought appropriate additional experience, and there was no recurrence of the problems.

> **As a medical leader you must remember one fact: when you are aware of dangerous practices, you yourself are as culpable as the offending clinicians if you do not act quickly and appropriately (guilt by association and knowledge). However, the actions taken have to be fair to everyone.**

The patient's welfare is uppermost; however, a witch-hunt against a particular clinician must be avoided at all times.

SITUATION 6.4
PEDIATRIC PATHOLOGIST DR CHARLES SMITH: *The Responsibility Issue, Part 2*

A great example of 'distributed' responsibility occurred in Canada in recent years, the case of Dr Charles Smith. Dr Smith is a clinical paediatric pathologist who developed an interest in forensics, becoming perhaps a kind of *CSI*-style pathologist. When a large number of high-profile paediatric cases were decided on the basis of his expert testimony, he became the darling of courtrooms and the press. Mothers, fathers, and others were convicted of child abuse or murder, fundamentally on the strength of his opinionated, sometimes condescending, and apparently authoritative opinions.

In the early part of the new century one case generated suspicion, and that ultimately led Chief Ontario Coroner Dr Barry McClellan to institute a formal review of many cases that had been assessed by Dr Smith. When details of the various cases were brought to light, it became clear that Smith had been guilty of proffering unsubstantiated judgments, erroneous opinions, false or misleading statements in court, bias, dogmatic opinions, sloppy retention of evidence, and at bottom an apparent arrogance and disdain for anyone who would question his judgment.

Many judgments and court decisions were eventually re-examined and reversed, and the Province of Ontario called for a formal review of these processes, under the supervision of Justice Stephen Goudge.[39] In his findings Justice Goudge stated, 'Dr Smith zealously believed that his role as an expert witness was to make the crown's [the prosecutor's] case look good. Innocent people had gone to jail, already grieving families were further shattered, and the credibility of the justice system was badly undermined' (*Toronto Star*). That was expected, but Justice Goudge went on to say that there was 'woefully inadequate oversight and undue deference to his perceived expertise' (Smith had no formal training in forensic pathology) and that this had 'allowed him to go unchecked for years, even as evidence of problems mounted.'

Justice Goudge specifically chastised Dr James Young and Dr James Cairns, the provincial chief and deputy coroners, 'for being lax, but also for misleading the College of Physicians and Surgeons of Ontario (CPSO) when a review of Dr Smith's activities was taking place. The story of failed oversight and Dr Smith's years is in large part the story of Dr Young's and Dr Cairn's failures and of the context in which that happens – the completely inadequate mechanisms for oversight and accountability.'

A letter from Dr Young to the CPSO, which was actually written by Smith's lawyer, defended Smith in response to a number of complaints that had been lodged against him. Judge Goudge felt that 'Dr Young's letter misled the CPSO. Dr Young told the enquiry that he sent this letter in an attempt to be fair to Dr Smith. He did so, however, at a cost to the public interest – the letter was not balanced or objective or candid. It was not a letter worthy of a senior public office holder in Ontario.'

The CPSO investigated Dr Charles Smith for professional misconduct, but because he no longer practised in the province, no significant penalties were expected, especially with respect to licensure. The point here for the medical leader is that the CPSO launched an enquiry into the conduct of the two coroners. These are honest, capable, and respected physicians who have been accused of having abrogated their responsibility to adequately oversee, as medical leaders, the activities they led.

The responsibility of a medical leader in a hospital is exactly the same as that of the physicians in the coroner's office. If as a medical leader you know of dangerous practice, you then become as responsible as the person directly guilty of the practice. 'What did you know, and when did you know it?' are questions the lawyers are going to pose. And if as a medical leader you don't know about dangerous practice in your department or division, you will be criticized for being a leader in absentia, and the hospital (or other organization in which you are a leader) will be criticized for not having adequate oversight systems in place.

What is your responsibility, as a hospital leader, in terms of monitoring the daily activities in your division? For instance, in a division of surgery should a leader know what kinds of surgery are being performed under his or her leadership and by whom? Yes, absolutely. The answer is that the division head is just as responsible as the individual surgeon who actually performs the procedure, if he has concerns about that surgeon's ability or experience. The head must know the capabilities and limitations of each of the surgeons in the unit, and accountability to the patient dictates that a surgeon is allowed to manage to the level of his or her expertise. That expertise is judged at the onset of an appointment and continuously thereafter.

Much of the foregoing is related to human error in our practice of medicine and surgery. However, it must be re-emphasized that the spirit of quality improvement in the present century mandates concentration on *improvement of processes*, rather than on blame to individual health care providers. In examining processes on an ongoing basis, organizations use failure modes and effects analysis (FMEA)[40] to identify and assess potential failures within the system. This is just another example of how the medical profession and the management of patients are becoming more and more aligned to practices in the manufacturing industry. This approach was originally introduced during the Second World War for military usage by the American armed forces and adopted by the aerospace industry during the Apollo space program. If these sectors can make astounding improvements in quality using such approaches, there has to be hope for medicine.

Continuous Quality Improvement and Patient Safety

Continuous quality improvement helps to avoid problems in the first place. So goes the obligation to minimize mistakes and poor or unexpected outcomes using the retrospective approach. But what about the more positive approach to continuously improving processes, using a system similar to the Six Sigma routine of Motorola?[41]

Although the health care industry has been enthusiastically engaged in improving its performance since 1999, other major industries have for decades adopted concepts such as the Six Sigma methodology, which is a registered trademark of Motorola and a way to improve work processes by eliminating defects, if not to zero, to a standard of 3.4 defects per million opportunities. If that standard had been achieved in the delivery of health care, imagine how the number of mortalities associated with the Institute of Medicine's report might have changed. A basic component of Six Sigma methodology is termed DMAIC:

- Define (specific goals)
- Measure (before and after a change to determine improvement)
- Analyse (all aspects to assess factors of causality)
- Improve (by changing processes to reach goals)
- Control (and stabilize processes to ensure future consistent performance)

Whatever methodology is used, the objective is the same: to achieve better outcomes by doing the right thing right for the patient, and that will include in future the right thing at an acceptable price.

The publication of *To Err Is Human*[9] called to action more than just the medical profession. President Bill Clinton's Advisory Commission on Consumer Protection and Quality in the Health Care Industry conceptualized the National Quality Forum (NQF) as a public-private collaborative venture in 1999. The objectives were to improve access and the patient experience, specifically the delivery of health care known to be effective, and to achieve better outcomes with enhanced patient safety. In late 2006, President George W. Bush signed the Tax Relief and Health Care Act of 2006 (TRHCA), which authorized the Centers for Medicare and Medicaid Services (CMS) to establish and implement a physician-quality reporting system. CMS then created the Physician Quality Reporting Initiative (PQRI) that not only articulated benchmarks for patient outcomes after specific treatments but actually organized incentive payments for those doctors achieving appropriate standards. The issue of incentives both for institutions and for individuals was introduced and continues to be a critical aspect of quality improvement. Bonus payments are made for good outcomes. Achieving these ends would require agreement on standardization, benchmarks, and a regular reporting system that would prove useful nationally. The federal government's Quality Interagency Coordination Task Force (QuIC) recommended that the National Quality Forum 'identify a set of patient safety measurements that should be a basic component of any medical errors reporting system.'

The practice of evidence-based medicine has been promoted by the Physician Consortium for Performance Improvement (PCPI), a product of the American Medical Association. The consortium comprises over one hundred national medical specialty and state medical societies and is open to anyone (organization or individual) committed to health care quality improvement and patient safety. In Canada the Canadian Patient Safety Institute (CPSI) and a dizzying array of provincial organizations are currently organizing efforts for quality of care and patient safety across the country. So there are dozens of organizations at various levels appropriately interested in quality of care and patient safety in North America, but what do you do in your own hospital to deal with these issues?

The delivery of safety and quality of care to patients is the *hospital's* mandate, with the challenge assigned, as stated previously, to an ever-changing and ever-increasing cadre of individuals. Just as the practice of medicine and surgery requires ongoing learning, so too does the hospital have to continually re-examine itself to improve its processes.

What about improvement in the *efficiency* of the organization's hundreds of processes devoted to patient care? Perhaps the best way to consider this is to recount the story of one patient, who on entering a hospital for the first time, was referred by a family physician to see a surgeon for the problem of an inguinal hernia.

SITUATION 6.5
MISTER P SEES A SURGEON IN THE HOSPITAL: *The Complex Journey of a 'Routine' Patient*

Mister P was a sixty-seven-year-old retired pharmacist who, at the time, was being treated for hypertension. He had had a myocardial infarction (MI) five years before this incident and until then had been a heavy smoker; after his MI, he quit the habit for good.

Mister P was being referred with an inguinal hernia to a general surgeon at the hospital. He went to the information desk in the lobby to find out where the surgeon's office was and discovered that she had an office in a building down the street (he had parked his car in a parkade adjacent to the hospital and had had to leave a twenty-dollar deposit).

Mister P walked down the street with some difficulty because of his uncomfortable groin and, after finding the doctor's office, was told that she couldn't see him until he had had a hospital card printed. So Mister P walked back to the hospital to the original information desk and was directed across the lobby where, an hour later because of a long line-up, he was issued with a hospital card. He then went back to the doctor's office and was seen by a very confident and competent surgeon, who conveyed to Mister P that he would need a pre-admission visit and an anaesthetic consultation before the surgery that she was going to perform, both of which were arranged for the following week.

At the pre-admission visit seven days later the anaesthesiologist arranged for a cardiogram, a thallium stress test, and a cardiologic consultation, all to be done subsequently on separate days in different parts of the hospital. The pre-admission visit lasted four and a half hours, and Mister P was ushered in and out of various examination rooms as he met with the pre-admission nurse practitioner, the anaesthesiologist, a technician administering an electrocardiogram, and an intravenous technician who took a number of blood samples that had been ordered by the surgeon at the original consultation.

Mister P then went back to see the surgeon in two weeks' time to have a discussion about the results of all the tests and further education about the indications, risks, benefits, and alternatives of the proposed operation. He decided to go ahead with the surgery and signed the consent form with the surgeon. The operation was scheduled for six months from that visit.

What's wrong with this picture? Obviously, almost everything.

If one starts with the patient and follows him or her through the experience of diagnosis and treatment, one is discouraged by the stories that the patient tells. And those patients with stories are usually very vocal, as they should be. If we look critically from the patient's point of view, we may have a glimmer of hope in improving a lamentable situation. Where do we turn but to the automotive industry, which has been the manufacturing key for so many countries in the past fifty plus years, even if in North America it has been suffering lately.

In the first decade of the twenty-first century Japanese carmakers, particularly Toyota Motor Corporation, have vaulted into the lead in quality of product and stock value, no doubt for a multiplicity of reasons. One major factor in the ascendance of Toyota has been deliberate attention to quality control and improvement on the production line. Recent events in the early weeks of 2010 indicate that even a company dedicated to quality and efficiency can experience issues of poor performance. That said, the quick response of Toyota to the sticky accelerator and brake problems is part of the process of quality improvement.

The Japanese concept of *Kaizen* ('change for the better' or 'improvement'; the modified English translation is 'continuous improvement') can be applied to medical processes as well as it can be to the car industry. Toyota is famous for supporting the generic process management philosophy known as lean manufacturing, which focuses on eliminating waste (*Muda*) and allowing for smooth, efficient, and variation-free activities in production.[42]

Returning to the saga of Mister P, the unfortunate patient with the hernia, we see a large number of problems and inconsistencies that are no doubt the product of processes that have developed over decades with the health care provider, rather than the patient, in mind. The following are all important issues:

1 Communication
2 Access to care
3 Scheduling
4 Coordination of care
5 Wait times for both investigations and interventions
6 Patient education

In the case of Mister P, these steps were all poorly executed. None of these glitches bothered any of the providers in that awful chain of events because the processes were designed years ago by doctors and nurses, at a time when the patient had little influence. But things have changed.

In a private system where the patients and their insurers support the profit margin, the patient must be satisfied, because happier and more numerous patients mean more profits. In a public system such as Canada's, the provincial government and the Ministry of Health listen to patients' concerns and monitor such quality metrics as surgical, radiologic, and emergency department wait times. The patients and the ministry must be satisfied, because the single payer holds the resources, and resources are increasingly assigned with volumes and quality in mind. In Canada, where patients now have high expectations and have 'prepaid' their medical care through taxes, and in the United States, where patients can give their business (and insurance revenue) to another organization, hospitals certainly are listening.

How do we get at the terribly complex array of inconveniences in Mister P's story? Unfortunately, just like a senior surgeon's habits that may have fossilized over decades, ingrained hospital practices may be hard to revise. We must break down that litany of unpleasant patient experiences into its parts. It's far beyond the scope of this volume to relate in detail those components of *lean manufacturing* that are covered in a much more comprehensive way in other publications. However, it might be useful to relate how one aspect of this story was dealt with at Community Hospital B. The approach used the following two techniques, which are critical aspects of lean manufacturing:

1 Value stream mapping (VSM)
2 Producing the rapid improvement event (RIE)

SITUATION 6.6
A COMMUNITY HOSPITAL IMPROVES PATIENT WAIT TIMES:
The Spaghetti Diagram Is Straightened Out

As you might expect, a problematic process that has evolved over years demands tremendous effort to correct. In Mister P's case (see situation 6.5), this correction involved direction from the hospital's information management services in order to manage the project, as well as commitment by the large number of stakeholders actually affected by the process.

One major problem identified was the time that patients spent in the pre-admission visit, which was thought to represent a major negative factor in patient satisfaction. Collection of data was undertaken through a survey conducted over ten working days. As predicted, the average time spent in the pre-admission clinic seemed excessive, at four and a half hours, for visits with two health care personnel (the nurse practitioner and the anaesthesiologist) and two technicians (for the ECG and the bloodletting).

Interviews with patients during the survey clearly showed that the inefficiencies and time wasted were sources of significant frustration for them. The actual time spent with the providers or technicians was only one and a half hours, so the remainder was devoted to waiting in the lounge area and moving from room to room to meet with the various personnel.

During a formal VSM process thirteen members of the pre-admission team, including nurses, technicians, IT specialists, and a project manager, met together for four working days, while extra staffing was provided in their area to meet the ongoing workload. Following were the objectives of the exercise:

1 Assess from the patient's point of view the journey through the pre-admission clinic

2 Define problems in efficiencies and delays

3 Suggest specific strategies for improvement

Performance metrics, including the following, were selected, discussed, and recorded:

1 Patient and staff satisfaction

2 Total time of the visit

3 Current and ideal 'maps' of the patients' experience

Everyone present had opportunities to express opinions, and all were watered and fed liberally (a necessary and productive perk in any hospital whenever you want cooperation and collaboration).

A patient value statement was devised in order to capture the mission of the project.

It's not hard to imagine how confusing that lengthy hospital visit was for Mister P. As a result of the pre-VSM survey, a complex diagram was sketched to indicate his movement from the registration desk to the waiting room, to the nurse examination room, back to the waiting room, to the room for the electrocardiogram, back to the waiting room, and so on. The use of the term *spaghetti diagram*, depicting all these travels, is obviously appropriate.

The movement of the patient was only one component of the *current state*, but there were others such as the unavailability of the anaesthesiologist at the appropriate time.

The VSM group turned its attention to the *ideal state*, which predictably focused on patient-centred processes, efficiency, collaboration, standardization, communication, and education of health care personnel. All of these were required if the selected metrics were to improve when changes were ultimately made.

All aspects of the current and ideal states were depicted on large flow charts pasted on the walls of the meeting room, which facilitated the recognition of gaps and the possible obstacles to correction of the flaws in the process. The *gap analysis* then led to proposals for possible solutions, some of which could be instituted the next day, while others required more time, effort, and possibly increased staffing to implement.

Of all the specific steps in this complex process that added to inefficiency, the patient movement was thought to be the most challenging and most culpable. A kind of experiment was then devised. The patient was placed in one room, and various events were directed to that patient in a single room, with minimal travel for the patient. This clearly demanded better coordination on the part of the health care personnel and may have seemed inconvenient for them at first, but in fact, after acclimatization, the time spent by the nurse practitioner, the anaesthesiologist, and the technician was no greater than it had been previously – and now they were all dealing with a much more contented patient because the whole visiting time had plummeted from four and a half hours to a consistent average of two and a half hours. This focus on a specific problem and the process to arrive at a solution is termed *a rapid improvement event* (RIE).

The element of time was just one of the pieces of Mister P's experience in this exposure to antiquated hospital practices. Nevertheless, the RIE had, with buy-in from a large number of interested hospital workers, produced significant gains.

VSM and RIEs are time consuming, but they can be very effective. The next question that you've undoubtedly already asked is, 'Yes, but is this sustainable?' In fact, one year later, the pre-admission visits continue to be monitored, continue to be more efficient, and are associated with improved patient and staff satisfaction. The changes have not led to more costs or inconvenience on the part of health care providers; they have simply represented a different way of doing things.

Now we can turn our attention to all the other glitches illustrated in that single patient's experience.

SITUATION 6.7
DR JOHN TOUSSAINT OF THEDACARE INC.: *A Culture of Quality Improvement*

Dr John Toussaint is the CEO of ThedaCare, Inc., a seven-county consortium in Wisconsin comprising four hospitals, twenty-one clinics, and other components of care including home care, hospice services, facilities for seniors, and behavioural health clinics. Previously the chief of medicine, Dr Toussaint has been in his current position since 2000 and has introduced and developed the ThedaCare Improvement System,[43] which is a direct descendant and medical derivative of the Toyota Production System. He claims that the approach of using VSM and RIEs as tools for continuous sustained improvement has been successful because

1 the system has a high and public profile in the organization,
2 numerous initiatives are under way simultaneously, and
3 ongoing results are posted for all to see and monitor.

The new culture of *sustained quality improvement* has obviously been established in this health care organization.

There are many local, national, and international quality control initiatives that are now being embraced by the medical and surgical communities. Most hospitals are involved in the Safer Health Care Now! initiative,[44] the Saving 100,000 Lives campaign,[45] the Protecting 5 Million Patients from Harm initiative,[46] the American College of Surgeons' National Surgical Quality Improvement Program (NSQIP),[47] and the Surgical Care Improvement Project (SCIP).[48] The SCIP focuses on surgical site infections; monitoring beta blockers for those taking the medication preoperatively; appropriate hair removal (*not* shaving, and preferably nothing); judicious and timely preoperative and possibly intra-operative administration of antibiotics; normothermia; and normoglycemia.

We are also seeing the development of the World Health Organization Surgical Safety Checklist project, in which eight centres around the world have collaborated in introducing a perioperative checklist (see situation 7.2). This is, in fact, an extension of the surgical timeout or 'surgical pause' that has become standard practice in most jurisdictions. The expansion of this concept is now taking place and really represents a vehicle that promotes the objectives of the other initiatives mentioned. It is discussed in more detail in chapter 7.

Through these organized approaches, hospitals are gradually finding more consistent ways of treating, for example, myocardial infarction or congestive heart failure and developing ways of avoiding such problems as nosocomial infections, central-line infections, ventilator-associated pneumonia, and mistakes in administering high-risk medications.

These generic initiatives promise to standardize patient care in ways never before implemented, and it is the medical leader's responsibility to ensure that all practitioners are on side.

> **Continued practice at a health care institution depends on strategies being carried out by every clinician to address these quality improvement concepts, and the medical leader must be the champion of such processes.**

In addition to the mandated initiatives, doctors and nurses are empowered if they can feel free to carry out local experiments designed to improve patient care – like the small groups on a Volvo assembly line, who can work and make suggested improvements independently. This is covered in more detail in the next chapter and involves methodology in which a team of professionals can analyse a perceived process problem and devise solutions that have demonstrable positive effects on their areas and perhaps, by extrapolation, on the whole organization.

Innovation

Monitoring the conventional treatment of problematic diseases is difficult enough, but how do you deal with the 'new and improved' or *innovative* treatments of a particularly dangerous disease state, and how do you as a medical leader respond to the creativity of a physician proposing a novel approach? Surely, the risks are greater to the patient, the practitioner, and the hospital.

SITUATION 6.8
NEW PROCEDURE FOR CEREBRAL ANEURYSMS:
Introducing Innovative Procedures, Part 1

In October 2008 a new procedure was proposed for the treatment of giant cerebral aneurysms. In the past, patients had either eventually succumbed to the rupture of such an aneurysm or they had been subjected to a massive operation that carried a high, and in many instances unacceptable, risk. A group in the Netherlands had reported early experience with the excimer laser-assisted non-occlusive anastomosis (ELANA) procedure.[49] This laser-based approach boasted the following benefits: improved efficacy, less risk in the face of high risk for stroke, and encouraging long-term outcomes.

Doctor N was an enterprising and audacious neurosurgeon at Community Hospital C in a large North American city. He immediately recognized the advantages of the highly technical ELANA procedure, and because of his expanding profile in the area of cerebrovascular disease, Doctor N had no shortage of patient referrals for such difficult care.

Doctor N submitted a proposal, in accordance with the rules of the innovation process in the organization, which required the presentation of the following:

- A review of experience in the field
- The rationale behind the procedure
- The likelihood of better outcomes than with more conventional treatment

---

That professional part of the process was assessed by the surgeon-in-chief and a small group of practitioners, who determined that this proposed procedure was not experimental (because there had been adequate experience elsewhere) and therefore did not necessitate a review with the Research Ethics Board (REB) of the hospital.

The more detailed components, that is, the operational steps, were then examined. The Dutch neurosurgeons who had devised the operation were invited to participate in the initial procedures, and the extensive processes of temporary licensure by the province were addressed. The technical equipment and, in particular, the nursing and anaesthetic familiarization had to be covered so that the Netherlands procedure might be duplicated as closely as possible. The Dutch surgeons came to Canada for a whole week, the length of time designed to conduct dry runs of the ELANA procedure for two days, followed by the real thing on two patients who had been fully informed and booked electively for this potentially lifesaving procedure.

Nurses, anaesthesiologists, and surgeons worked for two days to familiarize themselves with the operation of the laser, the steps of the operation, and the predicted 'glitches' that the Dutch surgeons had faced and overcome in their early experience. For an entire week, one of the neurosurgical operating rooms was transformed into a kind of active clinical research laboratory, and the theoretical became reality. The practice days came and went with precision, and two operations on local patients, thankfully, were performed with similar precision and with significant intensity.

The new procedures were carried out in Community Hospital C as planned and were made possible by the following:

- Examination of ethical concerns
- Careful preparation
- Expert mentoring
- Appropriate education of personnel
- The assembling of sophisticated equipment

That week, two patients were subjected to innovative procedures in a high-risk situation, and their courage may have led to many more patients like them being helped in the future.

Every certified doctor claims that he or she meets new challenges every day and that innovation is a part of practice. Every patient with a particular diagnosis is truly different in some way from every previous patient presenting that major problem. Therefore, fresh thinking must be brought to bear on the unique situation, based on education, a body of knowledge, experience, continuous professional development (also known as CME, continuing medical education), intuition, and common sense.

Sometimes a radical departure from the norm seems required to meet the demands of a particular patient case, and that judgment may well be examined in either educational rounds if the outcome was acceptable or in quality-of-care rounds if it wasn't.

What if a physician or surgeon wants to do something that is totally new to your institution and has the time to plan such a novel approach? Again, leadership must step in. As mentioned numerous times previously, the fundamental challenge facing you as a medical leader is to advocate for your reports, that is, the members of your division or department, and *at the same time* defend and follow the guidelines and principles of the organization (the hospital), management, and bioethical behaviour.

The four fundamental principles of bioethics must be observed:

- Autonomy
- Beneficence
- Non-maleficence
- Judgment

Patients must fully understand the implications of a proposed diagnosis and/or management and be confident that they are making the right decision(s) for themselves when they sign the consent form. However, the steps to be taken by the doctor are more far-reaching. The steps involved in the decision to pursue a new direction include asking the following questions:

- How will the new direction be pursued?
- With what preparation?
- Using what rationale?
- With what personnel?
- With what scrutiny?

Meanwhile, desperately needy patients, who it is hoped would benefit from a novel procedure or treatment, require all of the following in combination: the mindset of the doctors to innovate, the caring of practitioners to assist a fellow human being, complex preparation, and institutional commitment of necessary resources.

The program for considering novel approaches and treatments at our hospital is Enabling Innovation. It is so named because the organization's leaders recognized their mandates to innovate (as one of our stated values), avoid the stifling of creativity, be responsible to the patient, and adhere to bioethical principles.

SITUATION 6.9

A CREATIVE RESPONSE TO THE SHORTAGE OF DONOR LUNGS:
Introducing Innovative Procedures, Part 2

Somewhere between fifty and sixty patients waited on the lung transplant list in a large North American jurisdiction in early 2008. These people were in constant danger of dying before a viable lung became available through deceased donor avenues. The cadaver-donor rate in the jurisdiction is a shamefully low nine per million population per year, compared with about thirty per million in Spain, where the presumed-consent principle has been adopted. Presumed consent has not yet reached North America for a variety of reasons, including the mosaic of many peoples with differing cultures.

Thus, in North America, the situation for all potential transplant recipients is critical, particularly for those awaiting lung transplants because that organ is more sensitive to grafting than are others. One such unfortunate individual was Ontario Justice Archie Campbell, a noted legal mind and Renaissance man, who died of advanced pulmonary fibrosis while on the transplant list. (Justice Campbell had offered a learned report on the severe acute respiratory syndrome (SARS) crisis,[50] which is outlined in the section on disaster planning in chapter 9.)

At Community Hospital B, the organs of only one in four donors (fewer in other centres) are appropriate for transplantation at the time that they are being harvested. Grappling with the sad donor situation for years, Doctor O and her thoracic surgery team had come to the desperate conclusion that something had to be done to improve the donor rate. The obvious ways of doing so, of course, were to either educate the public to sign donor cards and instruct family members, or encourage government legislation to allow adoption of the Spanish presumed-consent approach.

Another option, however, might be to improve the less-than-adequate donor lungs to a level that they could be usable. Normally, the donor lungs are removed and flushed with a cold augmented saline solution prior to transplant into the recipient. However, these explanted lungs are heavy with extravascular water and a variety of inflammatory mediators that undoubtedly have a negative effect on their ultimate survival. So the team at Community Hospital B set out to explore ways to fine-tune these lungs after their removal from the donor. This was done in the laboratory by perfusing extracted donor pig lungs with a hyperosmolar high-protein solution for twelve hours at normal temperature, in the hopes that an unhealthy lung might eventually be rendered usable. Early experimental success was reported in the *American Journal of Transplantation*,[51] and preparations were made to extend these manoeuvres to the human context.

Unlike with the ELANA aneurysm procedure, however, this proposed plan involved *human experimentation*, as there was no evidence anywhere in the world that such a problem had been tackled in this way before. The hospital's Research Ethics Board examined the proposal, made some suggestions about clarification of the consent form, and essentially gave the green light to proceed with a human experimentation, provided that a large number of conditions were met.

Basically, the ex vivo perfusion procedure would take a donor lung that was of concern for its state of health and future transplantability, put it into a perfusion apparatus for several hours, and improve its function to the point that it could survive in the recipient. The rationale for the improvement lay in the postulate that the normothermic perfusion might remove the lung water and the inflammatory mediators.

The preparations in the operating theatre were just as detailed as those for the ELANA procedure. Anaesthesiologists and nurses became familiarized exhaustively with each proposed step, and this culminated in extensive practice runs carried out with every detail discussed, implemented, and recorded.

The first experience involved a double-lung transplant using acceptable lungs, one of which was perfused for four hours. This step was necessary to establish that the perfusion wasn't harmful to a normal lung deemed acceptable for transplantation, and indeed, in two patients who had these procedures, there was no discernible difference in the pairs of lungs that were grafted, and they functioned well.

The climax of this story came soon afterwards when a patient in urgent need of a double-lung transplant was presented, but the prospective donor lungs were *not* acceptable for harvesting: the X-rays, the perfusion, and the blood gases all indicated that the donor lungs were simply incompatible with future success. So the donor lungs underwent the novel ex vivo normothermic perfusion, the 'new and improved' lungs were transplanted, and the patient was extubated five days later with a promising future.

Comment: A creative approach was supported, and it may just lead to a change of practice in this critical area. An April 2009 press release from Royal Brompton Hospital in Britain[52] described the use of the technique with excellent results and thanked its Canadian colleagues for the generous transfer of knowledge and techniques.

If a unique medical or surgical approach, that is, a procedure that has not previously been done at your hospital (or, in some instances, anywhere), is proposed to be carried out electively at some point in the future, a more elective deliberate strategy should be adopted.

Every hospital must have a process that considers *innovative management strategies*. This is critical not only to ensure patient safety but also to protect the health care providers, while encouraging the creativity that every doctor protects and cherishes. (All surgeons would say that every operation is a little different and that they are innovating every time they hold a scalpel.) At the same time, such a process will ensure that novel techniques and equipment are known to all members of the team before a new operation is sprung on them. Gone are the days when surgeons came to the operating room armed with some new technology that they had just received from an enthusiastic equipment provider.

Sometimes the patient may require a risky treatment because without it death is certain. In other situations, an innovative treatment may be quite reasonable despite the risk because help for a particular patient and for future patients may be justified if the current patient is at no greater calculated risk than that of conventional treatment. Sometimes we must dare to implement change, dare to be better. That said, it will be the medical leader's job to monitor any innovative strategies or procedures so that innovation is encouraged but patient safety remains paramount.

In summary, when a surgeon wishes to introduce a new operation, careful attention must be paid to the following:

- The published results
- The experience of the surgeon in that particular area of endeavour
- The evidence of the training required and sought
- The education and practice of the nurses and anaesthesiologists involved

- The implications for operating room time and supplies
- The post-operative recovery requirements.

It goes without saying that the patient involved in this new procedure or treatment must be fully informed and educated and must understand the risks and benefits of conventional care as well as of the suggested innovation; informed consent is always critical, but even more so in this setting. Unfortunately, these many 'mundane' details may be the last things on the mind of the innovating surgeon, which emphasizes even more the need for standardized processes.

In our organization, as already mentioned, we use the term *enabling innovation*, an expression designed to encourage creativity and innovation but also to remind the proposing surgeon that appropriate preparations must be in place.

The subject of quality of care is indeed complex, but no topic is more important for you, either personally or in your responsibility as the medical leader to spearhead a team of like-minded professionals. While most of the foregoing is dedicated to minimizing risk to the patient, every practitioner knows that there is, and will continue to be, risk every time a medication is prescribed or an intervention planned.

7 Planning and Execution

Strategic planning, an essential but often painstakingly slow process, may be a relatively new experience for you, but if it's followed by execution of those plans and by measurable change, your sense of accomplishment and excitement will know no bounds. During your education in operations an acceptable knowledge of hospital finances is inescapable, and some extra courses may be required on your part.

Strategic Planning

For those people who like to get on with the job, and for whom keeping clear of the swamp's alligators is essential, strategic long-range planning usually prompts rolling of the eyes, a glassy-eyed stare, or a mild expletive accompanied by, 'Not again!' Planning is seen by some of us as time consuming, ineffective, repetitive, and a simple waste of the time that could be used more effectively in our day jobs. Planning may also be uncomfortable for some doctors because it may force them to take a closer look at the current state, drawing attention to disturbing shortcomings.

The bottom line is that planning implies impending change, and change in general is not welcomed. The majority of human beings are very content, if not thriving, on maintaining the status quo. They maintain a routine of doing, working, playing, and creating memories with friends and family, which gives them a feeling of contentment and stability and an inherent control of risk in their lives. Therefore, any change, especially one that is potentially substantive and will affect livelihoods, job processes, and ways of doing things, may add elements of unwanted risk and uncertainty.

A fundamental reality in the development of expertise in clinical medicine and surgery is uncertainty. As medical practitioners we all must learn to make decisions, and be comfortable making these decisions – which are sometimes significantly life saving or life threatening– in an atmosphere in which we're making educated guesses and where we may well be wrong. As the lawyers say, we're held to a common standard in the profession in which a practitioner will act in a reasonable way, and in a way that the profession would regard as reasonable. Just as we must accept risk in the clinical setting because more severe illness and possibly death are in the balance, so too must we accept risk in planning for the future, with mediocrity and the status quo in the balance.

Completing a long-range strategic planning process should not be regarded as the 'beginning of the end. But it is, perhaps, the end of the beginning,' as Winston Churchill is often quoted as saying in reference to the Second Battle of El Alamein. Long-range planning may not follow a prescribed format; it may simply answer the following questions:

1 What do we stand for?
2 Where do we want to be?
3 Where are we now?
4 What are the gaps?
5 How will we close the gaps?

Oversimplification may lead to an accusation of 'surgical thinking' on my part, but sometimes reducing a complex topic to simpler components is useful and certainly more engaging for a large number of colleagues.

Few areas of the business world have been sliced and diced more than the concept of planning. Studied at General Electric and in institutions such as Harvard Business School and Stanford University, strategic planning has been the lifeblood of many multinational corporations, a credit to countless CEOs who have written books and received gargantuan bonuses, and fodder for many prospective surgical leaders who, like myself, have dutifully traipsed to Harvard, Kellogg Graduate School of Management, or the Rotman School of Management to be transformed into the supposed management gurus of the future.

Planning *is* important. Planning is usually not convenient because most of us live our lives by riding a never-ending wave of activity. Our lives are so busy these days that smelling the roses may be relegated to a few specific days of the year when we try to make up for our short-comings in the rest of the year – and I know that I'm not speaking just for myself here. We all need to sit back and take time to think, to ponder, to look back with some satisfaction, and to look forward with anticipation and excitement. Peter Drucker, who died in 2006, fathered one of the best-known quotes about planning:

'The best way to predict the future is to create it.'

The futility that many among us feel about planning cycles likely comes from the experience of a lack of action, despite the many hours, sometimes days and months, spent in retreats and other strategic planning sessions. The declaration of 'same old, same old,' the looking back at work done or not done, and the feelings of frustration are unsettling. The other major factor, of course, is that serious exercises may have such long-range time frames that very few of the most interested and active individuals involved in strategy ever get a chance to see the fruits of their labours.

However, if one looks at these initiatives as an exciting beginning to the future, and if history in a particular organization shows that things *do* happen, strategic planning can be a truly exciting and inspiring activity.

Vision and Mission

Truly critical for the organization or group is a *vision statement* if the following conditions can be met:

1 The vision statement can be formulated by an appropriate segment of the membership, for example, a cross-section of all health care workers in a unit.
2 The vision statement is simple, short, and can be remembered.
3 The vision statement really *means* something to everyone who works in the unit or the group.

SITUATION 7.1
FATHER ATTENDS A WHITE-COAT CEREMONY: *Owning Your Future*

In the spring of 2007 I attended a ceremony at which all the new medical students were being introduced to a university in the yearly 'white-coat ceremony.' This involved the assembly of every one of the 147 new students,

a series of greetings from the faculty, and then the presentation of a personally monogrammed white lab coat to each of the neophytes. Very hokey to
be sure, but a highlight for the students and a time of bursting pride for the
parents, most of whom became amateur photographers for the day. What
impressed was the gesture of welcome, of course, but also the fact that the
president of each of the three more senior years in the medical school stood
and outlined for all to hear the vision statement of his or her respective class.

Each statement was a little different from the other, although the common theme was obvious, and the fact that the students in each class had
collaborated to produce something for which they stood resonated with the
parents, whose adult children had now become part of a unique society that
expressed such lofty but achievable goals.

A *mission statement* is simply a statement of what an organization is
doing to work towards its stated goals. Often a mission statement ends
up being repetitive and mundane, especially in the medical field.
Virtually every mission statement of an academic hospital, for instance,
refers to excellent clinical care, education, and research. Therefore, the
vision statement has the even greater challenge of being appropriate,
short, unique, and catchy. Many vision statements, however, really express the mission of the organization.

The following are some current examples of vision statements:

- *Massachusetts General Hospital*: 'As nurses, health professionals, and
  patient care services support staff, our every action is guided by
  knowledge, enabled by skill, and motivated by compassion.
  Patients are our primary focus, and the way we deliver care reflects
  that focus every day. We believe in creating a practice environment
  that has no barriers, is built on a spirit of inquiry, and reflects a
  culturally competent workforce supportive of the patient-focused
  values of this institution. It is through our professional practice
  model that we make our vision a demonstrable truth every day by
  letting our thoughts, decisions and actions be guided by our values.
  As clinicians, we ensure that our practice is caring, innovative,
  scientific, and empowering, and is based on a foundation of leadership and entrepreneurial teamwork.'[53]
- *Memorial Sloan-Kettering Hospital*: 'As one of the world's premier
  cancer centres, MSK cancer centre is committed to exceptional
  patient care, leading-edge research, and superb educational
  programs. The close collaboration between our physicians and

scientists is one of our unique strengths, enabling us to provide patients with the best care available today as we work to discover more effective strategies to prevent, control, and ultimately cure cancer in the future. Our education programs train future physicians and scientists, and the knowledge and experience they gain at Memorial Sloan-Kettering has an impact on cancer treatment and the biomedical research agenda around the world.'[54]
- *Johns Hopkins University Hospital*: 'The mission is to improve the health of the community and the world by setting the standard of excellence in medical education, research, and clinical care. Diverse and inclusive, Johns Hopkins Medicine educates medical students, scientists, health care professionals, and the public; conducts medical research; and provides patient-centred medicine to prevent, diagnose, and treat human illness. Johns Hopkins Medicine provides a diverse and inclusive environment that fosters intellectual discovery, creates and transmits innovative knowledge, improves human health, and provides medical leadership to the world.'[55]
- *Toronto's University Health Network*: 'Achieving global impact.'[56]
- *Toronto East General Hospital*: 'To be Ontario's leading community teaching hospital.'[57]

Which of the above can you remember, and which do you think the average hospital worker is aware of?

Ten Tips for Strategic Planning

As Ernest Hemingway said, all stories begin with 'the sheet of blank paper.' This is the excitement around major strategic planning. The piece of paper may have some baggage attached, threats of looming insolvency, and highly politicized interest areas all vying for the same resources. Nevertheless, here are ten general tips for the medical leader who will spearhead strategic planning at a hospital (or other institution):

1 Get a large number of people involved
2 Create some excitement around the exercise
3 Encourage active participation at various levels; this requires homework, research, and creative thinking on the part of the participants
4 Communicate the deliberations as you go along

5 Move towards a draft document that is short, to the point, containing clear recommendations and timelines, and noting the resources required
6 Seek feedback from all stakeholders before a final planning document is published
7 Celebrate the planning exercise and publish a final document with an executive summary containing specific recommendations
8 Most important, set in place specific *implementation plans* for each recommendation, with timelines, accountabilities, and the resources required
9 Focus on getting some quick wins
10 Review frequently the progress of the plans and achievements, and make in-course adjustments as necessary

How Long Does a Planning Exercise Take?

It depends. Some feel that retreats, which may last from one to three days, are more useful as team-building exercises rather than for arriving at crystallized thoughts about the future of an organization. Others prefer to conduct retreats with a specific subject in mind and a number of clearly stated objectives to work towards.

Professional facilitators can be useful in helping to move the conversations along because these individuals are presumably objective and have experience in creating consensus in the midst of controversy.

Another method is to have a series of shorter meetings over a few months. While this holds the risk of momentum loss, it has the advantage of sorting out and clarifying the issues that inevitably surface to complicate the discussions. Whatever the method used to plan, the objectives of the process must be stated at the outset – in particular, the clearly articulated responsibilities and expectations of all the players involved.

A hospital is a complex organization, and those in each area of interest must be given independence to present their own vision about where they see themselves now and in the future, not unlike what the medical school classes did in the white-coat ceremony described above. In the case of a complex medical or surgical department, for example, representatives of each group must have an opportunity to declare their own version of a SWOT analysis, that is, a self-assessment of their strengths, weaknesses, opportunities, and threats.

The SWOT analysis is perhaps an oversimplified and, some would say, antiquated approach to a complex topic, but sometimes an uncomplicated view is a good way to start. The process should take into account the internal and external factors affecting that group's situation. Representatives of a division or department must be able to articulate their current state, their desired state, and the perceived gap between the two.

In our own strategic planning process in surgical programs at the University Health Network, which was a process that lasted the better part of a year, there was one huge unexpected benefit: the education of all representatives of the various interest areas such as cardiac surgery, otolaryngology, and orthopaedics about the exciting things that were going on in every division and department. This served not only to create incentives for all those who had committed to present their cases but was a constant reminder that there were many other worthy horses at the same resource trough.

At the outset of the planning process, when the ground rules are being set, it's imperative to consider what other strategic planning is going on or has been completed in the recent past. In an academic setting a medical leader must be aware of the recommendations made in recent planning by the university as a whole, the medical faculty, the hospital, and other academic hospitals in the university family; these recommendations may weigh heavily on the deliberations in a specific division or department. There's no sense in reinventing a wheel or, in fact, creating a fifth wheel!

After all pertinent information has been put on the table, and all stakeholders have expressed their own hopes and dreams in the context of reality, a second crucial step in the planning process has to be taken. Through the documentation of all presentations, *common themes* will become evident, and the medical leader must undertake to collate the themes along with a personal vision. The leader must have a well-defined personal vision but not one that should or can be imposed if it is at odds with the majority of the stakeholders.

At this point, further articulation of strategy must be steered. This should be done by forming a number of task forces or subcommittees to address themes across divisions or interest areas. For example, in the case of surgery, the theme of minimally invasive surgery (MIS) may be of great interest, and an appointed task force would deliberate on the development of an MIS program across specialties, detailing the needs to achieve certain objectives in terms of personnel, capital, research, and educational programs.

In this way, the final planning document will be a reflection of both top-down and bottom-up developments of recommendations. I prefer to think of this process as the blooming of a flower, rather than as a distinctly hierarchal process. Leadership should really come from *everyone*.

As a medical leader you gently coach, organize, encourage, and distil – hopefully along lines that you can support without reservation.

The strategic planning exercises represent the very first step of change, with the real and most important challenge being everything that comes afterwards:

- Execution of the plans
- Follow-up
- Measurement of outcomes
- Resultant changes

These represent the real meat of the exercise.

Planning vs Execution: Taking a Step Backward and a Step Forward

Philip Orsino, as the president and CEO of the largest door manufacturer in the world, was a sought-after speaker because of his success and clear thinking. He repeatedly talked about his mantra of 'leadership, focus, and execution,' with the most important component, execution.[58]

The process of ultimately effecting change is like an iceberg: the tip that we see at the outset, with a few ethereal clouds above, is the strategic planning, and the 90 per cent lurking below the water is the real meat, the bulk of the overall job, the hard work, and the most difficult to effect.

Henry Mintzberg, the Cleghorn Professor of Management Studies at McGill University in Montreal, is a man of influence in the business world. He is well known to support the concept of on-the-job learning and training. 'The MBA trains the wrong people in the wrong ways with the wrong consequences,' he writes. 'Using the classroom to help develop people already practicing management is a fine idea, but pretending to create managers out of people who have never managed is a sham.'[59]

Mintzberg's approach is to recognize that our everyday experiences, whether they be in the operating theatre, on the ward, or outside our workplace, are the most valuable learning opportunities for each of us. Whether you are a recently graduated nurse, a seasoned veteran, a manager, or an academic physician or surgeon, your everyday experiences offer you valuable opportunities to learn.

How does Mintzberg think about organizations, in particular a large organization like an academic health sciences centre? Mintzberg identifies five basic subunits of a huge enterprise[60] (see figure 7.1):

Figure 7.1: The basic organization

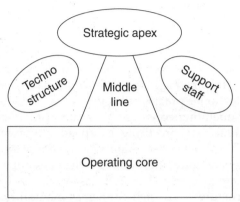

Source: Henry Mintzberg, *Structuring of Organizations*, 1st. edition, © 1979. Electronically reproduced by permission of Pearson Education, Inc., Upper Saddle River, New Jersey.

1 *The operating core*, consisting of the real people who are the lifeblood of the institution or organization, which in the hospital setting includes
   • the nurses,
   • the additional health care providers such as technicians and technologists, and
   • the doctors.
2 *The support staff*, including
   • human resources,
   • patient relations,
   • public relations,
   • payroll,
   • housekeeping, and
   • legal counsel.
3 *The technostructure*, which is becoming increasingly important to us, including
   • systems analysis,
   • information technology (IT), and
   • finance.
4 *The middle-line executives*, including
   • directors,
   • executive directors, and
   • vice-presidents with various portfolios.

5 *The strategic apex*, consisting of
   • the board of trustees and
   • the president and chief executive officer.

In the usual business sector company, the functional subunits look something like that. However, in a professional medical organization like a large hospital, in which we rely for coordination on the standardization of professional practice and the skills of all our health care providers, our operating core is seen as more prominent because we doctors and nurses are practising independently according to clear standards and benchmarks (see figure 7.2). The professional traditionally works independently of his or her colleagues but closely with clients or, in our case, patients. The standards by which we work originate outside our structure, with such entities as medical licensing bodies, credentialling organizations, and nursing associations. The strategies of this professional bureaucracy are largely those of the individual professionals within the health sciences centre as well as those of our professional organizations outside of it.

Why examine this apparently tangential concept? Because, in academic medicine at least, I don't think we want to be just this traditional type of Mintzberg professional organization at all. As all doctors are aware, we recognize and practise according to the externally imposed standards, but we're continually trying to push the envelope in our everyday practice, in our education, and in our research efforts. This creates a tension between creativity and progress on the one hand and established norms on the other, something that academic practitioners are attempting to encourage through innovation. Any innovative initiative might be regarded as an ad hoc process that hopefully stimulates innovation but at the same time ensures that the potentially stifling effect of traditional practice is nevertheless honoured and considered. In fact, Mintzberg not surprisingly has a basic organizational form for this type of situation, and he calls it *the adhocracy* (see figure 7.3).

> **In health science centres we must hire and give power to creative experts who can build on existing knowledge and skills.**

The other feature that Mintzberg emphasizes in the adhocracy is that individual academics must amalgamate their efforts and collaborate, unlike members of the professional organization who operate independently. In a hospital setting, different specialists must join forces

Figure 7.2: The professional organization

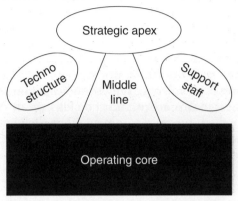

Figure 7.3: The adhocracy organization

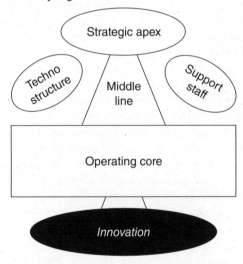

in multidisciplinary teams and programs. We have many examples of that in our modern hospitals, including our everyday teamwork in looking after patients, our programmatic structure, and specific multi-disciplinary collaborative groups such as those found in transplant, spine, hand, and head and neck surgery.

So our *academic* mandate, in Mintzberg's terms, is to be a professional organization like others but to constantly strive to be an adhocracy as we break new ground. That tightrope walk is a precarious existence because, of course, we risk failure, failure that is sometimes expensive both in terms of practice costs and, unfortunately, in terms of patient outcomes and stress on our colleagues.

How then does the Mintzberg philosophy affect our planning in the hospital setting? It means that we must be resolute in making our best effort to plan for the future in recruitment, in predicting trends in medicine, and in marrying our traditional practice of patient-centred care with technology-driven advances. Furthermore, we must take the 90 per cent of time required to execute these strategic plans, like the challenge of the iceberg below the water. But, to take the iceberg analogy one step further, we must always be ready to turn on a dime (something the *Titanic* could not do), be nimble enough to change direction, and innovate, based on the following:

- A must-have recruit
- A new technological development
- The demands of the population
- Fiscal realities

Until a few years ago, for example, who had given much thought to the development of multidisciplinary approaches to cardiac disease or to the embracing of surgery, image guidance, and physics as a critical way forward for the treatment of heart disease or cancer? Today many are engaged in the most exciting developments in years, with projects that marry into clinical armamentaria the concepts of innovation, intervention, and imaging and the implementation of experimental physics. These have been possible only because we were able to 'carpe diem,' to seize opportunities that presented themselves, and to turn a big ship on a dime.

Not every activity in an academic hospital lends itself to, or indeed requires, the formal lean manufacturing process to effect its implementation or improvement as described in chapter 6. A variety of strategies have been trumpeted to effect change, and all have some common elements. The eight-step John Kotter model of change management[61] consists of a sequence that includes the following:

1 Create a sense of urgency

2 Form a powerful coalition (a team for change)
3 Create a vision for change
4 Communicate that vision
5 Remove obstacles
6 Create short-term wins
7 Build on the change
8 Anchor the changes in corporate culture

Perhaps what should be further emphasized in that list is the need for *defining metrics* that will recognize the results of any changes made and stimulate either continued activity or in-course adjustments.

The Langley Nolan model of *plan, do, study, act* (PDSA)[62] is what might be called change on the run, which is appropriate in some cases where the following is feasible:

1 Just do it
2 Review
3 Pick up the pieces
4 Modify and continue

The attraction of this is implied in the speed of execution. Implementation of the surgical checklist described below might be a good example of this PDSA approach, and, of course, the notion of bashing ahead with an idea is seductive to a surgical mind.

As a surgeon I usually try to think in simple terms, and often I look at change management using what is referred to as my W6 approach, asking: Why? What? Who? How? When? Where? The *Where* might be included if there is a pilot project planned that may spread to other areas of the organization. (*How* doesn't begin with a W, but usually five out of six is a good result!)

1 *Why.* You as a medical leader must define the issue and the rationale for change. This is absolutely necessary for the requisite buy-in.
2 *What.* You need to identify what is the desired result and what is the action that has to be taken to achieve that result.
3 *Who.* You need to identify the players who will participate. Most times they should include individuals representing a cross-section of the organization, and not just managers.
4 *How.* In what manner will the information be assembled, and how will discussions be held and decisions made? How will the com-

munication issues be handled? How will you measure and be able to tell if you have succeeded?

5 *When.* What are the timelines, the deadlines, and the milestones – for discussion, decisions, implementation, and, importantly, monitoring and review?

6 *Where.* Which service, facility, or unit would be a good place to pilot the new process?

The six elements are all important, but the most important consideration is one of *team dynamics.* To achieve sustainable change with independent practitioners such as surgeons and anaesthesiologists, you must include them in that change management from the beginning. In the example of Mister P in the preoperative care unit, nurses as employees had to buy in to the changes; it is even more critical that *independent clinicians* have a say in the change management that affects them.

The specific approach is clearly not important as long as these common fundamental concepts are observed and followed in each case. However, think of 'planning for the expected, and preparing for the unexpected.'

Implementation

The institution of the WHO surgical safety checklist at the University Health Network is perhaps a good example of the implementation of a new process that was challenging, was not without its failures, and, in fact, remains a less than universally accepted initiative.

SITUATION 7.2
UHN AND THE WHO SURGICAL SAFETY CHECKLIST:
Implementing the Simple Can Be Complex

In 2007 the University Health Network in Toronto volunteered to be part of an international World Health Organization (WHO) initiative to improve and standardize preparations for surgical procedures. Representing one of two North American centres (the other being in Seattle), Richard Reznick, Chair of Surgery at University of Toronto, and I, as head of a hospital department, participated in discussions held in Geneva, Switzerland. These discussions led to the development of a universal operating room checklist as part of a safer-health-care megaproject of the WHO.

The objectives of the undertaking were the following:

- Improve patient outcomes
- Decrease infection rates
- Decrease medical errors such as wrong-side surgery
- Improve anticipation and therefore timely management of intra-operative and post-operative complications

The coordination of activities in the eight centres around the world was a formidable task in itself. The challenge we faced at UHN was the design and modification of a generic checklist to suit our own specific needs, which would presumably differ from those in Jordan or Tanzania (two of the other seven centres involved), and then the subsequent implementation as a brand new process in our operating room setting.

We were committed to design and execute a *perioperative safety checklist* that would be relevant for our varied surgical population. The checklist initially was to be applicable to all operations in specialties including multi-organ transplantation, complex cancer work, vascular surgery, and thoracic surgery.

A total of almost twenty-five thousand operations are performed every year at our three hospitals. How would we undertake the introduction of this new additional inconvenience to surgeons, nurses, and anaesthesiologists and then monitor and sustain it?

The perioperative safety checklist is a series of steps in the pre-, intra-, and post-operative experience of a surgical patient which have been designed to ensure that all important factors concerning diagnosis and treatment of a patient are known to every member of the perioperative team, thus maximizing outcomes and minimizing risk and untoward events.

In working on the surgical checklist, the *why* question was answered by the admission that we had daily untoward events that occurred around surgery, which were not unexpected when rather loose processes guided the performance of almost twenty-five thousand operations per year at UHN. We had intra-operative 'nuisance' events, such as blood products not being available on time, instrument trays not being fully equipped, and other issues that may not have directly affected the patient's outcome. But, unfortunately, as in every hospital, there were other more impactful events, including the following:

- The administration of drugs to which the patient is allergic
- Surgery being started on the wrong side (or, in the case of hand or spine surgery, on the wrong digit or level)

- Antibiotics not being given preoperatively at all or being given so early or so late that the blood levels at the time of incision are inconsequential, thus leading to a greater risk of infection
- Deep venous thrombosis (DVT) prophylaxis being forgotten until some time during the case

These are all issues that could very well affect the patient's outcome or, indeed, survival.

So the *why* question seemed a no-brainer, if we assume that a perioperative discussion confirming all those factors might avoid complications. For terminal sceptics, this type of initiative should not be introduced to our system without scientific proof that the steps taken have a certain chance of succeeding. To those like myself, such a scientific study would be analogous to a randomized, controlled trial of the parachute: if we are reasonably confident that this is good for the patient, and it costs little in terms of effort, time and money, let's just do it!

No one had ever shown conclusively that such a surgical checklist could improve care, but the intuitive conclusions seemed solid. In fact, we had had some experience with the concept in recent years. At one time an enterprising educational researcher had examined more closely the issues of communication in the operating room and had come to the conclusion after studying our vascular surgery division that a more complete discussion of the upcoming operation was a strong team-building exercise at the very least and perhaps influential on outcomes as well.

An ad hoc group of people consisting of representatives of nursing, anaesthesia, and surgery decided that we should go to the next step. The decision was made easier because the work with the vascular service had been reported, and UHN as a member of the University of Toronto family had been invited to join the WHO group interested in the same topic.

The *what* consisted of looking at a number of checklists, including the proposed WHO document, the previous list studied for the vascular service, and a Johns Hopkins version that significantly reduced the incidence of central-line infections in Michigan hospitals.[63] We then created a UHN surgical checklist that, in fact, reflected all those we had considered as well as specific entries that we felt were pertinent to our particular practice (initially at the Toronto General Hospital). This had to be instituted ultimately on a universal basis, but we thought that beginning with one site would be easier, and with the vascular service being at TGH, that site was the obvious place to start. The combined commitment of the university and the hospital to the WHO project added rationale and strength to the decision, even though sceptics obviously remained.

We ensured that Dr Barry Rubin, Chief of Vascular Surgery, explained to the other division heads how easy the checklist was to implement during each and every procedure and how little time it took.

The importance of champions, other than the bosses, in the success of an initiative cannot be overestimated.

Meetings were held to demonstrate the details of the surgical checklist, the importance of it, and the ways in which we were going to confirm its execution. It was our goal to address every provider in the perioperative area and to emphasize that the approach was patient centred, would likely decrease risk, would likely improve outcomes, and would cost little in terms of extra effort.

Repeated emails were sent to all surgeons and anaesthesiologists with electronic copies of the document to remind them of the impending introduction of the checklist.

In thinking about how we would present this in each operating suite, we decided that a visual presence would be extremely important. We therefore made multicoloured, plasticized reproductions of the checklist enlarged to a size of eleven inches by eighteen inches, and we hung them on the back of the main door of every operating theatre so that they could not be missed. (We saw subsequently that Seattle had gone further, with a reproduction that was large enough to be read from the next unit!)

It was stipulated that the ultimate responsibility of carrying out the checklist rested on the shoulders of *all* the stakeholders (nursing, anaesthesia, and surgery), with no fear of any of those individuals feeling as though he or she were the watchdog. Too frequently nurses have been placed in the position of policing processes in hospitals, and there is understandable resentment about that, especially when many of the doctors whom they remind feel entitled to do anything they want and are often inherently resistant to change (sometimes with resultant sarcastic and demeaning commentary).

The nurses were encouraged to enthusiastically participate in the process by giving their input in each case. Then they were to electronically confirm on the OR data-collection program that each of the three columns of the checklist (briefing, timeout, and debriefing) had indeed been carried out.

At first this did not happen consistently, presumably because of the feeling of surgical intimidation, but when a town hall meeting was held with all the OR nurses, and the omission was recognized, all were assured that the team as a group and individually would be supported in the execution and the monitoring functions.

Perhaps the key to successful implementation was the detailed attention paid by a research nurse and the surgeon-in-chief, who were constantly present to remind each member of the operating room staff of his or her collective responsibilities. This involved actually entering each operating room and, in a light-hearted manner, getting confirmation of each individual's participation in the 'new opportunity.'

We also had the advantage of having previously introduced the *incision-marking and timeout policy*, which was a critical step in the middle of the new three-columned checklist. (The timeout policy was reportable to the Ministry of Health through the Surgical Efficiency Targets Program.[64]) There were detractors to the concept of the timeout, but surgeons who continued to scoff were reminded that the new process was now part of our hospital's accepted surgical care (a *standard operating procedure*, or SOP). In other words, we had no choice with the timeout reporting to the ministry and simply had to implement it. When an activity becomes an SOP, people essentially have a choice (everyone must always have a choice); the choice was to operate at UHN and to do so with the privilege of participating in the timeout function or to find another hospital where they could ply their trade. However, the expansion of the timeout process to a more formal surgical checklist was not yet an SOP, and so the approach taken had to be subtle, stepwise, respectful, and understanding. The participants really *had to believe in what they were doing.*

After final implementation, checklist compliance records would be kept for each division and each individual surgeon and be posted for all to see periodically in the halls of the operating suite. The *when* coincided with the WHO project. We had a head start, of course, because the vascular surgery division was familiar with the experience, other divisions were familiar with the concept, and so there was therefore a kind of partial a priori buy-in. The plan was to introduce the checklist over the period of a month at Toronto General Hospital (9,000 operations per year), then two weeks later at Princess Margaret Hospital (3,000 operations per year), and a month after that at Toronto Western Hospital (12,500 operations per year); the whole spectrum of surgery including cardiac, orthopaedics, and neurosurgery would therefore be involved.

Meetings were held with all the nurses and anaesthesiologists at the second and third sites to explain the project, and the surgeons were repeatedly informed through their division heads at business meetings, by the email communications mentioned above, and personal visits.

The project was introduced according to plan. However, it did experience the anticipated bumps in the road. Reminding, cajoling, threatening, supporting, electronically confirming, and more reminding were all used to put into place what was thought to be just another small step forward in high-quality care and improved patient safety.

This kind of detailed process occurred in each of the eight international centres involved in the study but was not tightly controlled as to the specific processes in each site. The project was celebrated on 25 June 2008 in Washington, DC. This was a kick-off event chaired by Harvard's Dr Atul Gawande and was held to celebrate the WHO's Surgical Safety Checklist project with the hope that its implementation would spread internationally and finally prove with scientific rigour that it was the right step to take for all patients undergoing surgery.

The people involved in the implementation at UHN were basically all nurses, surgeons, anaesthesiologists, and other providers working at each site, but before the exact people plan was put into place, the concept was explained to and endorsed by the president and CEO of our hospital, who considered it reasonable that this surgical checklist would eventually become standard operating procedure. It was not the intent that a top-down decision would be enforced, but the elevation of the profile to the CEO level established the importance for the participating professionals, and the CEO's enthusiastic endorsement was one of the critical success factors.

At the time of the WHO's Surgical Safety Checklist study and subsequent implementation of the tool at all three hospitals in our UHN family, the previous evidence had not been so convincing that such a checklist could improve outcomes. We had relied on what we felt was a reasonable hunch that our intuition would bear fruit. Now that implementation is complete and consistent, our faith has been justified by the publication of the WHO's study in the *New England Journal of Medicine*.[65] After implementation of the surgical safety checklist in eight centres around the world, significant declines in operative mortality (in-hospital death within thirty days of surgery) and postoperative complications were recorded. As of early 2009, steps were being taken to examine ways to disseminate the surgical checklist tool to more organizations around the globe. (See also Atul Gawande, *The Checklist Manifesto: How to Get Things Right*, Metropolitan Books, 2009.)

Comment: The keys to the success of this project, which has now been sustained over time, were the following: executive support from the CEO, WHO participation, passionate leadership, persuasion, enthusiastic champions, dogged persistence, and electronic real-time confirmation.

Appreciative Enquiry

It seems evident that hospitals are taking a page from Toyota's lean manufacturing book, translating it into improved, efficient hospital processes. The proof is in the sustainability, and those like Dr John Toussaint have shown that the effects can be lasting as long as there remains staff enthusiasm and commitment. But are there other ways to skin the same cat?

The lean-manufacturing route might be viewed as a rather negative way of identifying problems, by defining current states, future desired states, and the gaps between them. The emphasis is on identifying the shortcomings and then devising ways to plug these holes. There is growing interest in a different way of doing things, which is rather like the positive reinforcement versus negative reinforcement of Pavlov's behavioural studies using dogs. The proponents of *appreciative enquiry*, which is rather like a business version of Norman Vincent Peale's power of positive thinking, believe that the best results come from looking at the bright side of an organization and extending that theme.

Instead of concentrating on negatives, employees and/or managers are presented with challenges like: 'Think back through your career in this organization. Locate a moment that was a high point, when you felt most effective and engaged. Describe how you felt and what made the situation possible.' Such an exercise might be asked of a number of pairs of individuals who work in the organization, after which they tell their individual stories to an assembled group. The results create pride, an enthusiasm for working in that organization, an inspiration to make things better, and hopefully an inherently improved sense of team.

Questions asked in such a way may explore issues of personal values, future wishes for the organization, ethics, customer service, interpersonal relationships, and so on. With the desired inspiration, the *team* is established first, and that foundation, rather than the systematic identification of shortcomings as used in the lean-manufacturing process, is then critical to the next steps. As Sue Annis Hammond says in *The Thin Book of Appreciative Inquiry*,[66] 'through a workshop format, the participants stir up memories of energizing moments of success, creating a new energy that is positive and synergistic. Participants walk away with a sense of commitment, confidence and affirmation that they have been successful. They also know clearly how to make more moments of success.'

One might draw the analogy of these two methods of change management (or, at least, change catalysts) to the half-full, half-empty glass. Lean manufacturing recognizes the half-empty glass and tries to replace the emptiness with technical and process improvements. Appreciative enquiry sees the half-full glass, glories in the positive, and stretches the positive to fill the glass. These are subtle differences in approach, but both can be successful.

SITUATION 7.3
THE GOALS AND OBJECTIVES PROCESS:
The Power of Stories

At two major teaching hospitals in Toronto, the Toronto General Hospital and the Toronto Western Hospital, the appreciative enquiry approach has been used for a number of years as the basis of a regular 'goals and objectives' process. Each year medical and surgical inpatient services work on various projects as part of overall quality improvement, and all initiatives are punctuated by stories of success. These are recognized and celebrated by scores of nurse managers and front-line workers, and many are stimulated by the success of others to reproduce successes in their own areas.

This fact points out the importance of *stories* in the daily operations of any big business, but especially in health care delivery. The power of stories is inestimable in helping to bring real life drama to statistics. If you move people, you have a much better chance of effecting change. The famous book of stories *What's Right in Health Care*[67] is full of moving accounts of the experiences of health care providers, patients, relatives, and, in fact, all the participants in the rich everyday life of the hospital. Some people find these and other anecdotes, in the Chicken Soup for the Soul series,[68] to be melodramatic and maudlin, but most of us have no problem in placing ourselves in the scenarios and thus are moved.

In 2008 Toronto General Hospital and its senior management published their own book, entitled *Moving Mountains*,[69] which is a collection of forty-two personal stories about patients, loved ones, and health care workers and how common goals were reached in novel and inspiring ways.

However quality improvement is achieved, it can only be achieved and sustained by the front-line workers who participate in the improvement process, take ownership of it, and, perhaps most importantly, are recognized for their efforts.

Positive Deviance

The *positive deviance* approach to solving problems arose out of the work of investigators at Tufts University's Friedman School of Nutrition Science and Policy. If a problem of process is identified in any industry, probably the best way to institute change and sustain that change is for the ideas and energy to come from the workers themselves.

In circumstances such as profound poverty in a Third World country the secret may lie in identification of those individuals (referred to as the *positive deviants*) who seem to have risen above the circumstances that their neighbours or colleagues have found oppressive or even hopeless. Those positive deviants are then studied to become the foundation for change within the ranks; the sustainability of such change is key and seen to be more reliable than the needs-based or top-down approach.

SITUATION 7.4
Coat Hooks for Better Patient Care: *Positive Deviance*[70]

A Philadelphia hospital identified a problem on a number of inpatient services: residents were not regularly visiting patients who were isolated with a variety of infectious conditions such as MRSA (Methicillin-resistant *Staphylococcus aureus*) and *C. difficile*, and the nurse managers were concerned that patient care was suffering.

When one manager asked her residents why they were neglecting these patients, who in fact required even closer scrutiny than many others, the residents replied that there was no place to hang their lab coats so that they could don gowns, gloves, and masks to see the patients; they would always say they would return to attend to those particular patients at the end of rounds but were frequently sidetracked by other emergencies.

In response to this disarmingly simple challenge, the nurse manager purchased a few hooks and installed them outside the rooms in question, and subsequently the residents' routine then included these abandoned patients.

The next step was equally important: what did the clinical directors do to spread the good word and good action to other services? Absolutely nothing.

The key to sustainability was to have the intent to change, and indeed the change itself, *come from within*.

Within six months, however, word had spread among the various inpatient services, nurse managers had themselves made the changes on each floor (all except one service), and coat hooks, strangely enough, became a sort of symbol of change, the management of which each group could be proud.

The example given represents a surprisingly simple step in a hospital setting where an idea came from one of the health care providers who had lived the problem, and the solution proceeded *laterally* rather than top-down.

Like appreciative enquiry, a positive deviance approach could be viewed as just another example of the many ways of skinning this change-management cat.

8 Data and Money

Data collection, and deliberate action on the basis of that collection, is at the core of institutional performance and health. Pay for performance (P4P) will depend on accurate and ongoing assessments of performance and the rewarding of good corporate behaviour.

Data Collection and Scorecards

To measure and improve performance – and to ask for more resources – you need to collect data and keep scorecards. Medical and surgical activity has not been actively measured and monitored in the past. The reputations of both individuals and hospitals have been made or broken on the basis of anecdotal evidence rather than reliable data. However, times have changed, and more important, patient expectations have changed immeasurably.

Most modern businesses have realized that the setting of short- and long-term objectives must be accompanied by an ability to measure ongoing performance. If one is making, distributing, and selling widgets, the pertinent data required may be fairly straightforward to collect and use for quality improvement. In the medical field the indicators may be more complex and difficult to measure, but they are no less important to the health of the organization and, ultimately of course, to that of the patient.

In the United States, hospitals are now compared and contrasted with respect to a number of parameters, and results are reported on the Internet for all to see. Although the instruments are reasonably blunt, they address enough high-profile issues, such as in-hospital mortality and surgical infection rates, that patients who are able to choose their institution can certainly be swayed by the data.

In Great Britain the results of a well-known study on hospital standardized mortality ratios (HSMR) prompted the Bradford Royal Infirmary to carefully examine all the factors that may have led to what was apparently an excessive hospital mortality rate in 2001 (see, for example, John Wright et al., 'Learning from Death: A Hospital Mortality Reduction Programme'[71]). The organization established a hospital mortality reduction group with senior leadership support. They paid special attention to the following:

- Clinical observations
- Medication administration
- Infection control, specifically
  - hand hygiene
  - ward-cleaning routines
  - antibiotic guidelines
  - increased surveillance and feedback of infection rates

A mortality audit revealed the following results:

- Suboptimal clinical observations in 61 per cent of cases
- Hospital-acquired infections in 23 per cent of patients
- Medication errors in 11 per cent of patients

A number of changes were made, and the mortality ratio subsequently dropped significantly, from 94.6 in 2001 to 77.5 in 2005. This translated into an estimated 905 fewer hospital deaths than expected, during the period 2002–2005.

In early 2008 the Canadian Institute of Health Information (CIHI) published for the first time HSMR, which varied tremendously from province to province and from hospital to hospital.[72] These figures were adjusted for age, complexity, and other factors of acuity and were reported on the front page of every newspaper in the country. As this will be an ongoing process, hospitals are taking the problem very seriously and examining in their own institutions those factors that can be controlled, in order to improve their following year's mortality ratings.

Many corporations in the business world such as banks and major manufacturing companies devote 10 to 14 per cent of their budget to the collection and management of data. Unfortunately, despite the importance of data in the medical field, hospitals generally spend closer to 3 to 4 per cent of budget in this critical domain. Fiscal pressures brought on by escalating costs of compensation, supplies, and progress in technology are often met by cutting back on the areas that don't appear to be directly patient related; therefore, capital, hospital physical renewal, and information systems often suffer the brunt of ongoing reductions and cost containment.

The importance of data collection must be better recognized.

As a medical leader you'd better resign yourself to becoming a bean counter and a financial being because that's where our profession is heading. Whether the payer is a health maintenance organization or a preferred provider organization (PPO) or a single provincial payer, accountability is the buzzword of the twenty-first century. You will need to justify your expenses, and you will need to produce outcomes and process efficiencies that demonstrate good practice in all dimensions.

The principal method of measuring business performance is the use of the *balanced scorecard* (BSC).[73] The scorecard is a concept linking actual performance with expected performance.

The BSC is broken down into a number of components that are meaningful and pertinent to each corporation. Critical success factors are declared to be important, and indicators must be chosen to track them. We must set into place metrics that can be followed on an ongoing basis, and when measurements of success factors continually speak to a problem, plans must be articulated to indicate expectations for action.

The development of the BSC process has coincided with the increased accountability of boards of trustees in every sector. If the members of boards are going to be more responsible for the reports and performance of organizations, lip service must be replaced by confirmatory facts and figures that meet predetermined expectations.

At Brigham and Women's Hospital (BWH) in Boston, Dr Michael Gustafson[74] was instrumental in creating a balanced scorecard, about which he says, 'The balanced scorecard has allowed our key strategic goals related to service, quality and safety, efficiency, staff satisfaction and development, and financial performance to be effectively measured, tracked and communicated to more than 1,000 staff members.'[75] There is a hospital-wide scorecard with supporting departmental and divisional scorecards, all of which are regarded as stepwise offspring of the organizational tool. These are interconnected in such a way that results raising concern are flagged and can be analysed further by drilling down to results that are more specific and offer explanations on the front line.

The trick, of course, is to operationalize a scorecard so that it becomes an integral part of every component of the organization and in such a way that results are regularly accessed, analysed, and acted upon; quality improvement is then truly continuous.

How do we elevate the profile of this tool? At BWH the balanced scorecard was placed as a regular item on the agenda of meetings of the Care Improvement Council. These meetings are attended by hospital executives, department chairs, board members, and others. It was hoped that departmental chiefs would address scorecard metrics in their annual reports, thus focusing more consistently on performance and gradually moving towards a pay-for-performance model.

Our own experience with a *surgical scorecard* at the University Health Network started with the development of a web-based reporting tool that simply organized all the perioperative data that we were collecting anyway. This site therefore was a repository for lots of metrics that, although relevant individually, were not organized particularly well. This included such items as OR utilization statistics, start-time accuracy, and cancellation rates.

Since its inception, we were aware that the frequency of use of the scorecard varied tremendously among the various division heads and business unit leaders, presumably in part because it was incomplete and because what we *did* report was perhaps less than user friendly.

We therefore set about to make additions and revisions that we felt would ultimately be more useful to the managers, and we ended up with an instrument that reported up-to-date accounting of specifics with regard to the following:

- Human resources issues
- Financial performance
- Volume targets
- Perioperative indices, in accordance with the provincial Surgical Efficiency Targets Program
- Wait-times targets for various elective surgical procedures, in cooperation with the provincial wait-times information system (WTIS)

We anticipate many more hits on this website with the improved usability, and ultimately we will have the kind of close to real-time statistics that will fit into the P4P model that the regional authority visualizes.

As a medical leader you are responsible for process issues and out-comes in high-quality care, and accordingly you will be part of the change towards more rigorous data measurement and responsiveness, with subsequent changes in measured performance.

Regional Variations and Performance

The performance of a single surgeon or physician is difficult to assess because metrics are not yet in place (as they should be) on a universal basis. Until information systems mature to the point that the collection, retrieval, and analysis of data can be in real time and responsive, we have to resort to cruder approaches.

Correspondingly, whole populations can be equally difficult to assess, but because regions have captured data on various interventions for some years, we now have access to abstracted information from patient files on a larger scale. The Institute for Clinical and Evaluative Sciences (ICES)[76] in Toronto has led the way in identifying regional variations in Canada for a variety of treatments, such as mastectomy for breast carcinoma and coronary artery bypass graft for coronary vessel disease.

Organizations such as ICES assess health care delivery, patterns of service utilization, health technologies, drug therapies, and treatment modalities, using anonymous population-based health information. Although these data may be helpful in pointing towards geographical variations and therefore posing questions about the reasons for such differences, the major steps in clarifying those reasons and finding solutions to problems are much more challenging.

SITUATION 8.1
VASCULAR STUDY GROUP OF NORTHERN NEW ENGLAND:
The Challenges of Regional Quality Improvement

One group that has taken extra steps towards quality improvement is the Vascular Study Group of Northern New England,[77] which consists of fifty surgeons in three states (New Hampshire, Maine, and Vermont) who have banded together, offered transparency of all their vascular experiences, and effectively championed improvements and the standardization of care. As the leader, Jack Cronenwett, reported, 'quality trumped ego' when all surgeons agreed to have their souls and their results bared for all to see.

This is a wonderful example of how transparency and honesty are the absolute sine qua non of improvement, perhaps analogous to the frank discussions at quality-of-care conferences that lead to change of practice in an institution. The Northern New England group has sustained the initiative for over four years, validated the data collected, and taken significant strides in improving preoperative medication usage, setting the stage for future potential standardization of care.

The medical leader of the twenty-first century must support such developments, push for accurate data collection pertaining to all activities at the hospital, and encourage participation in the interests of the wider region.

Another important area is the relationship of clinical volumes to performance and outcomes. The medical literature is now replete with information suggesting that, at least in the more complex treatments such as major cancer surgery, the various outcomes measured improve when adequate baseline volumes are performed. This has implications for a medical leader's department as a whole, but also potentially for each clinician. Is a general internal medicine specialist capable of managing a patient with complex congestive heart failure or diabetic coma, or must the knee-jerk response always be to call in a cardiologist or an endocrinologist? How many Whipple operations does a hepatobiliary surgeon have to perform (or how many CABGs a cardiac surgeon) to ensure the best results possible? There are no easy answers to these questions, but the division head has overall responsibility to ensure that his constituents are providing a standard of care that recognizes these volume-outcome relationships.

Data are essential for monitoring and improving performance and represent a critical feature in an equally important mandate, that is, by justifying more hospital resources to support a particular program or a new clinical initiative. Medical leaders must face the fact that there will *always* be financial challenges every year; we are continually being challenged to do more with less. In that setting, the introduction of a new program, which usually has financial implications, becomes even more challenging.

With the help of project managers and comptrollers the medical leader must become accustomed to assembling a *business case*, clearly stating how all aspects of a particular proposal will come together and how all the details of the financials have been considered. In some cases, *a proof of concept* or *a pilot project* may be an attractive way to initiate discussions before the organization commits to a larger notion. In times of fiscal constraint a collaborative regional approach that supports the concept of rationalization of services may create a win-win situation in which all organizations gain something, and no group has to sacrifice anything significant in terms of service or public profile.

Data lie at the heart of assessing the past and preparing for the future. However, again, don't forget the power of stories. Hospitals boast stories every day: stories that involve the trials, tribulations, and rich accounts of patients, of course, but also stories that may reflect the lives of the thousands of devoted health care workers that are essential to the hospital. While stories may not be instrumental in swaying a chief financial officer, they certainly validate the reasons that hospitals and health care workers exist and can be critical in fund-raising activities; stories may augment data in making a persuasive argument.

The Electronic Patient Record

The health care IT industry is exploding and promises to compete with hands-on patient care for health care dollars for the foreseeable future. At some point everyone came to the same conclusion; that is, doctors and nurses can be the most well-intentioned, educated and committed providers of health care and still make grievous mistakes that result in potentially calamitous complications for patients. Our patients have finally caught on to this realization as well; we providers are now officially off our pedestals, and we're trying to approach the topic dispassionately and with data retrieval in mind.

Realizing that ongoing data collection is paramount, most hospitals are now examining the institution of an electronic medical record (EMR), aka electronic patient record (EPR), as a means to improve accuracy, reduce redundancy, and enhance patient safety. Since the most important and frequent errors involve medication administration in a hospital, it's not surprising that initial forays into the EMR field have concentrated on computerized physician order entry (CPOE), computerized orders for tests (blood work and radiology), the reporting of those tests, and finally clinical documentation (doctors' and nurses' consultations and progress notes).

The whole process has proven to be challenging to say the least: it's very expensive, requires buy-in from groups of practitioners who are reticent to change, and involves a dizzying array of potential IT vendors, all of whom seem to have specific software that doesn't necessarily communicate effectively with the software in the next hospital. A recent online search concerning health care software IT vendors revealed a list of 178 companies ready to assist you with your hospital's IT needs! Many of the software packages are not web-based and therefore pose problems in interconnecting with the other systems that the patient may well be accessing (for example, concerning the community care that may follow a hospitalization).

In most countries high-level organizations have been set up to direct the development of a systemic approach that will integrate data across large sectors such as hospitals, states, and provinces; however, in my experience, the real advances are made by individual organizations that take it upon themselves to create meaningful electronic charting with specific objectives in mind. One such organization is Partners HealthCare (www.partners.org), which is a 'non-profit integrated health system founded by Brigham and Women's Hospital and Massachusetts General Hospital.' This group of hospitals strives to provide 'high-performance medicine by improving quality, safety and efficiency.' One such effort at Brigham and Women's Hospital was the scorecard referred to in the previous section, but the application of the computer to medical and surgical care is much broader than just the performance scorecard. In a study that was published in the *Journal of the American Medical Association*, Brigham and Women's decreased medication errors from 11 per cent to 5 per cent (a 55 per cent relative reduction) with the use of CPOE.[78]

When these steps are taken, patients are clearly less frequently exposed to human error; perhaps just as significantly, through a decision-support initiative, the physician and nurse may be helped with decisions about their treatment options by seeing reminder flags concerning appropriate medications, dosages, interactions among drugs, patient allergies, and the like. Currently, Partners HealthCare has thirty thousand order sets and rules in place, and the number is climbing. As one might imagine, this group is also extending a hand to the patient through the 'Patient Gateway,' whereby patients have access to their own medical records and are able to interact with the care providers.[79]

What's the meaning of all this to you as a medical leader? The message is that whatever the stage of EMR implementation in your organization, it's coming to your town, and it's here to stay. The obstacles are frequent and sometimes difficult, especially when your constituents would much rather scrawl an order and leave the ward, to have some unfortunate nurse decipher the handwriting and interpret the thought behind it. But your hospital must be committed to this process of the present and future, and you must be an enthusiastic proponent, an adviser, a coach, a mentor, and an example for your division or department members.

There is absolutely no doubt that accreditation standards in future will appropriately demand this utility, and you might as well be on the correct bandwagon to facilitate it. So learn how to use it, and if you're like most, after a period of walking in mud you will wonder how you ever lived without it for so long.

> **Institution of the electronic medical record will not be easy, but you must support this concept because it will be the basis of all your clinical documentation in future.**

Hospital Finances and Capital Investment

The subject of hospital finances and capital investment is not written in only paragraphs, sections, or chapters; it deserves full treatises and entire textbooks because it is the most challenging and complex area facing hospital management in the present century. Before 1980, in the United States, hospitals were (and usually are) profit-making companies; in Canada, where the single-payer provincial system was in place, any yearly budget overrun was simply covered by the Ministry of Health. In the past twenty years, however, the practice of medicine has become very much a business, with the same mandates of quality, finances, and workload that are reported by any major organization. Skyrocketing costs have been a direct result of innovation, newly developed treatments, expensive drugs, and the ever-increasing salaries of hospital employees.

Whatever the fundamental structure of your hospital setting and on whichever side of the forty-ninth parallel you reside, every manager and medical leader is going to have to pay careful attention to revenues; costing of cases; and delivery of efficient, high-quality, error-free care. The extent to which you wish to become involved in the finances of your institution will depend on the extent to which doctors participate now and also the level of your interest in such matters. It is my contention that you *must* be interested, and if you demonstrate knowledge and an aptitude, you will be much more useful to the organization and will quickly earn yourself a position of enhanced influence. Managers and hospital administrators *need* your clinical expertise to give them a medical perspective of their management decisions (if they're not doctors already), and if you actually understand the financial language they're speaking, so much the better.

The purpose of this section is to highlight some obvious concepts but also to give you further suggested reading opportunities because this particular subject is the most challenging – and potentially rewarding – that you will face as a medical leader.

> **The more that medical leaders know and understand about hospital finances, the more they will be able to have input into and influence decision making.**

> **The more that medical leaders can educate their constituents about hospital finances, the better their relationships with them will be, especially during the tough times.**

If as a medical leader you can educate your team members about the subject of hospital finances, and in particular the reasons for specific management decisions when service changes or reductions are contemplated, you will have better relationships with those on your team. This is especially critical in the surgical domain, where the clinicians are so dependent on hospital resources for their personal practice and incomes; generally, physicians can carry on a lucrative office practice without significant dependence on hospital activities (with the exception of procedure-based medical specialties like cardiology, gastroenterology, and nephrology).

> **You'll never have enough hospital resources to do the things you want to do.**

Creating revenues and trimming costs, even to maintain the same level of services that you enjoyed previously, will be an ongoing challenge for you, and you will never have enough hospital resources to do all of the things that you would like to do. Get used to the frustrations of 'doing the best you can,' which may appear to invite mediocrity, a state which should be abhorred.

> **The competition among programs will be always intense.**

When it comes to the competition among programs, you have a real opportunity to show your talents as a medical leader in the organization. In advancing the position that hospital resources should be assigned to your own areas of interest, be sure that your argument is accompanied by research and supported by the following:

- Demographics
- Advances in care
- Principles of patient-centred care
- Solid evidence showing that the hospital's mission is being promoted and furthered by your proposal

> **Always remember, the leadership you show must be corporation-wide and accommodate other interests as well; in other, words you must demonstrate a delicate balance between *entitlement, fairness,* and *greed*.**

Surgeons are notorious for always wanting more, and they don't do themselves any long-term favours when they disregard the needs of other groups who are competing for resources. Patient-care issues will always be used as a trump card when difficult decisions are made about resource assignment. While that in most cases is laudable and appropriate, it is also a trap because important infrastructure is frequently compromised too much and for far too long.

> **Patient-care issues will always trump other considerations.**

The following are the areas that tend to be short-changed when hospital resources are allocated in challenging times:

- Capital equipment
- Facilities maintenance
- Information technology

These three areas are vital to the health of a large organization, especially one that provides sophisticated service, and cannot be ignored. In particular, the concentration on information technology, which has been mentioned repeatedly in this book, will be a staple item in health care delivery generally for the foreseeable future.

When reliable systems that allow the seamless capture and transfer of information about specific patients are in place, perhaps the need for committing huge sums to IT will diminish; however, that time is likely a long way off, and the need won't abate any time soon.

> **By far the most expensive component
> of hospital costs is people.**

The most expensive component of hospital costs by far is *people*, and the salaries of people (most of whom are unionized) will continue to climb inexorably. It may be decided that less costly individuals may be sought for some kinds of care, for example, anaesthesia assistants instead of anaesthesiologists, and nurse practitioners instead of doctors; nevertheless, the overall proportion of the total clinical care costs in a hospital – exclusive of doctors' fees – that is attributable to providers of health care is about 67 per cent. Therefore, a reduction in the size of the hospital's workforce is the most attractive and the simplest method to cut costs. In real life, however, this approach can be disastrous.

In Ontario in the mid-1990s, the economic downturn led to a mandate to balance hospital budgets. The radical steps taken by a number of hospitals involved laying off large numbers of nurses, as a simple and direct cost-reduction strategy on the compensation line. That was certainly a quick fix to the budgetary issues, but the ramifications were problematic. The first nurses to be shown the door were the younger, newly graduated, promising nurses (as they had no seniority), and the resultant increased workload on the remaining cohort of nurses was stressful to the point that the ensuing early retirement, increased sick time, and compromised staff morale were inevitable. Hospitals that took this apparently responsible fiscal tack in favour of balancing their budgets achieved short-term objectives, but they suffered for many years subsequently. The critical group in the health care workforce, that is, the trained and certified nurses, were reluctant to choose a hospital that had a record of 'firing' its most valued employees.

As a medical leader mindful of hospital finances, with respect to the cost of *personnel* you will do the following:

- You will examine ways in which your staff may work more efficiently, such as in the pre-admission clinic where workflow was changed for the benefit of both patient and provider.
- You will consider changing the job descriptions of individuals who might multitask to make all patient care more efficient, with less waste.
- You will certainly want to safeguard against unreasonable workloads to ensure that overtime and sick time meet standardized benchmarks.

- You will try to make subtle changes in the daily habits of health care providers that will allow them more time with the patient and less time with chart work and documentation – after all, this is a service industry.
- You will learn to listen to everyone in the organization, because they're all trying to tell you something about what is wrong and, even better, what could be done to improve their lot in life.

You will be involved in all these possible changes, but keep in mind that your relationship with the unions is extremely important and must be supported and nurtured. Any alterations in the unionized workers' job descriptions must involve discussions with the union, and your ongoing relationship must be collaborative and seldom confrontational.

> **Even though the cost of supplies is about half the cost of compensation (people) in hospital finances, it's still a critical area of concern for the medical leader.**

As innovation remains the focus for every clinician, the commitment to advanced therapies involving expensive drugs and equipment is consistent. As a medical leader mindful of hospital finances, with respect to the cost of *supplies* you will do the following:

1 You will consider economies of scale that may include collaborations with sister hospitals in order to get the best possible price point.
2 You may agree to use specific new equipment provided by a creative company at prices that seem too good to be true – and if they seem to be, they likely are. If you renegotiate the deal when your staff has become used to the new product or device, you'll be in for a shock.
3 You will look for ways to minimize inventory and render stocking more efficient, for example, by using the clinical specialty supply chain model. In this way, you may reach the objectives of accounting accuracy, near-zero inventory, and improved ease of use by the average worker.
4 You will examine whether the leasing or the buying of expensive devices represents overall savings for the institution, using a healthy slice of guesswork when you see the exorbitant service contract of many inventions. You will need to be part of a concerted

effort to make a comprehensive long-term plan regarding all capital equipment, which speaks to important issues like obsolescence and the predictability of replacement.

5 You will, in the end, come to the realization that most proposals demand upfront costs with predicted long-term savings down the line. In practice, in my experience, the upfront costs are realized, but the long-term savings seldom hit the balance sheet.

The approaches to yearly challenges in financial management will demand all your creativity and your willingness to work closely with your operations directors and comptrollers. The financial subjects you study will be varied and complex, and you will be in a position to learn continuously about this critical area.

> **The financial bottom line to the hospital is certainly one of the bottom lines to your success as a medical leader.**

Capital Investment and Renewal

Most of our medical and surgical specialties are now dependent more than ever before on capital investment in such items as new technology, new hardware, or ongoing operating costs related to surgical instrumentation.

Unfortunately surgical divisions in particular have the ongoing costs of keeping up with technological advances, akin to the smaller and more powerful computers that we seem to find obsolete every eighteen to twenty-four months. However, while the costs of increased random access memory (RAM), processing, and memory have actually been going down, we have yet to experience that in the world of medical equipment. Most hospitals have compromised capital equipment for years in favour of keeping our operational heads above water. Hospitals must recognize that an infusion of capital investment is crucial to our moving forward, but the ongoing predicament in funding promises once again to stifle our capital renewal in favour of the more immediate, and justified, human priorities.

Surgeons know that innovation in our operating rooms requires the additional investment that many organizations simply cannot afford – from modernized operating rooms to the ever-increasing complexity of the surgical instrumentation required. Retention of hospital staff who are engaged in innovative work often is affected by the realization that innovation and just keeping up with trends is prohibitively expensive.

Clinicians sometimes forget the need for hospitals to spend significant resources on the plant itself. The upkeep of buildings, the fundamental but expensive processes of heat, light, and other energy sources, and the increasing safety concerns all combine to produce significant costs that the doctors in your division may not have been aware of.

Practice Plans

Owing to the fact that money is always at the centre of any discussion among independent medical practitioners, the concept of practice plans and the various ways that physicians are paid in a hospital setting are areas with which you are undoubtedly already familiar, but in your leadership position the level of your knowledge cannot be too great.

In most hospital organizations the doctors earn fee-for-service income, perhaps adding complexity and competition to the interactions among the medical staff. In my experience the doctors who profess, 'It's not the money,' when a particular personal financial subject is under consideration, really mean to say, 'It's *always* the money!'

This is an incredibly important, delicate, and sensitive issue that any medical leader must handle with great care. In a sense, independent physicians and surgeons earning incomes in apparent competition with one another may appear to invite discord. In most cases, however, this seems to work well in community hospitals in which the mutual support and the integration of care teams collaborate to offer seamless care. In the academic setting, institutional funding is provided primarily for patient care, and for academic activities to grow and innovate, additional funding is sought through arrangements in which doctors commit personal income to the academic mission. This commitment takes a variety of forms such as tithes or funds directed to the departmental chair and/or hospital physician- or surgeon-in-chief, tithes to the university, or formalized practice plans.

SITUATION 8.2

THE LANGER PRACTICE PLAN: *The Major Cultural Shift*

This is the story of how a major change came to the department of surgery at the University of Toronto in 1982. The central event occurred in the main lecture theatre at Toronto General Hospital (later this was called Banting Hall, and then in 2003 it was demolished to make way for redevelopment of the hospital). It was an amphitheatre in the old banked style, with a small

---

balcony at the back and a lectern and blackboards at the front. The principal dramatis persona was Professor Bernie Langer.

For some years the University of Toronto's department of surgery had been a recognized leader in North America in clinical surgery, with prominent names associated with the Hospital for Sick Children (now called Sick Kids), Toronto General Hospital, St Michael's Hospital, Wellesley Hospital, and other institutions. At the time, no fewer than ten teaching hospitals contributed to the University of Toronto School of Medicine.

Stories abounded of trips by Toronto surgeons to various venues to treat luminaries, and the 'outstanding clinician-teacher' was the highest accolade to which one could aspire. In fact, one of the world's first organized post-graduate surgical training programs, the so-called Gallie course initiated by Dr William E. Gallie, who was dean of the medical school in the 1930s, was, and indeed continues to be, the pride of the department.

An attempt between 1967 and 1972 to kick-start a serious commitment to surgical research and to develop a practice plan to support it had ultimately failed, and the term of the chairman of the department at that time was not renewed. In 1972 the position was filled by Dr Donald Wilson, a superlative clinical surgeon and teacher, who over the next ten years offered the department stability, a focus on clinical education, a spirit of cooperation and collaboration, and a moratorium on any discussion about practice plans.

In 1982 Dr Bernie Langer became the new chair of the department. On taking up his appointment, he recognized that, although the university hospital surgeons around the city maintained a credible profile as clinician-teachers with presumably acceptable outcomes (most conclusions about this were presumed in 1982), there was precious little commitment to any significant degree of research. By this was meant a level of investigation in clinical and basic realms that could be measured by grants held, manuscripts published, talks given at other academic institutions, and presentations made at formal organized conferences. But how was Dr Langer going to stimulate appreciation of the surgeon who wished to devote a significant time to investigation?

As a result of lamentable decisions made in the late 1960s, the amount of academic support coming from the dean of medicine to clinical departments at the University of Toronto had dwindled to the extent that the department chairs had very little financial influence. Almost all of the surgeons' incomes were derived from clinical earnings, and there was very little flexibility for the chair to award stipends to those new surgeons who were sacrificing considerable income to pursue their individual academic mandates. Moreover, Dr Langer was at the same time a hospital division head (of general surgery at Toronto General Hospital), so he didn't even have the influence of a hospital surgeon-in-chief, whose responsibilities include assignment of inpatient beds and operating time. He was clearly not playing with a strong hand.

In the 1970s only three divisions in the whole department of surgery in ten hospitals (out of over thirty divisions) had adopted an approach to this situation. The members of the divisions of general surgery at Toronto General and Toronto Western hospitals and the division of thoracic surgery at TGH (all comprising perhaps 10 per cent of the whole department of surgery at the medical school) had independently agreed among themselves to form income-sharing *practice plans* in their respective divisions in order to support the true academic enterprise. As academic (teaching and, in particular, research) activities were not being funded appropriately, some busy clinicians who by virtue of their remunerative activities earned substantially more than the surgeons who were in the lab or engaged in clinical research had decided to sacrifice income in order to contribute to academic growth.

In fact, the thoracic division, under the leadership of Dr Griff Pearson, had taken the extra step of forming an *equal-sharing arrangement*, which was unheard of at the time. All activities of all types in an academic environment therefore were valued equally in that pioneering division.

The problem for Bernie Langer was that all the other divisions and departments in the University of Toronto medical family remained on a fee-for-service income and, not surprisingly, were engaged only sporadically in meaningful research. How was he to change that?

With very limited support from other surgeons and leaders (with the exception of Dr Pearson, who in addition to being the division head of thoracic surgery at TGH was the surgeon-in-chief of that hospital), Dr Langer called a meeting of all surgeons at the University of Toronto to discuss the novel idea of practice plans across all divisions in the department of surgery in the ten teaching hospitals. The dean of medicine was also invited to support what was thought to be an inevitable concept.

Whereas spotty attendance had been the general rule at inter-hospital meetings, especially those discussing non-clinical matters, this auditorium in early February 1982 was packed. There was an air of excitement, resentment, and perhaps even revolution, at the idea that this new chair planned to invade the comfortable culture and stick his nose in areas that had previously been sacrosanct, that is, the surgeons' pockets!

In his soft-spoken but fiercely determined way Dr Langer recounted the origins of the department and outlined the importance of striking a new direction, which was the development of a serious focus on basic and clinical research to complement the long history of clinical excellence and teaching. He described the concept of income-sharing in order to promote sequestration of income to support academic endeavour in general, and the pooling of income among surgeons to recognize the non-remunerative activity of those clinicians who devoted significant amounts of their time to research.

Whereas in many universities a dean's tax or chair's tax was levied on clinicians to support the academic mandate, this had never been applied at the University of Toronto, and Dr Langer felt that it would be simply unworkable after such a long history of unfettered private practice.

He suggested, therefore, that the practice plan, later referred to (either affectionately or resentfully) as the Langer Plan, be administered to pool income, share a portion to recognize research and teaching as well as clinical productivity, and sequester a portion as academic enrichment funds (AEF) *in each division* so that no tithe would come to the chair; the only requirements were that the AEF were restricted to expenses for the support of teaching or research and that the divisions report on a yearly basis, documenting their compliance with the plan. Participation in a practice plan was voluntary, but he made it clear that departmental stipends would be paid only to individuals who signed on, that only surgeons who were members of a practice plan would be appointed to leadership positions in the department, and that all new appointees to the department would have to be members of a plan.

Since this could not be enforced by decree, the results were slow to develop, as one would expect; the divisions within some hospitals were quick to come on board, but others delayed and could not be penalized for their tardiness.

Gradually, over a number of years, the culture changed in the department, the surgeon-scientist program became known around the globe for enrolling and training approximately forty surgical residents each year towards a master's degree or a doctorate, and research became an integral part of the department's mission.

The point of this story is three-fold. First, the proposal forwarded by Bernie Langer that the practice plans be based in the local divisions so that funds would remain under the control of the members of the hospital divisions was a concession on his part, to be sure, but it was also a wonderful example of the kind of integrative thinking described by Roger Martin in his recent book *The Opposable Mind: How Successful Leaders Win Through Integrative Thinking* (2007).[80] (Martin asserts that effective, innovative leaders will assess a difficult situation, may recognize two or more obvious routes to take, and reject both in favour of a solution that is different from either approach, capitalizing on the best parts of each – thus our separation from our evolutionary ancestors with our 'opposable mind,' just like our opposable thumbs.)

Dr Langer was faced with a potentially intransigent group of surgeons and a shift in culture that he sensed would be clearly unpalatable if he were to institute a purely top-down, chairman-dictated approach. However, maintaining the status quo would never attract the kind of surgeon-scientists that would move the department forward. The middle ground was effective, albeit gradual, in reaching the goals of an academic department.

The second feature of note in this story is the length of time that the change took. It's fair to say that the number of divisions electing to adopt an income-sharing agreement grew quite slowly over the years (even though there was virtually complete compliance in one hospital), aided by the altruistic notion and the proof of recognized scientific advances that research was a laudable pursuit. However, it was not until almost twenty-five years later – when the dean of medicine decreed that an appointment at the university was dependent on any clinician having membership in a conforming practice plan – that the alliance of clinical and academic domains was complete in the whole university department. Occasionally, leaders have to compromise somewhat to effect change, and sometimes they have to resign themselves to a long-term implementation period.

Third, and finally, Dr Bernie Langer demonstrated that although control of resources can be a critical factor in effecting change, proposals involving a set of strong, shared values *do* have power and influence.

Another practical point comes to mind when discussing incomes of medical personnel: physicians and surgeons will accept fairly large variations in clinical income, which can be at the mercy of changing referral patterns, emergency department activity, and the like; however, for income that is related to such contributions as teaching, a decision to decrease an individual's stipend by as little as one thousand dollars can generate a cataclysmic response. I will not try to analyse this reaction but will just emphasize that it has been seen frequently enough to be of significant note.

It is worth noting that originally, with the practice plan, each surgeon had a gross income that included university and practice income, and deducted his or her own expenses of practice. From the resulting net income the surgeon would receive a base income, and the remainder would be partitioned into three segments: 50 per cent was retained by the surgeon, 30 per cent was pooled with his divisional partners (all of this segment to be returned if all partners earned the same), and 20 per cent was assigned to the academic enrichment fund, which provided for research and educational endeavours and to which all division members could apply according to rules set out in a formal agreement. The plan as described here remained in place for almost twenty years and has been modified since, using similar principles.

9 Other Important Issues

During the course of your career to date you may not have been aware of the various subjects that have occupied the time of your department or division head, other than the more far-reaching topics discussed in the last chapter such as planning and practice plans. The following is a potpourri of issues that are usually on-the-job lessons, akin to the topics in Mark H. McCormack's book *What They Don't Teach You at Harvard Business School: Notes from a Street-Smart Executive* (1990)[81] in relation to the business world.

You undoubtedly have either experience or opinions about subjects ranging from medical ethics to privacy issues to media relations to disaster plans, but if you assume a position of medical leadership, you'll have to switch gears. You'll become involved in these fields – you must become the go-to person in some, and certainly you must be an expert on related hospital policy in others.

Medical Ethics

If you attended medical school in the past fifteen years, you received instruction and attended classes in bioethics and its importance in the everyday life of a physician. If you graduated before that time, you may have flown by the seat of your pants, with the main guiding principles being those your mother imparted in your formative years. There has clearly been a lacuna in this education, not unlike in many other facets of medical life.

Hopefully, the aspiring medical leader will have been practising bioethical behaviour before ever considering any medical leadership position; if you don't adhere to the major bioethical principles, you can forget about the leadership position.

Bioethical behaviour is an absolute necessity for a medical leader, as well as for every capable clinician, educator, or researcher.

The bioethical principles of *autonomy, beneficence, non-maleficence*, and *judgment* should direct your every interaction with patients, colleagues, and any other person who comes into contact with you.

Despite, however, the clearly stated principles, you will often find that real-life situations are so complex that simple principles still rely on common sense and judgment before a final course can be plotted. What about, for instance, the elderly female patient whose family demands that the doctor *not* tell her of her diagnosis and can produce good evidence that a frank discussion about a serious diagnosis, in fact, would be counterproductive and harmful to this particular patient? For a doctor who wants to do no harm *(primum non nocere)*, this presents a dilemma with no easy resolution because the ultimate responsibility of the doctor is to the patient and his or her right to know.

Practising bioethical behaviour on a daily basis may not be straightforward, but medical chiefs must lead the way in supporting this concept and being the ambassadors of such behaviour. That should be easy because every decision must observe the four bioethical principles, whether the subject be patient, colleague, or process oriented. Reading materials are abundant, and opportunities for practice will occur daily.

Privacy Issues

SITUATION 9.1
PRIVACY ISSUES AND THE SURGICAL RESIDENT: *The Electronic Patient Record and Confidentiality*

In 2005, Dr John P was a fourth-year resident in the postgraduate training program and just beginning a six-month senior rotation at Community Hospital B. He went through the usual orientation to the hospital's processes, but as he had been there on a previous more junior rotation, Doctor P regarded the orientation as rather repetitive and, to a degree, unnecessary for him.

The hospital's electronic patient chart had been developed over a period of five years, and there was much left to be done prior to the achievement of a truly paperless record. Patients' files were, therefore, hybrid (part electronic and part paper) and would remain so for a number of years.

Doctor P had heard that two prominent individuals, former prime minister Brian Mulroney and Toronto Maple Leafs former hockey coach Pat Quinn, had been admitted to this hospital a few weeks before he had arrived for the rotation, and the newspaper reports had been very mysterious about the characterization of their illnesses, other than the fact that they were 'undisclosed.' Doctor P accessed the electronic record of these patients, and with his curiosity overriding his good sense, he ignored the notice 'Recording chart access – do you wish to proceed?' Thus, Doctor P learned a great deal about the personal affairs of these particular high-profile individuals.

Doctor P clearly committed a serious breach of confidentiality, an act that, in 2010, is career threatening. One of the hallmarks of current medical care is patient confidentiality, and there is zero tolerance for transgression of this principle. Doctor P was lucky because this was in the early developmental stages of keeping electronic health records (EHRs) and because the hospital's processes could arguably have been called into question even despite a confidentiality contract; thus, his future remained effectively unimpeded.

However, a couple of principles came to light as a result of this incident. First, any signed document such as a confidentiality agreement has to be confirmed with *education*, something that Doctor P received as a remedial activity and as a condition of the solution to his problem. In addition, the issue of *transparency* was important in this case, because the hospital freely admitted the flagrant breach, and the incident was subsequently reported prominently in local newspapers.[82] However, as in most similar cases of daily news, this story lasted for about one day in public, but it led to a more rigorous sustainable approach to confidentiality at the medical institution.

> **Always maintain strict confidentiality with respect to patients' illnesses and records. However, when the activities of the *hospital* and its *health care providers* are brought into question in the media, disclose with unlimited transparency.**

Media Relations

You may well have an opportunity in your institution to receive some media training, which is well worth the time and effort. Much about how to interact with and, indeed, use the media is foreign to doctors and may be considered superfluous to the noble activities of caring for patients, but, make no mistake, the current era of communication is critically important. Media relations can be vital in saving your bacon in some instances and in helping you achieve your objectives in others. I assure you that this training will be interesting, regardless of the eventual need. You will be coached on the following topics:

- Your appearance (for a man, your socks must be long enough and your suit dark enough; for a woman, your skirt should be just the right length for the times; and other apparently frivolous issues)
- Your demeanour (authoritative, serious, sincere, human, but not wooden)
- Your vocal communication, or the way you phrase your answers and comments, just as you would be on the stand (that is, answer the question, don't make gratuitous comments, and concentrate on sound bites that you have formulated in advance)

SITUATION 9.2
THE MEDIA AND ANAESTHESIA SHORTAGES IN TORONTO:
Your Important Media Relationship

In 2003 there was a crisis of anaesthesia shortages in Toronto. Many elective cases had to be cancelled because of the lack of anaesthetic services, and the chief of anaesthesia, David Bevan (who was also the university chair of anaesthesia), found himself in front of the cameras, trying to explain the rather tough position that had been taken.

Essentially, the practice of anaesthesia has become multifaceted in the past decade, and it involves much more than 'passing gas' at the behest of surgeons in a variety of specialty areas. Anaesthesiologists are involved in education, research, pain control, ambulatory surgery, intensive care, risk assessment, and many other areas of critical concern to patients.

In the academic setting, where teaching slows down the pace of surgery and anaesthesia, academic anaesthesiologists simply cannot generate the kind of fee-for-service income that they can in the community setting. Therefore, the challenge of recruitment and retention of outstanding clinicians in this vital department is always present.

Dr Bevan had to face the media with the truth and with the dexterity to indicate that this apparently well-heeled group of clinicians, in fact, had a just argument and they had to be recognized for their expertise at least as well as their community counterparts were. He was treading on thin ice in this endeavour because the public was not likely to sympathize with a group that they might regard as 'fat cats,' and even his own surgical colleagues might see this as a threat to their *own* livelihoods; their cases were being cancelled.

Surgery was brought into the fray, and, in summary, our stance was to try to support both the patients, whose surgery was being delayed, and our close anaesthetic colleagues, on whom we depended daily. There were no accusations, there were positive comments about the return to normalcy, and the crisis died down in about forty-eight hours.

The lessons in this story were the default positions:

1 The patients come first.
2 Colleagues are with us forever.
3 Crises will usually pass after a very short time.

The messages had to be short and to the point, and if an emotional twist could be added, so much the better.

Your public relations director will look forward to the times that you can spread the good word (that is, the 'gospel') about something that you *wish* to broadcast. These opportunities may come all too infrequently, and they should be capitalized on. Such opportunities might involve issues like the following for your institution:

• A favourable HSMR rate (see 'Data Collection and Scorecards' in chapter 8)
• A 'first'
• An improvement in wait times
• A unique and innovative treatment
• A fund-raising coup

These must all be trumpeted with appropriate fanfare but with professionalism, great care, and as much planning as your most intricate medical or surgical regimen. And don't do it alone! Just as in the practice of medicine and surgery and in the management of a hospital, relationships among living, breathing people represent the bedrock of public relations. Your director or vice-president of this important interest area has many long-standing associations based on personal trust, and you must rely on these to get any messages out.

Take the best advice, and play by the rules that are set by others; if you improvise or go it alone, you will be playing a game for which you're not prepared and by rules that you don't understand.

Fund-Raising

Most hospitals identify fund-raising as an important priority for its clinicians. Thanks to our intimate relationship with patients, we are in an unusual position of trust as well as a very sensitive position with regard to donations for research or capital equipment.

In the past there have been too many stories that relate sleazy approaches of unfortunately tying patients' generosity to the care they receive. This is not only odious but borders on manipulation and fraud. However, if the two domains of patient care and fund-raising can be separated, the grateful patient and/or family is a tremendous potential source of progress for a medical organization.

Some physicians and surgeons feel uncomfortable with the concept of approaching patients, but this can be done in a very moral and bioethically acceptable way. At the very least, clinicians should be responsible for putting patients together with professional fund-raisers who can be trusted to keep personal medical issues at arm's length.

In addition to the physical improvements in an institution, the core budget of any research activities usually must be supported because granting agencies don't always fund those costs.

The Community of Your Hospital

The clientele of your division may vary widely, from street people to Wall Street people, and you have to recognize the difference. Although we all contend that every patient who comes in the door receives the most consistent and best treatment that we can offer, the exact mode is dependent to a great extent on patient expectations.

The management of the professionals in your organization must be based on principles and policy, and the interaction must reflect sensitivity on the part of the medical leader as to the needs of the individual doctor and his or her mindset and values. So, too, is patient management and interaction dependent on the mindset and values of the individual patient. The attending doctor and the medical leader must offer exemplary care within the framework of that patient's reality.

The hospital's community, therefore, must play a role in operations and planning at every step. Some achieve this end by inviting patient advocates and representatives to be members of various planning and operations committees, and others organize actual community advisory committees whose members, it is hoped, represent a cross-section of the institution's clientele and who can, on a regular basis, provide feedback on how that hospital is performing.

The most common way of assessing community acceptability is by the use of *patient satisfaction surveys*. These are detailed questionnaires that probe the level of acceptance by patients of the various people and processes in a health care delivery organization. While some clinicians object to the apparently miniscule variations from hospital to hospital being considered seriously in public reports, the methodology has been validated and is here to stay. It will be one of your main responsibilities as a medical leader to monitor these results and devise ways to strive towards continuous improvement in the eyes of the patients. The eyes of your CEO will be on the case, to be sure.

Accreditation of Your Hospital

Every hospital must prove intermittently that it meets the standards expected of it by the appointed governing body of a particular country. In the United States the Joint Commission on the Accreditation of Healthcare Organizations (JCAHO)[83] is the accrediting body to which all hospitals must answer. In addition, the National Committee for Quality Assurance (NCQA)[84] monitors activities in institutions that deliver health care. The board of directors of JCAHO consists of representatives of the following organizations: American Medical Association, American Hospital Association, American College of Physicians, American College of Surgeons, American Dental Association, nursing representatives, and non-medical business members.

Essentially, to gain accreditation a hospital must be able to verify that every staff member at the institution is able to describe and demonstrate proficiency and receive a performance evaluation based on his or her job description. Currently, hospitals submit to the accreditation process every three or four years, are evaluated, and gain recognition as being 'fully accredited.' If glaring deficiencies are found, they face another review sooner than the end of the next three- or four-year period.

In future, it is expected that the process will involve *unannounced surveys*, which it is hoped will confirm the ideal practised by a given institution on a daily basis.

In Canada the accreditation process is administered by the Canadian Council on Health Services Accreditation (CCHSA), recently renamed Accreditation Canada.[85] The council's tagline is 'Driving Quality Health

Services.' The focus of accreditation practices has changed over the years, and currently it relates to a *tracer methodology* that concentrates on processes from the patient's point of view. In other words, survey team members wish to know how a patient is treated and managed from the moment he or she gains access to the hospital as a patient, and how each interaction, test, or intervention is handled with compassion, efficiency, effectiveness, and safety in mind. The surveyors focus on the front-line staff and patients for information – not just on the managers and directors, which was the past accreditation practice.

As a medical leader, not only must you take responsibility for your section in practising according to the standards of the accrediting body, but also you must ensure that the members of your team are prepared for the survey. The current process in Canada is now directing efforts towards the assessment of how a hospital really works, by carrying out a massive *organizational effectiveness survey* – a survey of the people who do the work – and judging to what degree there is an effective link between management and the front lines.

The whole process of accreditation may be regarded as a nuisance that periodically interferes with patient care and other more 'necessary' activities, but it is an essential part of a hospital's future well-being. Learn all about the details of this important and mandatory process.

Disaster Plans

We all yearn for order in our lives and for a sense of predictability that leads to a modicum of control. Most doctors are energized early in their careers by the unexpected and drawn by the lure of the life-and-death, moment-to-moment existence of an ER doctor or an ICU physician. While some maintain that mindset throughout their careers, most doctors come to prefer a more stable, predictable environment and a more elective practice.

Hospitals and other medical institutions must have the capacity on a grand scale to respond in the most timely and efficient way possible to internal and external disasters. A disaster-preparedness or emergency-preparedness plan must be in place and practised intermittently, not unlike the conduct of a periodic fire alarm in an elementary school to heighten awareness of a possible future disaster. Don't forget that the medical and nursing population of a hospital usually need as much instruction and awareness as do those fifth graders in preparation for such an occurrence.

Disasters may take many forms, from the acute (such as 9/11 or the London subway bombing) to the less acute (such as the SARS crisis in Toronto in 2003 or the swine flu pandemic of 2009). The preparations on the part of management and medical personnel are detailed, time consuming, and exhaustive, and it is hoped that it will never be necessary to put them into operation. However, unexpected events in any hospital such as outbreaks of infection, the breakdown of circulating fans (and other facilities issues), bomb threats, and violent patients provide occasional practice on a smaller scale for the times that may necessitate all hands on deck.

Most hospitals are required at the management level to periodically engage in 'tabletop exercises' that are mock enactments of a disaster. Such activities might seem trite at first, but they are invaluable for familiarizing managers with command centre set-up, communication issues, and the like. If you are a medical leader, jump into these exercises with both feet and both arms (head also recommended); this is the ultimate team effort and one with personal reward.

SITUATION 9.3

THE 2003 SARS CRISIS: *The Coordinated Emergency Response*

The SARS disaster in 2003 proved to be an exercise that drew many Toronto hospitals together, fine-tuned organizational practices, promoted teamwork throughout the system, and likely curtailed what could have been an absolutely calamitous and generalized outbreak. In the end, 44 people in the Toronto area died, and another 330 were struck down with serious lung disease.

Justice Archie Campbell, in his subsequent review,[50] liberally complimented the health care workers on their dedication and selflessness, as well as the leadership of the provincial response in the person of Dr Sheela Basrur. But he also had much to say about the organizational activities between the two. His report contained eighty-three recommendations, and although he concluded that the outbreak was not preventable, more could have been done to protect the safety of health care workers: 'If the commission has one single take-home message, it is the "precautionary principle" that safety comes first, that reasonable efforts to reduce risk need not await scientific proof. Ontario needs to enshrine this principle and to enforce it throughout our entire health system.' Specifically, the problems that Justice Campbell identified included the following:

- Poor internal and external communications
- Inadequate preparation and planning for an outbreak of a virulent disease

- Accountability issues
- Inadequate attention to worker and patient safety
- Poor infection control
- Inattentive surveillance
- Lack of independent safety inspections
- Lack of application of the precautionary principle

All of Justice Campbell's recommendations with regard to the SARS crisis in Toronto in 2003 point to the necessity of an emergency-preparedness plan for every institution and to the mandate that all medical leaders must be aware of, accountable for, and responsible for the execution of that plan by all of their reports.

You as a medical leader, therefore, must be acutely aware of the algorithm of the emergency response in your hospital and have the contact coordinates of all of your division or department members with you at all times.

The transfer of this responsibility is also extremely important when you are away, just as is the transfer of responsibility of care for specific patients.

The ALC Patient

The patients who are given the designation *alternate level of care* (ALC) represent one of the most challenging issues in hospital care today. Defined as patients who no longer require an acute care hospital bed, they unfortunately do still need attention that cannot be adequately provided at home.

A multitude of factors affect each person's situation, and these may include the following:

- Weak support systems, such as friends and family
- Inadequate resources
- Particularly problematic chronic disease states

Sometimes patients are even dropped off at an emergency department, and the 'chauffeur' disappears, leaving an unstable patient with no apparent outside-world connections at all. Frequently retirement-home staff may find themselves barely coping with a patient, who then predictably develops a more serious problem, and the capabilities of the home are vastly exceeded. In many cases, healthier patients may endure a serious illness and require a longer period of convalescence than had been expected, and they must simply wait for a bed at another, more appropriate facility.

This conundrum is not new, but it now comes at a time when the number of inpatient beds has been reduced significantly (these reductions are often related to the high cost of compensation for hospital personnel, and thus the reduction of staff) and the acuity level of the patients who *should* be there has escalated remarkably. So we now have the paradoxical situation of hospital wards filled with patients who are extremely ill and require high-level care, juxtaposed with patients who should be in some other institution.

The knee-jerk conclusion is that there simply aren't enough convalescent and chronic care beds available. While that may be true in some settings, the *coordination* of such accommodation may be the more pivotal factor. The medical leader must be very active in this domain. It is your responsibility to seek out alternative arrangements for the patients on your service, look for community liaisons, and work with senior management on strategies that involve a variety of institutions.

On a daily basis as well, it is your responsibility to ensure the efficient throughput of patients on your service. Daily rounds must be carried out early enough for blood work to be done and X-rays taken, if necessary, in order to confirm a patient's ability to be discharged.

Discharge planning must start before the patient is admitted electively, not at some point when the attending staff finds that a bed is desperately needed. There should be incentives put in place to encourage *all specialties* to actively plan for the ordered investigation, treatment, and future discharge of each patient. Surgery has that incentive because the next day's elective list depends on discharges of home-bound or ALC patients. Other services need incentives to act with similar urgency.

Palliative Care

> Guérir quelquefois, soulager souvent, consoler toujours.
> [To cure sometimes, to relieve pain often, to comfort always.]
> – Inscription on a statue of Dr Edward Livingston Trudeau
> at Saranac Lake, New York

Edward Livingston Trudeau was a New York State doctor who, in 1882, founded the Adirondack Cottage Sanitarium at Saranac Lake for the treatment of tuberculosis. He devoted his whole professional career to the study of the disease, and the above quotation on his statue appropriately captures his dedication to palliative care.

Doctors are seldom educated to give up their dogged determination to preserve life, always acceding to the principle that *length* of life is sacrosanct. In the Western world that sentiment is shared by patients whose expectations seem to accelerate each year. With medical miracles publicized constantly in the media, the public generally feels a sense of entitlement to the most modern treatment available.

The issue of chronic disease management, particularly in view of our aging population, has also become an overriding concern with any funding agency interested in health care, and it threatens to break the health care bank. There are countless examples of elderly patients receiving high-risk interventions that were not dreamed of a few years ago; how could we refuse aggressive treatment for the eighty-five-year-old patient who has a CABG procedure and has a reasonable prognosis thereafter, or for a seventy-five-year-old diabetic who is quite comfortable on home dialysis for his renal failure? In these settings the precise definitions of curative and palliative treatment become blurred.

In the management of many chronic diseases, treatment is palliative by nature because interventions and medications are directed at relieving symptoms but not eradicating the condition. When we treat solid cancers, our chemotherapeutic regimens are frequently palliative in nature. They are administered with the confidence that scientific proof supports the practice. For example, often the use of cytotoxic agents has been proven scientifically in randomized controlled trials (RCTs) to lengthen life, when compared with patients not receiving the said drug(s). But if the evidence shows improvement in survival by only weeks or months, with the survival accompanied by noxious effects of the treatment, are we really providing patient-centred care? Some would say, 'I may not be living longer, but it sure *seems* longer!'

Some hospitals in North America, especially those that deal with severe and chronic illness, may have as many as 30 to 40 per cent of their inpatient beds occupied by patients who are not only palliative in nature but, in fact, could be regarded as requiring end-of-life care. It's surprising, therefore, that it wasn't until recently that this field became a major subspecialty in health care.

The spectrum of palliative care is broad, and it involves not only pain and symptom management but also social, psychological, cultural, emotional, and spiritual support. The support also extends to the family and friends of the patient and most certainly to the caregiver as well.

Palliative care may be perhaps the model of patient-centred care in a bioethical environment.

SITUATION 9.4
GYNAECOLOGIC ONCOLOGY AND PALLIATIVE CARE:
On Death and Dying

One of the busiest divisions of gynaecologic oncology in North America practices at Community Hospital B. Inherent in that specialty is the fact that many patients require palliative or end-of-life care at some point, and in 2007 the hospital recognized that more focus was needed on this important area.

Approximately twenty members of the team, including surgeons, nurses, house staff, and other providers, engaged in a value stream mapping (VSM) process and a rapid improvement event (RIE), as described under 'Continuous Quality Improvement and Patient Safety' in chapter 6. The objectives of the exercise were the following:

- Identify at an early stage those patients who require palliative care
- Immediately establish lines of communication and education with the patient and the patient's family
- Consult with the palliative care team and social workers
- Study the options that best suit the needs of the patient

Patient satisfaction had previously been measured using standard benchmarking, and the length of stay of such patients in the acute care setting was known to be excessive. It was hoped that as a result of introducing the above objectives patient satisfaction would improve and patient transfer to a more comfortable hospitable setting would be facilitated.

After new processes were put in place following the execution of the RIE, patient hospital stay was decreased from twenty-one days to seven days (a 66 per cent reduction), and the hospital stay of those patients who were transferred to a palliative care unit was decreased from thirty-four days to seven days (a 79 per cent reduction). More important than these impressive early results is the fact that the reductions have been sustained ever since, and they have been accompanied by patient and family acceptance.

As a medical leader you will have to embrace this field because it is proper and moral to do so and, from an efficiency standpoint, it just makes sense. If an appropriate process is in place, patients and families will receive timely and compassionate support, and they will likely have a better opportunity to die in their familiar home surrounded by their loved ones.

Like so many other examples in health care, a palliative care process can be not only more *efficient*, but also more *humane*.

On a final note, if you want to read an exceptional manual on how to sensitively interact with the terminally ill patient, *How to Break Bad News: A Guide for Health Care Professionals* (1992) by Robert Buckman,[86] with contributions by Yvonne Kason, should be in your library. This practical account of the whats and hows, written by an unusually gifted medical oncologist who is now at Princess Margaret Hospital in Toronto and whose early years were spent with the Monty Python comedy group in Britain (strange bedfellows, to be sure!), is tremendously insightful and helpful.

The Addicted Physician

The good news is that medical doctors and nurses are knowledgeable about and have access to restricted medications. The bad news is that medical doctors and nurses are knowledgeable about and have access to restricted medications. All doctors are human, overworked, often fatigued, frequently under stress, and just as subject to addictive behaviour as is the average human being; however, doctors have access to substances to which others do not have access.

The rate of doctor addiction to alcohol and/or drugs is disturbingly high and, if truth be known, is likely to be significantly higher in reality than is revealed in published figures. It is estimated that over a professional lifetime the likelihood of *anyone,* including doctors, developing a treatable addiction to alcohol or drugs may approach 9 per cent, and the proportion may be higher for those specialists who have easier access to drugs.

Every leader of a large medical organization can relate poignant stories of experiences in this field, because the response to such a problem in an individual can be either life saving or life destroying. In my thirty years' experience I've had the opportunity to be involved in several such incidents that have required intervention of the sort that has temporarily taken an individual out of active practice. Although the details cannot be related, respecting confidentiality, let me say that I have never witnessed nor participated in more satisfying or memorable events in my career than those that led to the successful rehabilitation of professional colleagues.

Five Things You Need to Know about the Addicted Physician

1 Physician addiction is more pervasive than reported.
2 Physician addiction is insidious and can sometimes involve the last person you'd expect. Prepare to be surprised.
3 Your decision about confrontation and intervention with an addicted physician will be the most difficult step you will ever take.
4 Implementation of the plan for rehabilitation must be decisive, precipitous, forceful, and directive, giving the individual no choice. You will risk a personal relationship with your colleague, but you must act in this way.
5 A successful outcome will result in your gaining an experience you cannot talk about, an unparallelled level of satisfaction, and an extremely appreciative friend for life.

You must therefore be on the lookout for such problems, explore rumours or reports, and be acutely aware of the local organizations that manage these problems, including medical associations, psychiatry and psychology groups, and social organizations.

Relationships with Industry

In the 1950s the name Alan Freed became famous for being involved in a rock 'n' roll scandal.[87] He was accused of receiving payment for broadcasting specific songs on the radio, while implying that the songs were part of the usual music fare. Interestingly, a subsequent change in the law suggested that such payments *could* be legal but only if they were disclosed on air – perhaps foretelling similar situations in relationships between industry and medicine.

As a medical leader with some experience in the marketplace, you are undoubtedly very familiar with the relationships of clinicians with pharmaceutical and medical instrument companies. In the not-too-distant past, suture representatives were seen hovering around, or even *in*, operating theatres, plying their trade. Many pleasant meetings, punctuated by lavish food and drink, were held to extol the virtues of a new antibiotic or a more effective proton pump inhibitor. Expensive dinners, travel to industry-sponsored conferences, free samples of the latest and greatest drugs, or tickets to sporting or entertainment events were the rule rather than the exception. Some doctors who had a hand in helping to devise new instruments or treatments even enjoyed lucrative contracts with related companies.

Over the years, concerns about these relationships have led to an evolution towards academic or educational meetings sponsored by industry, but in a relatively arm's-length way so that no direct promises by practitioners can be inferred.

Manuscripts now accepted for publication must be accompanied by clear declarations about the source of financial support for the published work. We're currently involved in an evolutionary process that is increasingly under scrutiny and will surely become better defined in future. Promiscuity was followed by selective mutually consensual relationships, and it now appears as though absolute separation and celibacy may be inevitable in many collaborations![88]

Bioethical behaviour has become a hot topic in all curricula, and so recognition of these potential conflicts of interest naturally follows. Public interest was stimulated by recent events in the U.S. court system. The orthopaedic implant industry is a lucrative one, leading not surprisingly to a spate of kickbacks, which take a variety of forms, including consulting fees and attractive travel assignments. In September 2007 four such companies (Dupuy Orthopedics; Biomet; Smith and Nephew; and Zimmer) paid fines of $310 million, and new rules were put into place that mandated transparency when doctors are paid by providers. Public declaration is the first critical step in the ensuring legitimacy of such support.

There is now a growing trend for hospitals, universities, and physicians' organizations to articulate strict codes of conduct that are designed to guide ethical business relationships with companies who themselves have even developed similar policies.

Today, in 2010, we live in interesting times with regard to this important issue; some like Stanford University have outlawed *any* form of support from industry (and have therefore set a clear example), but others recognize potential virtues in collaboration and have given qualified support to the concept as long as transparency is present. The latter groups posit that a mutually supportive relationship may ultimately assist patients with enhanced research support.

The challenge here is maintaining strict bioethical principles at a time of extreme fiscal restraint. Research funding is always scarce, and in times of recession it is expectedly compromised even further; under such circumstances, perhaps meeting somewhere in the middle is a more realistic approach than the Stanford model. If you have an opportunity to participate in this discussion in your organization, take it because you will at the very least learn a lot and maybe even have a hand in formulating policy that will in the end improve patient care in a way that respects ethical principles.

As a medical leader you will have to carefully assess your organization's position on this crucial issue and either follow the principles fastidiously or be a part of developing a more progressive policy. Whatever stance you and your division or department take, you as a medical leader will have to be front and centre in the development of policy and in the implementation and close monitoring of your written guidelines with respect to these important associations.

These are just a few of the issues that may be somewhat new to you with respect to either your knowledge of them or your responsibility as a medical leader to deal with them. Suffice it to say that there will undoubtedly be many others that you will face and that will prompt further study, consultation with your colleagues, or the occasional decision made on the basis of your gut feelings and common sense. Just as we always return to basic principles when we manage a medical puzzle that we haven't seen before, so too must the medical leader, when stymied, return to the basic principles, values, and policies of the organization. But also, as in the clinical realm, there should be no hesitation in

- asking for advice,
- buying time, and
- making the best decision.

Your decision will not always be the eventual right decision, but it can be the best one you are able to make at the time, justified by the information available to you.

10 The Character of a Leader

Now I would like to offer you some miscellaneous bits of unsolicited advice. Over the past twenty-five years I have admittedly developed ways of being, of doing things, and of working with the people in my environment. Every person alive has various effects on different people; there are character traits that may be attractive to some and at the same time repulsive to others.

You won't please everyone all the time, and your actions will certainly not be welcomed either universally or continually. Nevertheless, I have developed some habits and biases that I personally feel have made the journey a little smoother and more effective, for me anyway.

The Way You Are

Be Positive

You will face many challenges, and some days you will appear to be flitting from one crisis to another. This is the ultimate challenge of a medical leader – to keep your eye on the ball while the fans in the stands are hurling a variety of objects onto the field, trying to disrupt the game. My old anaesthetic colleague David Bevan labelled these people *bomb-throwers*, referring to individuals who from the back seat of a lecture hall will often hurl insults or controversy, from a distance, always ready to make a quick exit. As a medical leader you must remain optimistic and forward thinking despite interruptions; after all, your responsibility is to move towards the vision. While you are being optimistic, however, you must be frank and forthcoming; your colleagues have a right to know the truth about the challenges that face you, them, and the organization.

There's also something to remember about the perceived negativism of some colleagues. Excellence has a price, and to achieve excellence we must always look for areas of improvement; as we strive to improve, we may sound as though we're discontented.

We will always be unsatisfied with our current lot because that's how we progress, but we must remember that the discontent, if managed appropriately, can be a positive catalyst for change. A good medical leader will appreciate those reminders of potential improvement and should let the disgruntled know that their continued input is valued.

Be Consistent, Truthful, Honest

I hesitate to document such obvious characteristics as consistency, truthfulness, and honesty, which are really attributes that every person on the planet should profess and strive for. The reason for articulating them here is that without them you will fail miserably as a medical leader.

I have seen superbly talented doctors who continue to succeed and be recognized nationally and internationally for their outstanding contributions, but who lack total honesty and truthfulness and who certainly have not been consistent in their behaviour. On the international stage where individuals are seen intermittently, their prominence may not be affected by their inconsistent behaviour back home. But the medical leader who is on the job 24/7 and is not true to these character traits will not last a month in maintaining respect.

When respect is lost, effectiveness is lost.

Be Appreciative

As a medical leader you will have a lot to be thankful for, and you should show that thanks every time you get a chance. At meetings, verbal acknowledgments of the contributors, including the organizers, are much appreciated and may even be a factor in a person's willingness to put in the same time and effort the next year.

Frequent email recognition is the easiest way to thank someone and should be encouraged to a degree. Remember, however, that a repetitive method that is copied to many begins to sound vacuous and meaningless, so you should try to think of more novel ways to thank your colleagues. A small token such as a book, a tie, a scarf, or a bottle of wine, depending on the recipient's habits, may be just the right way to say, 'A job well done,' or 'Much appreciated.'

I personally favour the handwritten note. If I receive a note that has taken time, thought, and effort, I am inclined to save it, simply because I value it so much. To me, this gesture ranks up there with the hand-written messages that acknowledge wedding gifts, in that they are the most personal expressions of feelings and appreciation. Unlike the wedding example, however, a handwritten note from a medical leader is entirely unexpected and, therefore, all the more poignant.

Be Human, and Admit It

> In the course of my life, I have often had to eat my words, and I must con-fess that I have always found it a wholesome diet.
>
> – Winston Churchill

You will gain tremendous trust if you repeatedly confirm the fact that you are human. Look for the counsel of others, from the first meeting with each of your colleagues to every meeting with the CEO. If you have done something egregious, or made a bad decision that could have been avoided, *say you're sorry.*

A well-known study in Detroit[89] looking at the propensity of patients and families to enter into lawsuits found that a policy of saying 'I'm sorry' for an unfavourable clinical outcome resulted in a significant de-cline in the number of lawsuits brought against that organization. Just as patients forgive and accept apologies, so too do colleagues. The re-cent changes in law have stipulated that saying you're sorry does not constitute an admission of guilt or culpability.

Know Your Facts

As a medical leader you are being watched and listened to constantly, oc-casionally with admiration, sometimes with resentment, often with the most critical eye. Despite the fact that you shouldn't be afraid to show your ignorance, there are some facts that you should have at your fingertips and ont the tip of your tongue. The following should be your mantras:

- The mission
- The vision

- The values of your organization, and of your department or division if they differ slightly from the larger expressions

If your hospital places a value on patient-centred care (which one doesn't?), you should be able to regurgitate every dimension of that care. The coloured emergency codes in your hospital should be obvious to every living being who works there, but you have to know them instantly if asked. The responses to fire, such as the acronym REACT (Remove occupants, Enclose area, Activate alarm, Call emergency number, and Try to fight fire) for the evacuation routes, and the building-related issues all must be second nature to you.

You must know the geography of your institution and be able to direct patients wherever they want to go. You should tour the hospital intermittently to familiarize yourself with areas that you seldom visit; this is in some ways *your* home, and your interest in knowing a lot about it is a reflection of the pride and responsibility you have for it. You should know apparently insignificant details like the cost of parking, and the members of the food court and their contributions to your organization – they all count.

Be Impartial, but Not Too Impartial

You start as the leader of a specific group of clinicians, and you are an inveterate supporter of and an advocate for that group's welfare. As you take on more senior responsibilities, you're faced with the problem of favouring your home team, be it endocrinology, general surgery, orthopaedics, or hematology.

SITUATION 10.1
NEW CEO: *Be Fair, but Not Too Fair*

In 1998, near the end of Doctor D's tenure as president and CEO of UHN, there were concerns about the ability of the Neuroscience Program to adequately and safely care for its growing referral base of complex neurological patients who required intensive care. Doctor Q, the head of neurology, and I, in my then role of acting director of surgical services, analysed the patient flow, the needs of the program, and the overall expenditures in Neurosciences, which was one of our so-called priority programs of the organization at that time (along with Transplantation, Oncology, and Cardiac Sciences).

We discovered not only that there was a definite need for more level-two ICU beds, nurse practitioners, and clinical associates, but also that the

Neuroscience Program received a significantly lower level of funding than all the other programs.

Doctor Q and I went to Doctor D with a carefully laid-out plan describing all the needs and long-term implications, along with the financial comparators of the other programs. We were delighted when he signed off on the spot, realizing that he had probably disadvantaged, unwittingly, the Neuroscience Program in comparison with other programs.

Doctor D had been an internationally prominent academic neurosurgeon and chair of the university's division of neurosurgery for ten years prior to coming to UHN.

Occasionally, as a medical leader you will advantage yourself, and that is clearly unacceptable, as demonstrated in the story of the division head who assigned himself more operating time than anyone else. More often than not, however, medical leaders are so worried about the optics of what they do that they place at a disadvantage the interest areas that they're concerned about favouring, as was the case with Doctor M (in situation 5.1).

What You Do

Don't Be Afraid to Show Your Ignorance

Ask questions incessantly. Everyone in the organization knows more than you do about some subject. You didn't get to the leadership position by knowing everything.

It goes without saying that in areas for which you have direct responsibility you must study, read, meet, call, and go to any lengths to gather and store information, becoming an expert in the areas you need to be an expert. In addition, there will be numerous opportunities for you to demonstrate your thirst for knowledge and your desire to learn something from a colleague, and as a result to enrich your relationships with others in the hospital organization.

Nothing is more appreciated than a medical leader saying to someone, 'Thanks for telling me that. That's very useful information.'

Listen to People: Everyone Is Smart

Don't be afraid to take someone else's idea and run with it. It may even be a vision that results in substantive change.

Your Daily Habits

As a medical leader you certainly don't have to be the best at everything, and you aren't expected to be, but you must demonstrate some of the behaviours that you expect of others. Many of these have been implied in the sections on living your values, answering emails, et cetera.

If punctuality at meetings is valued, you must be early – particularly if you are the chair. Frequently, you may have overlapping commitments and have to attend more than one meeting in a given hour; in such circumstances you should inform the chair of your late arrival or early departure and make it clear why you're not on time.

Many medical leaders arrive very early in the morning, not only because that is a standard to be emulated but because before seven o'clock a lot of work can be accomplished without the interruptions from telephones, locating operators, and the like.

Be Visible

Be visible as a medical leader, what some refer to as *management by walking around:*

- Visit the various inpatient and outpatient clinics.
- Drop into the operating room.
- Stand in coffee lines with your colleagues.
- Above all, enjoy meeting and greeting people.

This may sound somewhat contrived, but when you *learn the names of the people* who work in the hospital organization at a variety of levels, you will receive repeated feedback that will make you want to learn even more names and more about your colleagues.

It also makes everyone in the organization more comfortable with coming up to you in the hallway, saying, 'Hello,' and giving you a piece of their mind. As long as you maintain your healthy thick skin, this can be a very useful tool in keeping your ear close to the ground.

Prioritize Your Energies Every Day

The well-known Serenity Prayer, written by Reinhold Niebuhr, should be on every medical leader's wall and should direct every day's activity. There are so many obligations and so much tugging coming from every direction that a daily prioritization of energies is mandatory.

'Lord grant me the serenity to accept the things
I cannot change, the courage to change the things
I can, and the wisdom to know the difference.'

Any person who works in an organization will recognize also the eighty-twenty rule, where 80 per cent of one's time ends up being devoted to 20 per cent of the area, people, and/or programs.

As a medical leader you must learn to sort out these competing forces every day and decide how best to approach them in an economical and effective way. Some problems don't need a decision right away, and some will sort themselves out given enough time; in these situations, procrastination can work in your favour, but you must decide which problems to manage in that way.

Some problems are insoluble and can simply be mitigated for the present, and then managed repeatedly in future. One such issue is the clinical problem of the escalating complexity of patients and their inexorably increasing requirements for resources in a hospital setting. We will continue trying to ease this tension brought on by patient expectations and doctor ingenuity (that is, there are never enough resources to offer the care we need to), but it will never be solved. We will strive for ever more efficient care and attempt to develop novel revenue streams, but we will have to be content with the best we can do, rather than the ideal.

TURN OFF THE ENGINE

One other point about practising serenity: I have no solution for the practitioner or medical leader who wakes up at three o'clock in the morning thinking about administrative problems, patients and their post-operative complications, or how the quality presentation to the board of trustees will go this week. Virtually every medical leader to whom I've talked about this subject laments the difficulty in turning off the engine. Despite that difficulty, one must continue to strive for the separation of work and private time in the interests of personal and family health.

Take Time to Think

You must confer with your executive assistant and map out the kind of day or week you want to pursue. Innumerable people will want a piece of you, and it's imperative that you plan your day, week, and month in ways that will meet your ultimate objectives.

It is important to control the kinds of what I call *passive activities* in the medical field that usually fill a day:

- Patient calls
- Clinic visits
- Scheduled meetings
- Unscheduled meetings with people whose subjects 'just can't wait'

Some of these can't easily be controlled, but control them you must.

PLAN DOWNTIME

You must plan downtime, time that your executive assistant regards as sacrosanct, and unless there is a dire emergency, that time is for you alone. During that hour, half-day, or day, you must turn off the phone ringer, shut off the cellphone and beeper, and devote time to concentrating on the problems you face, the visioning, preparing the next planning exercise, and/or setting out details of a family vacation.

Leadership jobs, because of multiple demands, complexity, and the paucity of time, can become black holes of activity with little time for contemplation. If you don't have this time, you will find that all your activities are directed at extinguishing brush fires; that is, you will be an ineffective manager and a poor medical leader.

Get It Done

Some medical leaders have wonderful vision, can make a cogent plan, can start a process of change, but nevertheless in the long run they fail to finish the project. This speaks once again to the notion of implementation so enthusiastically espoused by Mintzberg. To reverse the old adage, why do tomorrow what you can do today?

There has always been a tendency for grant applications in the medical field to be submitted the day before a deadline. In medical leadership the task should be done now – your standing will increase with the most important people, those whom you lead. The completion of projects, however small, and their subsequent celebration represent crucial steps in the overall success of any leader.

When participating people are applauded for their success and thanked for their contributions, there's tremendous incentive generated for starting and finishing the next project.

Use Power, and You Lose It

The majority of medical leadership positions don't come with any cheque-writing ability. You won't be making any major organizational decisions without the collaboration and assistance of many others. That said, you will have to distribute the hospital resources that are available to your colleagues in a way that is fair, equitable, and *seen* to be fair.

Rather than power, which might be paraphrased as the ability to make unilateral decisions, you will have *influence*, which implies that your position and counsel will be heard and considered. To the extent that you do have decision-making power, you should be very careful how you exercise it. Owing to the fact that you lead independent practitioners, any show of power risks the loss of trust.

Don't Forget to Mow the Lawn and Take Out the Garbage

This book is about focusing on the important things and not letting little bothersome issues dominate your life. However, *every* job on the planet is made up, at least in part, of mundane activities that may seem to be 'below' the incumbent. Family doctors may see twenty patients who complain of sniffles, and even the most accomplished general or colorectal surgeon may have to band haemorrhoids or fix an inguinal hernia. The medical manager is in the same boat, and the perception may vary with the job and the tolerance of the individual. Some doctors find a one-hour meeting to be interminable, others answer emails with obvious disdain, and still others compose supportive promotion letters with virtually no enthusiasm.

> **Be warned that in every medical leadership position there are menial tasks to be performed.**

As a medical leader you will have menial tasks to perform, perhaps typified by signing yearly letters of reappointment for scores of colleagues. But be prepared, and plan on achieving the same sense of accomplishment that you have when mowing your lawn. You may not enjoy it, but it's part of the job, and when the task is finished, there is indeed a sense of achievement (however muted).

Some doctors literally can't stand the thought of this type of endeavour, and if you're one of those, best not apply.

Your Colleagues

Recognize Stress

Stress and potential burnout are constant companions of health care providers, and if they are not, these unwanted visitors are often knocking at the door. Today's most senior physicians represent the baby boomers of the post–Second World War period, and most of us have adopted a work ethic that was at one time thought to be noble, but now is considered somewhat stupid and arcane.

Controllable workload, diverse interests, attention to personal health and fitness, and nurturing a family are becoming more important in the lives of today's future doctors;

I suspect that the elements of stress and burnout will be less common in the future than they have been in the past. Gone are the days of 100-hour work weeks. These are now quickly being replaced by group practices, time away from work, legislated workloads for nurses and doctors generally, and a more wholesome and sensible approach to life.

That said, we still have a generation of senior doctors and many younger doctors who remain under constant stress. The stress is exacerbated in our particular service industry, in which patients and families often deal with sudden tragedy, and if we are good doctors who offer patient-centred care, we truly participate in and feel that tragedy.

Early in a career a young doctor is often seduced by highly stressful situations and high-tension medicine and surgery that revolve around emergency departments, intensive care units, and operating rooms, but a steady diet of such activity can have insidious and long-lasting effects. This may be exacerbated by the baby boomers now facing the care of their own parents, along with their professional life, and, of course, financial troubles that may add to the complex situation.

RECOGNIZING BURNOUT

Frustration, depression, withdrawal, and a feeling of emptiness may represent burnout, and the last person to recognize this condition is the victim. Therefore, as a medical leader you must be on the lookout for the stressed or burned-out physician, just as you have to be on the lookout for the addicted one (see 'The Addicted Physician' in chapter 9). Note unusual behaviour, subtly pursue rumours that may be circulating, and feel free to get together for coffee and a chat about business issues (and the other ones that will undoubtedly come up). Once again, having a strong personal relationship to begin with makes this approach much easier.

One of the paradoxes of medicine is that we deal with the dark side of life so much that we likely build a kind of immunity to these feelings, and we may, in fact, be less likely than the average person to recognize them in ourselves.

In an interesting book entitled *Nothing to Be Frightened Of* (2008),[90] Julian Barnes points to the medical profession as being less capable of accepting the concept of death, when compared to other people. This is not surprising when you consider that we tend to develop a very clinical view of the subject of death, so we have no time for it personally.

REVERSING BURNOUT.
It is far beyond the scope of this effort to more than remind you of this trap – the inevitable vortex of intensive service activity. Reversing the end stage of stress, that is, the emptiness of burnout, usually requires intervention, understanding, a lot of support, and considerable time.

Ironically, all postgraduate residency programs, in fact, have appropriate initiatives in place to assist residents who are under great stress, but the recognition of the problem and the inclination of more senior clinicians to seek help have lagged behind. Every hospital organization currently, however, has an appropriate function available to the stressed worker, and there should be no hesitation in capitalizing on that service.

Share the Leadership

The most flattering thing for you as a medical leader is to have people lining up to apply for your job when your term is finished (which may be seen by the pessimist as buzzards circling the still-warm body). This implies that the job is worth doing and that you have added to or maintained a feeling of respect for it.

How did you land in that enviable place? You did this by *giving up the leadership* continually during your mandate. There are countless opportunities for clinicians with leadership aspirations to show their worth, if the leader is willing to do the following, for example:

• Assign tasks to good people
• Appoint chairs of task forces to bring a fresh perspective to new challenges

- Share responsibility in decision making
- Reward those future leaders with recognition for jobs well done
- Create meaningful management positions with meaningful titles

Sharing leadership is also important to afford people the chance to see *outside* their own area of knowledge or expertise. Any individual aspiring to a more senior managerial post has to come to the realization that the whole frame of reference will change. That person has to 'abandon' to some degree total parochial allegiance to a specific area and become committed not only to that area but also to many other areas and the whole organization at the same time.

Epilogue:
Some Final Thoughts about the Success
of Your Leadership

When you leave your post, you want to be regarded as having been a success in your position as a medical leader. Here are some of my general principles, distilled along my road in various positions as a medical leader:

1 Never forget for whom you work. While it's true that you officially report to your chief of department and the CEO (also the chair and the dean in an academic centre), you really work for your constituents, that is, the professionals in your section who report to you (your reports).

2 Never flaunt your position. You are still one of the guys or girls, and when you are in the clinical domain you have no more special rights than others have. You must be governed by processes at arm's length, and therefore your share of resources must be equal to or less than that of others. If you ever throw your weight around for personal favours or gain, you might as well resign from the leadership position; you are done.

3 Your legacy, if you believe in one, will be in the people you brought on and in *their* success, not in your own personal accomplishments. (That said, don't forget the reasons you were recognized as a potential leader in the first place – you still should pursue continued personal development.)

4 You will be remembered for *the fun and the achievements* you brought to the division or department and whether others looked forward to coming to work. In the midst of jockeying for resources, the resulting

competition among clinicians can be healthy, but also potentially destructive. Strive every day to encourage healthy competition and avoid 'competition for scraps.'

5 You will be remembered less for the institutional successes and more for the way you *cared* about the individual people you led.

6 If you did all the above, and nurtured others to assume leadership with the appropriate principles and values in mind, you shouldn't be missed when your mandate comes to an end. You should have helped set the stage for further progress, excellence, and excitement. Go back to join the group for celebratory parties, but don't try to have any influence after your departure, either in the choice of your successor or in future operations. Mind your own business!

7 'When the going gets tough, the tough get going!' This is a hackneyed phrase inscribed over every football team's dressing-room door. The reason athletic team players remain friends for life is that they dream together, have common goals together, experience emotional events together, and endure pain together (although the presentation of NFL games as a war with accompanying Wagnerian music probably goes a little too far). If the same kind of concentration, focus, and commitment can be achieved in the medical domain, patients will benefit, and those running the show will have the time of their lives.

References

1. Porter, Michael E., and Elizabeth Olmsted Teisberg. *Redefining Health Care: Creating Positive-Sum Competition to Deliver Value*. Boston: Harvard Business Press, 2005.
2. Doctors at Community Hospital A. Personal communications.
3. Drucker, Peter. *The Effective Executive*. New York: HarperCollins, 2006.
4. Segal, Steven. *Business Feel: From the Science of Management to the Philosophy of Leadership*. New York: Palgrave Macmillan, 2004.
5. Drucker, Peter F. *The Five Most Important Questions You Will Ever Ask About Your Organization*. New York: John Wiley and Sons, 2008.
6. Goleman, Daniel. *Social Intelligence: The New Science of Social Relationships*. New York: Bantam Books, 2007.
7. Gerteis, Margaret, Susan Edgman-Levitan, Jennifer Daley, and Thomas L. Delbano, eds. *Through the Patient's Eyes: Understanding and Promoting Patient-Centered Care*. New York: Jossey-Bass, 1993.
8. *Patient-centred care*. www.ihi.org/IHI/Topics?PatientCenteredCare/ PatientCenteredCareGeneral (accessed 27 January 2010).
9. Institute of Medicine. *To Err Is Human: Building a Safer Health System*. Ed. Linda T. Kohn, Janet Corrigan, and Molla S. Donaldson. Washington, DC: National Academy Press, 2000.
10. www.humanmetrics.com/cgi-win/Jtypes2.asp (accessed 27 January 2010).
11. Collins, Jim. *Good to Great: Why Some Companies Make the Leap, and Others Don't*. New York: HarperBusiness, 2001. *Good to Great and the Social Sectors:* A Monograph to Accompany Good to Great. New York: HarperCollins, 2006.
12. Goleman, Daniel, Richard Boyatzis, and Annie McKee. *Primal Leadership: Realizing the Power of Emotional Intelligence*. Columbus, OH: McGraw-Hill, 2004.
13. Gladwell, Malcolm. *Outliers: The Story of Success*. New York: Little Brown, 2008.

14. Interview with Chris Langan. http://www.youtube.com/results?search_query=christopher+langan+part+1&search_type=&aq=0&oq=christopher+langan (accessed 27 January 2010).
15. Leadership Styles. http://www.changingminds.org/disciplines/leadership/styles/leadership_styles.htm (accessed 27 January 2010).
16. Peter, Laurence J. *The Peter Principle*. Cutchogue, NY: Buccaneer Books, 1996.
17. Lehrer, Jonah. *How We Decide*. Orlando, FL: Houghton Mifflin Harcourt, 2009.
18. Gladwell, Malcolm. *Blink*. Boston: Little Brown, 2005.
19. *Webster's Dictionary of the English Language*. New York: Lexicon Publishers, 1991.
20. Wageman, Ruth, Debra A. Nunes, James A. Burruss, and J. Richard Hackman. *Senior Leadership Teams: What It Takes to Make Them Great*. Boston: Harvard Business School, 2008.
21. Tuckman, Bruce. Developmental Sequence in Small Groups. *Psychological Bulletin* 63, no. 6 (1965): 384–99.
22. Schein, E.H. *Organizational Culture and Leadership*. 3rd ed. New York: Jossey-Bass, 2005.
23. *Electronic Data Systems: Horsemen Herding Cats in a Wild West Setting* http://www.youtube.com/watch?v=YdwrYiNJc_E (accessed 27 January 2010).
24. Trilla, Antoni, Marta Aymerich, Antonio M. Lacy, Maria J. Bertran. Phenotypic Differences Between Male Physicians, Surgeons and Film Stars: Comparative Study. *BMJ* 2006, no. 333: 1291–3.
25. Dreikurs, Rudolph. *The Challenge of Parenthood*. New York: Plume, 1992.
26. Sutton, Robert. *The No Asshole Rule: Building a Civilized Workplace and Surviving One That Isn't*. New York: Warner Business Books, 2007.
27. College of Physicians and Surgeons of Ontario. *Guidebook for Managing Disruptive Physician Behaviour*. CPSO/OHA, 2008. http://www.cpso.on.ca/uploadedFiles/downloads/cpsodocuments/policies/positions/CPSO%20DPBI%20Guidebook(1).pdf (accessed 27 January 2010).
28. Friedman, Richard. Sounding Board: Fantasyland. *New England Journal of Medicine* 308, no. 11 (1983): 651–3.
29. Maintenance of Certification in Canada. http://rcpsc.medical.org/opd/moc-program/index.php (accessed 27 January 2010).
30. Beard, Jonathan D. Education and Training Committee of the Vascular Society of Great Britain and Ireland. *European Journal of Vascular Endovascular Surgery* 30, no. 2 (2005): 215–18.
31. *Alberta Physician Assessment Review (Par) Project*. http://www.par-program.org/ (accessed 27 January 2010).

32. Mark Auerman. Personal communication.

33. Reason, James. Human Error: Models and Management. *British Medical Journal* 320, no. 7237 (2000): 768–70.

34. SelfCounseling.com. *http://www.selfcounseling.com/help/personalsuccess/personalvalues.html* (accessed 27 January 2010).

35. Henry M. III, Robert. *Robert's Rules of Order Newly Revised in Brief*. New York: Perseus Books, 2004.

36. Fisher, Roger, William Ury, and Bruce Patton, eds. *Getting to Yes: Negotiating Agreement Without Giving In*. New York: Penguin Books, 1981.

37. Sanborn, Mark. *High Impact Leadership: How to Move Beyond Manager to Leader*. Toronto: Monarch Books of Canada, 1995.

38. Baker, G, Ross, Peter G. Norton, Virginia Flintoft, et al. The Canadian Adverse Events Study: The Incidence of Adverse Events among Hospital Patients in Canada. *Canadian Medical Association Journal* 170, no. 11 (2004): 1678–86.

39. The Honourable Stephen Goudge, Commissioner. *Inquiry into Pediatric Forensic Pathology in Ontario: Report*. http://www.attorneygeneral.jus.gov.on.ca/inquiries/goudge/report/ (accessed 27 January 2010).

40. *Procedure for Performing Failure Mode Effect and Critical Analysis*. U.S. Military Procedure MIL-P-1629. November 1949.

41. Motorola University. *What is Six Sigma?* Motorola.com/content.jsp?globalObjectId=3088 (accessed 27 January 2010).

42. Ohno, Taiichi. *The Toyota Production System: Beyond Large Scale Production*. Productivity Press, 1988.

43. The ThedaCare Improvement System. http://www.createhealthcarevalue.com/about/thedacare/ (accessed 27 January 2010).

44. The Safer Health Care Now! Initiative. http://www.saferhealthcarenow.ca (accessed 27 January 2010).

45. Gosfield, A.G., and J.L. Reinertsen. The 100,000 Lives Campaign: Crystallizing Standards of Care for Hospitals. *Health Affairs* 24, no. 6 (Nov.–Dec. 2005), 1560–70.

46. The Initiative to Protect 5 Million Patients from Harm. www.ihi.org/IHI/programs/campaign/Campaign.htm?TabId=6 (accessed 27 January 2010).

47. The American College of Surgeons' National Surgical Quality Improvement Program (NSQIP). http://acsnsqip.org (accessed 27 January 2010).

48. Surgical Care Improvement Project (SCIP). www.ihi.org/IHI/Topics/PatientSafety/SurgicalSiteInfections/Resources/SurgicalCareImprovementProject.htm (accessed 27 January 2010).

49. Tullekin, C.A., R.M. Verdaasdonk, H.J. Mansvelt Beck. ELANA: Non-occlusive Excimer Laser-Assisted End-to-Side Anastomosis. *Annals of Thoracic Surgery* 63 (1997): S138–S142.

50. Campbell, Justice Archie. *The SARS Crisis.* www.health.gov.on.ca/english/ public/pub/ministry_reports/campbell06/online_rep/index.html (accessed 27 January 2010).
51. Cypel, M., M. Rubacha, J. Yeung, S. Hirayama, K. Torbicki, M. Madonik, S. Fischer, D. Hwang, A. Pierre, T.K. Waddell, M. de Perrot, M. Liu, and S. Keshavjee. Normothermic Ex Vivo Perfusion Prevents Lung Injury Compared to Extended Cold Preservation for Transplantation. *American Journal of Transplantation* 9, no. 10 (2009): 2262–9.
52. Press release from Royal Brompton Hospital in Britain. April 2009.
53. Vision statement of Massachusetts General Hospital. http://massgeneral .org/pcs/about/vision/aspx (accessed 27 January 2010).
54. Vision statement of Memorial Sloan-Kettering Hospital. http://www .mskcc.org/mskcc/html/512.cfm (accessed 27 January 2010).
55. Vision statement of Johns Hopkins University Hospital. http://www .hopkinsmedicine.org/about/mission.html (accessed 27 January 2010).
56. Vision statement of Toronto's University Health Network. http://uhn.ca/ About_UHN/index.asp (accessed 27 January 2010).
57. Vision statement of Toronto East General Hospital. http://www.tegh.on .ca/bins/content_page.asp?cid=8-14 (accessed 27 January 2010).
58. Philip Orsino. In *Wikipedia*, http://en.wikipedia.org/wiki/Philip_Orsino (accessed 27 January 2010).
59. Mintzberg, Henry. *Managers Not MBA's: A Hard Look at the Soft Practice of Managing and Management Development.* San Francisco: Berrett-Koehler Publishers, 2005.
60. Mintzberg, Henry. *Structuring of Organizations.* Upper Saddle River, NJ: Pearson Education, 1978.
61. Kotter, John P. *Leading Change.* Columbus, OH: McGraw-Hill, 1996.
62. Langley, Gerald, Ronald Moen, Kevin Nolan, et al. *The Improvement Guide: A Practical Approach to Enhancing Organizational Performance.* New York: Jossey-Bass, 2009.
63. Pronovost, Peter, Dale Needham, Sean Berenholtz, et al. An Intervention to Decrease Catheter-Related Bloodstream Infections in the ICU. *NEJM* 355 (28 December 2006): 2725–32.
64. Ontario Ministry of Health and Long-Term Care. The Ontario Surgical Efficiency Targets Program (SETP). http://health.gov.on.ca/transformation/ wait_times/providers/wt_improv_mn.html (accessed 27 January 2010).
65. Haynes, A.B., T.G. Weiser, Bryce Taylor, A.A. Gawande, et al. A Surgical Safety Checklist to Reduce Morbidity and Mortality in a Global Population. *NEJM* 360, no. 5 (29 January 2009): 491–9.

66. Hammond, Sue Annis. *The Thin Book of Appreciative Inquiry.* 2nd ed. Bend, OR: Thin Book, 1998.

67. Studer, Quint. *What's Right in Health Care: 365 Stories of Purpose, Worthwhile Work, and Making a Difference.* Austin, TX: Greenleaf Book Group, 2008.

68. Canfield, Jack. *Chicken Soup for the Soul: 101 stories to Celebrate, Honor and Inspire the Nursing Profession.* Deerfield Beach, FL: Health Communications Inc., 2001.

69. Multiple contributors. *Moving Mountains to Make a Wish Come True.* Toronto: University Health Network, 2008.

70. Dr Michael Gardam. Personal communication.

71. Wright, John, et al. Learning from Death: A Hospital Mortality Reduction Programme. *Journal of the Royal Society of Medicine* 99 (2006): 303–8.

72. *HMSR: A New Approach for Measuring Hospital Mortality Trends in Canada.* http://secure.cihi.ca/cihiweb/dispPage.jsp?cw_page=AR_1789_E (accessed 27 January 2010).

73. Kaplan, Robert S., and David P. Norton. *The Balanced Scorecard: Translating Strategy into Action.* Boston: Harvard Business School Press, 1996.

74. Michael L. Gustafson, MD, MBA. http://www.brighamandwomens.org/CenterforSurgeryandPublicHealth/Documents/Dr.%20Gustafson%20Revised%20bio.aspx (accessed 27 January 2010).

75. *SAS Customer Brigham and Women's Hospital Wins National Health Care Award.* Press release. http://www.sas.com/news/preleases/030806/news1.html (accessed 27 January2010).

76. The Institute for Clinical and Evaluative Sciences (ICES). www.ices.on.ca.

77. Cronenwett, Jack, Donald Likosky, et al., Vascular Study Group of Northern New England (www.vsgnne.org). A Regional Registry for Quality Assurance and Improvement: The Vascular Surgery Group of Northern New England (VSGNNE). *Journal of Vascular Surgery* 46, no. 6 (2007): 1093–1101.

78. Bates, David, Lucian Leape, et al. Effect of Computerized Physician Order Entry and a Team Intervention on Prevention of Serious Medication Errors. *JAMA* 280, no. 15 (1998): 1311–16.

79. Glaser, John. *Improving Care Quality Through Electronic Health Records: The Experience at Partners Health Care.* ISQua 26th International Conference, Dublin, Ireland, 13 October 2009.

80. Martin, Roger. *The Opposable Mind: How Successful Leaders Win Through Integrative Thinking.* Boston: Harvard Business School Press, 2007.

81. McCormack, Mark. *What They Don't Teach You at Harvard Business School: Notes from a Street-Smart Executive.* New York: Bantam Books, 1990.

82. Berger, Earl. Attitudes to Privacy, Health Records and Interconnection: Implications for Healthcare Organizations. *Healthcare Quarterly* 5, no. 4 (2002): 40–45. http://www.longwoods.com/product.php?productid=16671 (accessed 27 January 2010).
83. Joint Commission on the Accreditation of Healthcare Organizations (JCAHO). www.jointcommission.org (accessed 27 January 2010).
84. National Committee for Quality Assurance. www.ncqa.org (accessed 27 January 2010).
85. Accreditation Canada. www.accreditation.ca (accessed 27 January 2010).
86. Buckman, Robert. *How to Break Bad News: A Guide for Health Care Professionals.* Toronto: University of Toronto Press, 1992.
87. Alan Freed biography. http://www.alanfreed.com/biography.html (accessed 27 January 2010).
88. Association of American Medical Colleges. *Financial Conflicts of Interest in Academic Medicine.* AAMC policy. www.aamc.org/research/coi/start.htm (accessed 27 January 2010).
89. Robbennolt, J.K. Apologies and Legal Settlement: An Empirical Examination. *Mich Law Rev* 102 (2004): 460–516.
90. Barnes, Julian. *Nothing to Be Frightened Of.* Mississauga, ON: Vintage Canada, 2009.

Index